Black Women
Taught Us

Black Women Taught Us

An Intimate History of Black Feminism

Jenn M. Jackson, PhD

RANDOM HOUSE

NEW YORK

Published in the United States by Random House, an imprint and division of Penguin Random House LLC, New York.

RANDOM HOUSE and the HOUSE colophon are registered trademarks of Penguin Random House LLC.

LIBRARY OF CONGRESS CATALOGING-IN-PUBLICATION DATA
Names: Jackson, Jenn M., author.
Title: Black women taught us / Jenn M. Jackson.
Description: First edition. | New York: Random House, [2024] |
Includes bibliographical references and index.
Identifiers: LCCN 2023012455 (print) | LCCN 2023012456 (ebook) |
ISBN 9780593243336 (hardback) | ISBN 9780593243343 (ebook)
Subjects: LCSH: African American women political activists—History. |
African American feminists—History. | African American women—
Political activity—History. | African American women—Social conditions. |
African Americans—Social conditions. | African Americans—Civil rights—
History. | United States—Race relations—History. | Jackson, Jenn M.
Classification: LCC E185.86 .J332 2024 (print) | LCC E185.86 (ebook) |
DDC 305.48/896073—dc23/eng/20230907
LC record available at https://lccn.loc.gov/2023012455
LC ebook record available at https://lccn.loc.gov/2023012456

Printed in the United States of America on acid-free paper

randomhousebooks.com

9 8 7 6 5 4 3 2 1

First Edition

Book design by Diane Hobbing

Contents

Introduction

Black Women Taught Us

Every Wednesday as I grew up, our tiny two-bedroom home became a concert hall for a majestic group of gospel singers. Auntie Donna Faye (no blood relation to me), a tall woman with a perfect asymmetrical bob, long curved fingernails, and a no-nonsense glare, was the alto who always rested right in the vocal pocket. Auntie Barbara (also no blood relation), who was the oldest of the group but would never share her actual age, always wore a big curly wig and bright-red lipstick. She was a soprano from another generation of Black singers. Sharon was a quiet, sarcastic woman whose baritone voice could rumble the whole house when she murmured an *mhmmmmmm* along to any song. Sometimes, I would tiptoe into the living room during rehearsal just to hear Sharon's *mhmmmmmm*s and sneak back out before my mom noticed. My mother's sister, Deborah, was one of the greatest voices I had ever heard, a soprano whose vibrato made you feel like you were lying in a blanket fresh out of the dryer. I also thought she was the *A Different World* actress Jasmine Guy for most of my childhood because she resembled the actress so closely. Cassandra, the group's pianist and vocal arranger, would glide into the room with her deep voice and thick-rimmed glasses every week. She was such a quietly powerful presence.

Then there was my mother, Cynthia. An unassuming woman standing at five foot five, she was always in a battle with her weight. She was, and still is, a beautiful, brown-skinned woman with a perfectly placed mole nestled at the base of her philtrum, the area right below the nose that some people call the Cupid's bow. My mother could sing anything and exuded so much charisma when she performed that most audience members got excited just to see her open her mouth and to bask in her gifts.

As a child, I always looked forward to seeing this awe-inspiring group of women, who would crowd into our living room for their Wednesday rehearsals, circling our upright piano, singing all manner of gospel songs. Cassandra named the group "Majesty" before I was born and, just as it was for her kids, it was one of the first words I learned.

Majesty toured Oakland and the rest of the San Francisco Bay Area throughout the eighties and nineties, performing traditional gospel hits. They were known for their vocal embellishments that stemmed from years of listening to and studying the greats, like Shirley Caesar and the Clark Sisters. Singing high into the rafters and deep into the vocal valleys was common for them. The members of Majesty were different from the singers my church community and family saw on *Bobby Jones Gospel* every Sunday afternoon: They were our mothers, aunties, grandmothers, church leaders, and Sunday school teachers. They were the women who raised us, cooked for us, put on our Band-Aids, and scolded us for crossing the street without looking first.

They were *ours*.

"Fill my cup, let it overflow. Fill my cup, let it oh-ver-flow. Fill it up! Fill it up! And let it oh-oooh-oooh-oh-ver-flow. Let it oh-oh-oh-ver-flow, with love," they would sing while forming their lips into perfect "O" shapes. They also sang "12 Gates to the City" by the Famous Davis Sisters. The harmonies that emanated from that living room sounded like they were ordained by God, likely because they were. Meanwhile, in my room, I'd be entertaining the kids. Sometimes, Auntie Barbara would bring a grandchild or two, and Sharon would do the same. I would immediately shift from being a usually lonely only child into a makeshift hostess and pseudo-mother for the younger kids. I'd set up the little ones with video games so that I'd be free to style the hair of my younger "cousins": Esther, Lee Lee, and Lizzy, Cassandra's three little girls. She had five children in total, but the boys were usually as far away from my makeshift hair salon as possible. We all had a nickname or two at that point. The house was only ever full like this on rehearsal nights and holidays. They were some of the most joyful nights of my young life.

To prepare for these evenings and my weekly hosting duties, I taught myself how to cook. I wanted to offer something, a small gift, to these women who brought so much warmth to my home. Rehearsal was at the end of the day, often after they had been working for hours and caring for children. Feeding them seemed like a kind and necessary gesture. By around the age of four, I could scramble eggs. At age eight, I tried my hand at baked chicken.

"Cynthia, this chicken is raw in the middle," Auntie Barbara told my mom one week as she pulled the meat from the bone, exposing the red vertebrae and tendons that were clearly undercooked.

"Jennifer, be careful," my mom scolded.

"Yes, Mommy," I replied, feeling deflated.

"Don't be too hard on her, Cynthia. The chicken is seasoned so well," Auntie Barbara told her. "You did good, baby. Just cook it a little longer next time and poke it with a knife to see if blood comes out, okay?" she said as she leaned over to me, her lipstick bright and smudged from the chicken.

"Yes, Auntie Barbara," I said, feeling determined to do better, as though this was an assignment for me to conquer.

Like my Auntie Barbara and the other members of Majesty, my mother, grandmothers, and my extended community of Black women and queer folks would often offer me lessons, teachings from their own lives—lessons that they had struggled to learn themselves, but that had likely saved them time and again. Auntie Donna taught me about navigating the world in a tall, large-bodied frame. "Don't ever get dressed up and put on lipstick without throwing on some earrings, girl!" she would tell me at church. I still chuckle about this lesson whenever I see the collection of spare earrings on my desk. Sometimes the lessons were harder and carried more weight, like when my grandmother, an outspoken, ambitious, and headstrong Black woman, warned me, "Baby, people like us spend a lot of time alone, so you just have to find the people who love you and love them right back." I was eleven years old when she said that. At the time, I didn't understand what she meant by "people like us." I understand now.

This informal knowledge network and storytelling community introduced me to the central tenets of Black Feminism before I had the language or the training to utter those words in that sequence. But no one tells you—at least, no one told me—that these quiet, quotidian experiences, these everyday Black feminisms, matter, or that they contain essential wisdom and knowledge for living. The recipes, the dating advice, the movement work, and the church and community organizing. Instead, just like most of the world, I failed to see these women's work in my life as nuanced, different, significant, or deeply rooted in an ongoing fight for liberation and freedom. It wasn't until I was surrounded by whiteness that these lessons became clearer to me.

I grew up in the highly segregated Oakland Bay Area, which means that I didn't have many interactions with white people until I left for college. Even while my childhood overflowed with Black women and Black feminisms, I wasn't impelled to think about Black Feminism in an academic or even a formal sense. In truth, I just wasn't aware that any of this literature existed. I attended an elite private institution, but I never took a course on Black Feminism because none were offered. During undergrad, I had only one Black woman professor. I had no idea that race, gender, and LGBTQIA+ scholars and researchers had been waging a decades-long battle against universities and their donors to make room for the study of diverse people on these campuses. The predominantly white campuses I gained access to successfully obfuscated the lack of willingness and desire to center Black Studies, and especially Black Feminism, in their curricula. And while my mother had done her best to teach me about the intersections of race, gender, class, and disability, she did so out of a need to survive. She had no college degrees or personal studies to equip her with the theories, concepts, and teachings of Black women thinkers and activists. Rather, she spoke from the experience of growing up poor in Berkeley, California, living in dilapidated homes with her mother and two younger siblings, learning to outrun her abusive and alcoholic father, and surviving a world full of rejection: rejection of her shapely Black body, her thick lips, her wide-set nose, her kinky hair, and her brown skin. She taught me that these experiences were both the poison and the fuel that she used to raise me.

In 2007, I was working at Disneyland as a Workforce Analyst, which is a fancy way of saying that I was using math to make hiring and staffing more efficient for my employer. For years I struggled with being paid less than many of my peers, facing daily subtle racist comments and gestures, and being constantly reminded that I was different from everyone else on my team. As far as they could tell, I was both Black *and* a woman (at the time, no one knew I was polyamorous, queer, and genderflux—not even me). Sometimes, during busy work meetings, white women would loudly declare, "Jenn, this is my favorite of your hairs!," and they'd sometimes touch it without my permission. While I recognized these as racist *and* sexist actions, I didn't know how to interpret them, and I couldn't understand where they stemmed from or how to eradicate them altogether.

Then, in 2009, in the wee hours of the morning on New Year's Day, twenty-two-year-old Oscar Grant was killed by BART police officer Johannes Mehserle at the Fruitvale BART Station in Oakland, California. I was only twenty-four years old at the time. That was a station I had frequented growing up. It was no more than ten minutes from my grandmother's house and served as a key thoroughfare for many young people growing up in East Oakland. Oscar's death was so personal, so intimate. It was the first time a police killing truly shattered me. The next year, seven-year-old Aiyana Stanley-Jones was killed by Detroit SWAT in a "botched raid." She was lying on the couch in her grandmother's arms when gunshots erupted. She was killed instantly. It was another heartbreak. I was a mother by that point. The loss of Black children hit me differently. It hurt in a way I had never encountered before. My desperation in my work life and the ongoing violence against Black people I was witnessing online catalyzed a deep hunger in me to learn more about myself, my foremothers, and my larger Black Feminist community. My own evolution as a Black woman and parent to a Black child sent me on a voracious trek to find answers. I wanted to understand why these things were happening and why it felt like it was my responsibility to end them.

I called my mom first, as I typically do when I have burning questions about Black life.

"Mama, who were the Black women who wrote those books on your shelf back at our house in East Oakland? Tell me their names."

"Who? Like, Alice Walker? Terry McMillan?"

I wrote down the names on a sticky note. "Yes! Alice Walker wrote the one about female circumcision in Africa, right?"

"Yep. *Possessing the Secret of Joy*."

That was it. I had to find that book. I knew that if I did, I could find others like it.

On a balmy Saturday morning in Orange County, California, I went to Borders, hunting for the titles and voices I had seen on my mother's shelf. In my frantic search, I came across Melissa

Harris-Perry's *Sister Citizen*. The cover was immediately striking: It featured a Black woman's face—her eyes closed, her head
shaved—with the American flag overlaying her skin. I had to
know what was inside. This was my first encounter with a book
that was expressly written to interpret and frame Black women's
unique experiences in the United States. Though I had grown
up reading the fiction of Zora Neale Hurston, Sister Souljah,
and Toni Morrison, it had never dawned on me that these stories
resonated with me *because* of my own experience as a poor Black
girl living in a world that saw Blackness as a cardinal sin.

In *Sister Citizen,* Harris-Perry wrote about the "crooked
room" where Black women's identities are often contorted to
fit the desires and expectations of others. Harris-Perry explained that the crooked room stems from stereotypes like the
Jezebel (the hypersexual Black woman), the Mammy (the asexual Black woman caretaker), and the Sapphire (the angry
Black woman). I read the book. I cried into the book. I read the
book again. Harris-Perry said that Black women should endeavor to stand upright in that crooked room. This was the
first time an analogy rocked me to my core. I imagined having
walked around the world for twenty-seven years hunched
over, shaped like a lowercase "F." I reflected on the crooked
rooms I'd encountered at work and at school. And I cried once
more, overwhelmed by the force of recognition.

During this time, I began digging into Black Feminist literature because of the conditions of the world around me. The
first Black president had been elected, and a beautiful Black
woman was living in the White House with two Black girls.
President Obama's message of hope had excited me and drawn
me toward social action in a new way. Simultaneously, I be-

came increasingly aware of racial injustice in the United States. When my co-workers whispered to my boss about me being unapproachable and angry, and my white colleagues at school avoided working with me in study groups because they assumed I was only at USC because of racial quotas, I realized that these individual experiences were related to the forms of oppression that my mother and larger community had already encountered. It was clear to me that the abusive treatment from Black men, the discrimination from white people, the classist surveillance from rich folks in the segregated neighborhoods of Oakland, and the fatphobia from within our own community were all connected. They were microcosms of the larger systemic problems of white supremacy, anti-Blackness, and what Moya Bailey and Trudy call "misogynoir"—the gender-specific racism faced by Black women. I began to see that all of these systems were connected to the issues I had witnessed my whole life, like the mass incarceration of my family and friends, police harassment of my brother and cousins, and anti-Black violence all over the United States.

Then I became angry.

I recalled how, in high school, we weren't taught many lessons that focused on the contributions of Black women in history, and when we were, our schools were selective in what they taught. Harriet Tubman was the only Black woman I came across in my history class: They told us she was a fugitive slave who freed hundreds of enslaved Black people via the Underground Railroad. But they didn't tell us that Tubman was a military leader in the Civil War. They never taught us that in 1863, Tubman led soldiers along the Combahee River with Colonel James Montgomery to raid the South Carolina rice plantations. They never told us that "General Tubman" was a Union spy and recruiter. Instead, the interpretation of Tubman's otherwise radical life that they taught us was co-opted and watered down—effectively erasing the parts of her story that threatened our nation's preference for stories about nonviolent resistance. Rather than frame Tubman as a fierce and persistent abolitionist whose work was animated by a deep commitment to ending chattel bondage (the enslavement of Black people under the supposition that they were property akin to cattle) and carceral logics (the larger surveillance state that resorts to criminalization and punishment to eradicate anyone the State deems "deviant") across the United States, they sterilized her legacy and taught us that she "helped free the slaves."

I began searching for women who were writing about our varied Black experiences. What I found was that many of the books I had voraciously read at the foot of my mother's bed growing up were out of print, hard to find in local bookstores, or simply inaccessible due to the printing press's high costs. It often took several searches, calls to bookstores, and waiting lists to get a chance to purchase books by prominent feminists. Luckily, after 2004, the advent of social media platforms like Facebook, Twitter, and Tumblr gave us access to the world and to Black feminists on every continent. Those of us who had been avid readers of Alice Walker, Toni Morrison, and bell hooks were now being introduced to people just like us on the Internet who were sharing their lived experiences with anti-Blackness, policing, gender discrimination, and everything in between. *Racialicious, Crunk Feminist Collective,* and Trudy's blog *Gradient Lair* were early platforms that worked to consolidate our experiences and translate them in critical and nuanced ways. I realized, too, that Black feminists were everywhere. Just like my mother and the women of Majesty, young Black women in my communities at the intersections of queerness, movements, education, social work, and the like were putting words to the experiences I had witnessed and endured. And, while much of that work had not been published on mainstream websites, printed in books, or highlighted on the evening news, that work was resonating with all of us.

In taking in all of this literature on Black women's theorizing and activism, I had found a mirror of my own realities and those of the women I had encountered as I grew up. Having now discovered parts of myself that had been neglected and had grown over with insecurities, I became obsessed with understanding myself, society, and the potential for a more just world, so I kept reading, following Harris-Perry's bibliography like it was the yellow brick road. First, I read bell hooks's *Feminism Is for Everybody,* a guidebook on introducing feminism to men and other non-women who don't understand its implications for their lives. Next, I read Audre Lorde's essay "The Master's Tools Will Never Dismantle the Master's House." The short essay snapped me out of the idea that assimilation was ideal (or even possible) for Black women who believe in freedom. Lorde wrote,

> Those of us who stand outside the circle of this society's definition of acceptable women; those of us who have been forged in the crucibles of difference—those of us who are poor, who are lesbians, who are Black, who are older—know that survival is *not an academic skill.* . . . It is learning how to take our differences and make them strengths.[1]

In Lorde's words, I heard my grandmother's voice telling me about how lonesome it would be to be one of "us." It was through Lorde's confrontation with the master's tools that I began to confront the ways in which I had internalized white supremacy, anti-Blackness, homophobia, classism, and ableism in my own life and heart. I realized that, by chasing whiteness, I was hustling backward in a game I was never set to win. As a queer and trans person who was also navigating multiple disabilities—anxiety, depression, Marfan syndrome (a congenital heart disease), and blindness—I was coming to see that so many of the phobias and antagonisms I had held in my body were antagonisms I was holding about myself.

Then George Zimmerman killed Trayvon Martin in 2012. I heard the 911 call. I sobbed, crying over another loss. The heartbreak felt unbearable this time. When the verdict in the Zimmerman case came down, I was the mother of two small children, with my third child on the way. I was sitting in a convention center in Washington, D.C., at the national conference for Delta Sigma Theta, Inc., a service-oriented sorority serving predominantly Black women. This room, packed with thousands and thousands of Black women, sat in silence when we learned that Zimmerman was found not guilty. Then, some of us sobbed. Others sat quietly in reflection. Others verbally expressed rage. We sat together, tired and in mourning. I will never forget the silence that fell over the room as we all raised our phones, lighting the space, to honor the life of this young boy and to remind one another that we were present together.

In the coming weeks and months, young Black people all over the country began mounting directed campaigns in support of Black lives. Like so many others, I shifted course. I believed intrinsically in President Obama's message of hope, but I also felt invigorated by the growing coalition Movement for Black Lives, which directed legitimate critiques at him and his use of presidential power. I left corporate America for good. I returned to school and committed myself to the study of race, gender, and politics full-time. I chose to study Political Science because I wanted to study power. I wanted to understand the systems and institutions that made all of these experiences not only possible but prevalent. I wanted to know why I was never taught about my forestrugglers, why people in other communities had rights and privileges I did not, why a young boy could be shot down for carrying iced tea and candy, and why the whole country wasn't enraged by it. But it wasn't my readings of the "canon" of liberal philosophers like John Locke, Thomas Hobbes, and Jean-Jacques Rousseau that helped me answer these questions. Black women taught me.

What I have come to learn over the course of my nearly forty years is that the difficulty I faced in trying to find Black women's voices, work, and contributions wasn't a matter of its existing or not. It was a direct result of the systems in place that diminish Black women and erase them from history while co-opting and appropriating the very work they have produced. For example, Fortune 500 corporations tout their diversity and commitments to building racial equity while the number of Black women CEOs among them is an astounding two.[2] Megastars like Kim Kardashian caricature Black women's features for money in campaigns meant to "break the Internet" while never having any serious dialogue about the forms of violence their imagery and modeling choices enact on Black women.[3]

This phenomenon is not isolated nor is it just a contemporary problem. Black women's bodies have long been caricatured and commodified for white Americans who viewed our bodies as animalistic and nonhuman. The earliest example I learned of was Saartjie "Sarah" Baartman, born in South Africa's East Cape in 1789.[4] In 1810, after years of hardship, including the deaths of her parents and her infant child and the murder of her partner, Baartman signed a contract with an English surgeon who intended to take her to London and Paris for shows. There, she was billed as the "Hottentot Venus" and marketed to onlookers for her large buttocks and supposedly disfigured genitalia. According to *The New York Times,* "When she arrived in London in 1810, this young woman from South Africa became an overnight sensation in London's theater of human oddities."[5]

Baartman's experience in the "freak shows" of the nineteenth century was one of the most prominent examples of Black women's bodies being consumed as objects rather than regarded as human beings. Clad in a flesh-colored, skintight bodysuit, adorned with feathers, and propped up on a stage in Piccadilly, Baartman became the object of obsession, disgust, and fascination. The show itself played on the ways that Baartman's image emerged in the white imagination. *The Guardian* notes, "In London, the act consisted of her emerging from a cage like a wild animal. In Paris she was sold to an animal trainer and paraded at high society balls."[6] Baartman's economic and sexual exploitation was central to her life in the colonial world. She had little to no personal freedom and relied on alcohol to self-medicate in her later years.

Baartman died in 1815, at which time her body was dissected, her brain and genitalia preserved in formaldehyde, and her skeleton saved. A painted cast of Baartman was displayed at the Musée de l'Homme until the 1970s. And it wasn't until 2002 that her body was returned to her homeland.

Baartman's exploitation and hypersexualization connects directly to the ways that Black women and girls are stereotyped and caricatured today. Mikki Kendall writes of this when she discussed the issue of the "fast-tailed girl"[7] trope wherein little Black girls in their teens and adolescence are often sexualized as their bodies develop naturally, seen by older men as sexually available and, often, policed by older Black women who are all too familiar with the dangers of the male gaze on a Black girl's developing body. Family health professionals refer to this process as "adultification," which is one of the ways that young Black Americans are perceived as older than their true age. This is linked to emotional and social issues for Black girls.[8] These dangers include stigmatization and shame but they also include increased rates of sexual assault and rape, which are compounded if Black women and girls are bisexual, incarcerated, disabled, low income, or HIV-positive.[9]

This is our reality: Black feminists, organizers, and scholars have a long intellectual tradition rooted in defining themselves outside of the systems that oppress us. That tradition includes specifically identifying the ways that Black women's unpaid community labor is usurped by charismatic male leaders like Martin Luther King, Jr., naming our work within movements. It includes theorizing about systems that facilitate the oppression of all Black people and, critically, those among us who have the least. This tradition articulates a picture of what a liberated world looks like even though we have never once seen it. From these traditions have emerged a whole host of words and gestures referring to the connections that Black folk build with one another and how we should create modern movements, communities, families, and relationships. Black women have given us guidebooks on how to be better humans. In fact, they have often done it for free.

Many of our path breaking Black Feminist writers, theorists, and organizers have struggled in their lifetimes to have access to adequate healthcare, payment for their labor, nutritious food to eat, and supportive communities to ensure their safety and comfort in the sunsets of their lives. Many of them suffered from the destructive consequences of disabilities, cancer, and other ailments before their deaths. In many ways, they gave so much to us that there was sometimes little left for themselves. Why does Black Feminist teaching require so much of its teachers? What is it about us, as students, that allows us to be apathetic to the lives and livelihoods of the Black women and foremothers who have sacrificed so much so that we can be a little more free?

Listening to Black women requires that we center, engage with, and become challenged by the parts of their teachings and lessons that uproot us the most. In this book, I focus on those voices that are too often overlooked, imagined away, watered down, and simply ignored by white people, institutions, and the authority of the State. I write each essay as a love letter to the women who led me back to myself. The women who built our movements and taught us how to love ourselves whole.

Black women taught us how to listen and work. It's time we do both.

Black Women
Taught Us

CHAPTER 1

Harriet Jacobs Taught Me About Freedom

The dream of my life is not yet realized.

—Harriet Jacobs

we are each other's
magnitude and bond.

—Gwendolyn Brooks

On display at the National Museum of African American History and Culture in Washington, D.C., is a reconstructed slave cabin—a small, one-story rectangular shack from Edisto Island, South Carolina. It was my first time visiting and walking through a slave cabin, and the doorframe was so tiny that I could barely fit through it with my six-foot-four frame. I had to tilt my head to the side and hunch my shoulders to get in. Inside, the floor was sturdy but uneven. I peered through the wide openings between the walls' worn wooden slats. "This was it?" asked the other visitors at the exhibit. Except for the occasional murmur, a thick blanket of silence and reverence covered everything in the space.

Preservationists had brought the structure from South Carolina after it was donated by the Burnet Maybank family, owners of the Point of Pines Plantation where the cabin once stood, housing enslaved people.[1] The cabin dates back to the 1850s and is typical of the tiny buildings that enslaved Black people once called home on land that never felt like *home*. As I stood there in the middle of the cabin as a free Black woman, I still felt the weight of bondage. The space was small and cold. I felt like I was walking through an empty closet where nightmares lived. The visceral horror I experienced in that space intensified when I thought of the enslaved people, like Harriet Jacobs, who used these spaces to plan and execute their escapes from their enslavers. I may have felt claustrophobic in that moment, but I tried to remember that I was also standing within a space that once offered solace to Black slaves amid unspeakable violence. While the outside world was nothing but shackles and surveillance, these cabins were, in many ways, the first stops along a complicated road toward a freedom that almost none of them had ever seen. It was a freedom that they had to imagine and invent for themselves.

For Harriet Jacobs, that road from enslavement to freedom was preceded by blissful ignorance. In her now canonical *Incidents in the Life of a Slave Girl* (1861), Jacobs—who wrote under the pseudonym Linda Brent—begins by explaining, "I was born a slave; but I never knew it till six years of happy childhood had passed away."[2] She had been cared for by her grandmother, a fair-skinned slave woman who was able to use her seniority and moderate power to protect her five children from the typical drudgery and violence of slavery. It was only when Jacobs's mother died that she realized that she—and her family—were enslaved. Jacobs writes, "My mother's mistress was the daughter of my grandmother's mistress. She was the foster sister of my mother; they were both nourished at my grandmother's breast. In fact, my mother had been weaned at three months old, that the babe of the mistress might obtain sufficient food."[3] Jacobs was treated kindly by her mistress until the woman died when she was twelve years old. At that time, Jacobs was bequeathed to her mistress's five-year-old niece, while her grandmother's surviving children were auctioned off to other owners. Reflecting on the sale of her kin, Jacobs writes, "These God-breathing machines are no more, in the sight of their masters, than the cotton they plant, or the horses they tend."[4]

As a young woman, Jacobs faced the constant threat of sexual assault, violence, emotional abuse, and intimidation. Her slaver, Dr. Flint, took special notice of her and frequently sought to coerce her into a sexual relationship. As slaves had no rights to property, to their own children, or to their own bodies, Jacobs, by law, could not be raped because she was the property of her slave owner. Slaves could not be witnesses in a court. They were not allowed to bring evidence in support or defense of themselves. To be unfree in the era of slavery meant to be unfree in every way possible.

With nothing protecting her from the whims of her slavers, Jacobs's time under Dr. Flint's roof was filled with constant anxiety, paranoia, and fear. She shuddered at the mere sound of his footsteps. Jacobs says that slavery prematurely introduced Black girls to "evil things." She writes, "She will be compelled to realize she is no longer a child. If God has bestowed beauty upon her, it will prove her greatest curse. That

which commands admiration in the white woman only has-
tens the degradation of the female slave."[5] Dr. Flint wanted to
control Jacobs's love life and whom she married. He dangled
freedom in front of her, claiming that if she gave her body to
him (a body that he technically owned, mind you), he would
give her something akin to freedom: accommodations that
would set her apart from other slaves, equivalent to her having
her own quarters on the plantation land, but only under the
condition that he would have constant access to her body. Jacobs saw the lie at the heart of this Faustian bargain: She knew
that "freedom" wasn't her own rooms on *his* land, nor anything else he could give her. Instead, freedom was something
she would have to fight for—something she would have to
take for herself and her family.

Jacobs seized what little agency she could when she gave
herself not to Flint, but to "Mr. Sands," a white man who she
believed loved her. Flattered by his kindness and friendship,
she felt that her relationship with Sands gave her a glimpse
into what freedom could look like: "It seems less degrading to
give one's self, than to submit to compulsion. There is something akin to freedom in having a lover who has no control
over you, except that which he gains by kindness and attach-
ment."[6] For Jacobs, her relationship with Mr. Sands was an
opportunity to reclaim herself and her sexuality from a system
that sought only to possess and erase her identity. While this
exercise in personal and physical freedom animated Jacobs's
maturation and movement into adult life, it also reminded her
of her compressed autonomy and limited authority in determining her own fate.

After giving birth to two children, Jacobs was concerned that Dr. Flint's obsession with her would only worsen and that he might punish her by selling her children away. She resolved that her escape would require her to leave her children in the care of her grandmother. She had faith that Mr. Sands would eventually save her children from slavery (in time, he did). Then, nineteen-year-old Jacobs began her harrowing escape from slavery along the Underground Railroad. She hid on the plantation, nearly in plain sight, afraid that if she took to the woods on foot, she would be recaptured by slave patrols and returned to Dr. Flint. As she prepared for her quest toward the North, she took refuge by hiding in the "attic" of her grandmother's slave quarters on Dr. Flint's plantation. As large as a crawl space, this attic wasn't large enough for Jacobs to stand in, let alone move around in. In the section of her autobiography entitled "The Loophole of Retreat," Jacobs describes the space:

> A small shed had been added to my grandmother's house years ago. Some boards were laid across the joists at the top, and between these boards and the roof was a very small garret, never occupied by anything but rats and mice. It was a pent roof, covered with nothing but shingles, according to the southern custom for such buildings. The garret was only nine feet long and seven feet wide. The highest part was three feet high, and sloped down abruptly to the loose board floor. There was no admission for either light or air.[7]

She would remain there in hiding for seven years. It was there that the calculus of escape became clear to her: By running away, Jacobs would have to give up the few freedoms she knew—freedom to be with her children, freedom of movement, freedom to see the sun and be outdoors—for a freedom beyond slavery that was neither guaranteed nor known.

When Jacobs slept at night, she felt rats and mice running over her body. Sleep and peace evaded her. At times, she found herself frightened, running from her crawl space into the dead dark of the night. She was bitten by hidden predators, which hissed and snapped at her as she tucked herself away from potential slave catchers. The bites from rats, mice, and snakes left Jacobs disabled, and she walked with a limp. Her body became weaker every day that she was forced to remain crumpled and contorted in a space not built for humans. For Jacobs, the deep loneliness and isolation were only exacerbated by the awful conditions she endured to survive. But it was in that space that she started to feel what it meant to be free.

Whenever I teach the "Loophole of Retreat" passages from *Incidents in the Life of a Slave Girl,* students inevitably challenge me on the idea that Jacobs found freedom in that attic. There's no way, they say, that being *that* secluded, that mentally and physically shut off from the world, could feel like freedom. In today's terms, certainly, this may look more like imprisonment than anything else, but the freedom that Jacobs captured during those seven years was in her ability to exercise autonomy. She made plans to escape the plantation after ensuring her children would be protected by her grandmother. And she utilized her agency over her own body to see that choice through to the end. She decided to step out from underneath a slaver who watched her every move and into a darkness where she could never be seen nor found. This was a prison of her own choosing. She made a choice to become invisible during a moment when her visibility was a constant threat to her safety. There is freedom in choosing. There is freedom in the in-between, too.

It's at this point that I remind my students that there is the concept of being free *from* and being free *to*. Freedom from oppressive structures and from situations that limit our mobility and autonomy requires that we become familiar with unfreedom, that we learn what oppression looks like so that we can define a freedom outside of it. Freedom to become something otherwise requires our imagination. It requires that we have the mental and emotional wherewithal to envision transformative changes to our existing conditions. While being free from a situation, person, or institution of power might be all the freedom we need in a given moment, being free to make decisions on one's own behalf and in the name of developing one's own life outcomes is wholly different. When we focus only on being free from the oppressive structures and people that hold us back, we don't focus enough on the process of *getting* free to become our full selves. To dream. To imagine. To be otherwise. Jacobs's escape from slavery demonstrates how she got free from the physical barriers that imprisoned her body so that she could be free to become the woman and mother she had only imagined.

Indeed, it should come as no surprise that Jacobs titled the section of her book concerned with her escape from slavery "The Loophole of Retreat." After all, a loophole is a hidden way out (or, perhaps, a hidden way in). In legal terms, it can denote an inadequacy in a law or set of statutes that allows for one to legally achieve a goal that is otherwise not permitted. No matter the context, it's universally understood that loopholes can offer you an advantage over a system that is likely overpowered. It grants the person who has discovered it an opportunity to win when faced with loss. Jacobs's title acts as a double entendre conveying the small holes through which she could peer at the outside world while she crouched quietly, and the literal legal loophole she hoped to exploit to get free. She knew that if she just made it to free soil, she would be free, too. The Fugitive Slave Acts of 1793 and, later, 1850, were efforts by Southern states to enforce the capture and return of runaway enslaved people. However, many Northern states abolished slavery and refused to enforce the laws, making themselves safe havens for enslaved people seeking refuge.

Many Black Feminist writers have accounted for these experiences of fleeting freedom. There are profound parallels between Jacobs's account of the attic and the literary critic Hortense Spillers's narrative of the horrors of the Middle Passage. In her canonical essay "Mama's Baby, Papa's Maybe," Spillers describes this treacherous journey as a process of both doing and undoing, of being "unmade" and "exposed." It is the passage across the sea in the bowels of slave ships via the transatlantic slave trade that fundamentally marked Africans in America. Forced to leave behind their families, their communities, their spiritual practices, and even their names, enslaved Africans en route to America entered the in-between space of the Middle Passage. In Spillers's terms, they were "suspended in the oceanic": "Removed from the Indigenous land and culture, and not-yet 'American' either, these captive persons, without names that their captors would recognize, were in movement across the Atlantic, but they were also *nowhere* at all."[8] Like Jacobs's attic, the Middle Passage was a place where time stopped and the enslaved body lay in wait for some future state of being. In this way, becoming a Black American was a process of suspension and transformation and of moving into the unknown.

Spillers explains how the Middle Passage was an expedition of disconnection and disjunction as much as it was a process of rewriting and reentry. To be nowhere at all is to exist in a space that is not named by dominators because it is not deemed valid or critical enough to compel recognition. When enslaved Black people existed in this liminal space, they existed as vessels into which white supremacy sought to pour new meaning. In the bowels of ships, chained to one another, enslaved Black people were considered nameless cargo, objects with no origin. They were crucibles within which capitalism and the oppressive nature of race-making combined to write and rewrite history. This experience was different for men, women, and children who made the journey across the Atlantic. The enslaved woman's body was a site of forced reproduction wherein slave masters could increase their wealth and accumulation through rape. This was an intentional aspect of the institution of slavery. The enslaved man's body was akin to chattel, the recipient of chain and whip, a tool of the plantation meant to be beaten down and expended like a horse or an axle on a buggy. Every child born to an enslaved woman took on the enslaved condition of its mother. This juridical loophole allowed for slave masters to father children with enslaved women against their will and include their own children among their property. The entire system was rooted in dehumanization and objectification of enslaved Black people's bodies. This was the nature of racial capitalism during slavery.

In the Middle Passage, Africans were packed so densely that they often could not move. They would often be starved to death, sick from the filth and moisture in the deep cavities of the boats, and when other captives died in transport, captors would leave the dying and decaying bodies among the living, spreading disease and worsening the conditions for other Africans. This process removed African people from communities and from their tribal families. It cemented their roles as property and possessions, thereby discouraging insurgence and resistance. From the outset, the goal was to demoralize. It was to wash away the richness and prominence of the African tribal heritage and indigeneity that these folks brought along with them. Once captive Africans landed on the shores in the West Indies, the Caribbean, and North America, they were sold off into bondage, given new names, frequently branded with insignias identifying them as the property of their slavers, and chained like farm animals and equipment.

But slavery and the harrowing escape from it were not the full story. For enslaved Black people, the possibility of freedom and the dream that it would one day come were enough to buoy them for years, sometimes even lifetimes, of being unfree. Slavery itself, for enslaved people, was a form of in-between. It was a stop before liberation and an obstacle to personal salvation. Freedom would never be absolute, nor would it come in one sonic boom. The accounts from General Toussaint Louverture (the most prominent leader of the only successful overthrow of slavery in history, which secured Haitian independence from France) and other freedom fighters during the Haitian Revolution show that enslaved Black people knew that it would take the efforts of many people over many years to dismantle and formally dissolve the peculiar institution of slavery. And, in revisiting the narratives of freed and escaped slaves like Frederick Douglass and Sojourner Truth, many Black Americans believed that even after the institution fell away, Black people would still have to fight to be recognized as full and equal citizens in the United States.

Like these long struggles, Jacobs's journey along the Underground Railroad and her time in the attic were analogous to what it means to constantly struggle toward freedom. There are moments when we find ourselves cast in a deep cloak of darkness, overrun with pests and unknown nuisances that seek to gnaw at us and eat away at our bodies. At other times, we can do nothing more than sit in the stillness and quiet, awaiting a freer day in the sun, in the light that we know is sure to come. Freedom is not always about the moments of celebration, the pomp and circumstance, or the big proclamations, declarations, and statements. It doesn't always come after a war or due to a march, protest, or the violent overthrow of a corrupt political leader. Freedom also rests in the quiet moments when nothing seems to be happening at all. In the waiting and strategizing. Freedom comes in the revolutionary choice to be unmoved by the State, to remain still, grounded, and planted in the truth that we each deserve to be fully recognized and respected in our bodies, beliefs, and objectives. Freedom comes when we are not even doing anything but continuing to live despite a world that does not want us to exist.

Toward Freedom

> Oh, freedom, oh, freedom
> Oh, freedom over me
> And before I'd be a slave
> I'd be buried in my grave
> And go home to my Lord and be free.[9]

The song "Oh, Freedom" likely gained mass popularity among churchgoing folks after the end of slavery. It reemerged as a rallying cry for Black Americans during the civil rights era of the 1950s and 1960s—a period marked by calls for desegregation of lunch counters, trains, buses, and other public spaces; school and public integration; and mass protests against macabre anti-Black violence all over the country. The idea of "freedom" in the song signifies the deeply Christian idea that we will all be free after death. It also signals that, for the slave, a newfound freedom lies on the other side of captivity. While there was no certainty about what that "other side" looked or felt like, there was certainty that it was not the captivity with which we had become so familiar.

Freedom as a Christian concept has long been connected to death and rebirth, mimicking the journey of the Savior Jesus Christ, who was born to the Virgin Mary, killed by the Romans, and raised from the dead by the Holy Ghost three days later. For enslaved Black people, who have had few other stories, rituals, and traditions through which to connect to this new world, Christianity often became a singular path to this notion of freedom. Through the persecution of the Israelites at the hands of stronger, wealthier, and more formidable races of people, many Black people have connected our long struggle for liberation to that of our biblical ancestors. Meanwhile, the stories of our most immediate family and those who passed on only generations ago tell a similar tale of constant struggle. They echo the narratives of patient long-suffering, perpetual oppression, and the specter of being the "other" for the duration of our lives on Earth.

For us, Black diasporic people, struggling for freedom has involved those biblical notions: having the faith, keeping the faith, hoping for the things we have never seen, and believing even when we have little evidence that our faith will result in anything of substance. We, the collective Black "we," have had faith and works, but so far, little to no real freedom. In my own childhood, the Christian messages I learned from the Bible and in church told me that the struggle meant I was doing it right. This intersected with my own Blackness because I was constantly struggling to be seen, acknowledged as equal, and respected like many of my non-Black peers. In its place, constrained forms of liberty and justice have been stand-ins for a freedom we've chased for generations. In the United States, the era of chattel slavery was followed by apartheid-style laws barring Black Americans from full citizenship or public movement. Debt slavery and the exploitation of Black sharecroppers reintroduced many newly freed Black people to modern forms of shackles and bondage as they were targeted for labor with little to no pay and burdened by flimsy legal structures that never intended to secure their rights as free citizens. With the failure of Reconstruction, lynching and the terrorization of

Black people became the status quo throughout the American South and in some areas in the North. In the generations since, Black Americans have collectively built countermovements to eradicate anti-Black violence and white supremacy. Black collective struggles like the Black Power movement and the Black Panther Party for Self-Defense have followed generally along these contested lines.

The freedoms we've enjoyed have often come to us after immense political struggle. For example, the Voting Rights Act of 1965 passed after the culmination of over two decades of civil rights confrontations led by Martin Luther King, Jr., Ella Baker, and members of the Student Nonviolent Coordinating Committee, like the late Rep. John Lewis. Even now, voting rights for Black Americans have been contested in many Southern states after that very same act was gutted in 2013 by conservative forces. This struggle has endured.

In thinking of this conundrum, I'm reminded of events like that on the Edmund Pettus Bridge on Sunday, March 7, 1965, when state troopers violently beat six hundred Black protestors, including Lewis, as they marched across the bridge to demonstrate in the name of Black people's right to vote.[10] The violence on "Bloody Sunday," as it is now remembered, was televised across the country so that U.S. citizens, especially white people in the North, could witness the vicious violence descending upon the peaceful protestors. Lewis's skull was cracked open that day. The Voting Rights Act of 1965 was passed two months later.

Bodily harm. Mental and emotional violence committed against our communities. Compromises to our own health, safety, joy, and peace. This is the price that Black Americans pay for freedom. Our freedom is fraught.

Lewis lived with the memory of the trauma and violence he confronted on that bridge until his passing in July 2020, which occurred during the same season that the world protested in response to the police killings of Breonna Taylor and George Floyd. Mass uprisings in cities around the globe were the hallmark of an already contentious summer as Black people were dying disproportionately from COVID-19, incarcerated populations were unable to socially distance from the virus, and houseless people were left with little scaffolding to address the effects of the pandemic. Lewis's passing in this moment was another reminder of the long struggle that continues even after our heroes pass on. His body was carried over the bridge one last time at the close of his memorial, a symbolic display of gratitude for his service to a country that almost killed him. But when many Black people saw this display, they reacted with disappointment. Why? Because it reminded Black folks once again that, even in death, the time when we should be truly free, we might still be marred by the violence, racism, anti-Blackness, and stereotypes that plagued us on this side. We may never escape it at all.

We see this time and time again. When Sandra Bland was killed in police custody in 2015, she was posthumously blamed for the conditions of her death. They suggested that her mental health resulted in her dying by suicide. Police authorities released videos of her traffic stop to suggest that her demeanor and "attitude" warranted harsh treatment. Even in death, she wasn't free from the binds of white supremacy. One thinks, too, of Trayvon Martin, whose hoodie was blamed for his murder, and Michael Brown, whose body size and his being "no angel" were used as justification for killing him. Korryn Gaines was blamed because she had a weapon to defend herself. Charleena Lyles was blamed for her death because she had a knife in her hand. Time and again, it remains clear that even on the other side, Black people are not allowed to rest. Freedom still comes with the terror and violence of white supremacist naming practices and the efforts of the State to absolve itself for its constant attacks against Black people of all shapes, sizes, skin tones, abilities, immigration statuses, genders, and sexualities.

For many Black women today, even in the wake of BLM and anti-racist discourse, freedom comes not only with terror and violence but also with the horror of physical assault, racial and gender discrimination, and personal threats. Black women are still punished by their employers for their physical features and body choices, such as natural hairstyles that are considered "unprofessional." Black women are still paid less than white men and women for the same work. Black women's bodies are frequently caricatured in mass media and depicted as being hypersexual and "unrapeable," perpetuating myths that Black women are stronger, impervious to pain, and available for public use and consumption. This is illustrated in the recent case rapper Megan Thee Stallion brought against Tory Lanez after he shot her in 2020.[11] During the trial, Megan was scrutinized in the court of public opinion while Lanez used his assault of the rapper to gain cachet among fans who cared little about the experiences Megan shared. Lanez was found guilty and convicted on three counts associated with the shooting.

In August 2023, Lanez was sentenced to ten years in prison.[12] Despite the court's findings, many have debated online about the validity of Megan's claims about the shooting.[13] This brand of gaslighting and denial stems directly from the idea that Black women are out to get Black men rather than reality that many Black women suffer at the hands of intimate partners, family members, community leaders, and other men they know. The perception that Black women's bodies are perpetually available, unprotected, and uncared for leaves so many exposed to senseless violence.

The conditions are even worse for Black women who are incarcerated.[14] These struggles pepper the landscape of the United States. They are the soundtrack Black women hear and experience as their lives play out. Even as "free" Black women today attempt to navigate the social world in their bodies, they are frequently under attack for their mere existence. So, what is freedom then? And how will we know it when we see it?

The concept of "freedom" has always eluded us as a people. While millions of Black people lived in bondage, fifty-six delegates to the Second Continental Congress of what would be the United States of America wrote these words in the Declaration of Independence: "We hold these truths to be self-evident, that all men are created equal, that they are endowed by their Creator with certain unalienable Rights, that among these are Life, Liberty and the pursuit of Happiness." For these middle-class, heteronormative, propertied white men, "we" referred only to other white men like themselves, and the life, liberty, and happiness they deemed "unalienable rights" applied only to white men who looked, believed, and behaved like them. Their conception of freedom was contingent upon the ways that people's identities were defined, recognized, and accepted into a larger society for whom slavery was not yet understood as a "peculiar institution."

For those of us committed to liberation and justice for all people, freedom is still a horizon upon which we have never cast our eyes. It is a promised land uncharted. Freedom is a theory, a land we've imagined that's full of abundance, where we no longer cry out for what we need and we no longer struggle to survive. It's a place where we are made whole. Or at least we hope. But freedom, like anything else, doesn't come in absolutes. It isn't a constant state of being nor is it a place, like the Garden of Eden or the land of milk and honey. When we—as citizens, as individuals fighting for a better world—conceptualize freedom as an endpoint, we fail to realize that freedom comes through the process of obtaining it. Every generation discovers this truth. It is the freedoms secured by the preceding generation that build an arc to the possibilities for freedom in the next. Every little freedom won by our forestrugglers has set us on a path toward new freedoms today.

Singer Nina Simone once said that freedom was living with "no fear." Angela Davis wrote a book called *Freedom Is a Constant Struggle*. In "Letter from Birmingham Jail," written in 1963, Dr. Martin Luther King, Jr., wrote that "freedom is never given voluntarily by the oppressor; it must be demanded by the oppressed." It is this last narrative on freedom that most succinctly sums up what it means to work toward getting free.

In many ways, unfreedom must exist for us to both understand and cherish what freedom truly is and has the potential to become. Black American history has shown us that freedom comes to us in feelings, moments, and contexts. It visits us, sometimes momentarily. We have to work hard to hold on to it. For us Black people, freedom has never been given, only worked for, earned, and taken back.

Over the years, students and audience members at talks have asked me questions like: How do we chase a freedom we've never seen? How do we know when we are truly free? What exactly is freedom? In response, I often jokingly tell them, "Well, maybe we'll just know it when we see it."

While my response is mildly facetious, I say it because, over my years in teaching, organizing, and political education, I've asked many people what freedom means to them and heard many different answers. Some have told me that freedom is about agency, choice, autonomy, self-control, simply doing what you want, or living on your own terms. For others, freedom is corporeal and about the ways in which they have been repressed or denied the ability to truly express their authentic selves. There is also a freedom that is rooted in mental health, emotional centering, and spirituality. They want to feel free within themselves so that they will feel aligned with their full lives. All these concepts of freedom are correct to some degree, especially because it's important to be able to define freedom for ourselves. Yet it's also time that we abandon a need to define what freedom is or isn't. Instead, I take from Jacobs the lesson that we must focus on and explore the fact that though we have never seen freedom, we continue to fight for it anyway. That's what the narratives of enslaved Black women like

Jacobs teach us: that we struggle toward a freedom we have never experienced and may never achieve in our lifetimes. It's through the act of getting free that we find our grounding and move toward the dreams of freedom we hold for ourselves, our children, and our communities.

Jacobs's narrative instructs us that freedom does not come easily. When it appears simple or straightforward, we should confront it with skepticism and critique because getting free requires a great deal of intention, care, and strategy if it is to be actualized. This is a process of personal responsibility. Every one of us must decide what freedom looks and feels like for our own lives and livelihoods. We must all take full responsibility for our own entanglements with white supremacy and anti-Blackness so that we can adequately account for our complicity in the systems that make others unfree. And, in exercising our own autonomy and agency, we each have accountability to others who may experience unfreedom at our hands. So, how do we "get free"? Taking Jacobs's guidance as a directive, I have organized my notion of freedom into four suppositions. These are by no means exhaustive, but they are an earnest start.

1. My freedom can never be contingent upon someone else's unfreedom.

After attending class together one day, my colleague and dear friend Uday Jain once explained to me that freedom and unfreedom work in a state of symbiosis much like dystopia and utopia. He told me how people's commitments to living in excess frequently mask their similar commitments to denying the basic needs of others. People are so committed to having their "slice of the pie" that they don't realize that freedom is infinite. It isn't a pie at all, he said. It isn't a limited resource. Rather it is unlimited, fully accessible, and available to everyone who simply believes that we don't have to hoard our way into happiness. After this conversation, I not only started to think more intentionally about what it means to do justice to myself and to others, but I also started to think more dynamically about what freedom is, how it manifests in our lives, and how we imagine freedom as inherently tethered to the permissions we give ourselves and others.

Unfortunately, our conceptions of freedom have often been reserved for the wealthy, the able-bodied, white Americans, heterosexuals, cisgender people, and religious zealots who have frequently used their group membership and elite status to alienate others and delimit other people's access to public spaces. Because of this, defining freedom for ourselves has often meant well-to-do people whisking their friends and loved ones off to swanky resorts on remote islands where tourists have exploited local Indigenous peoples, hoarding land that should be returned to the people to whom it first belonged, gorging themselves on food while others live in food deserts, and demanding that the State provide them welfare in the form of tax cuts while increasing the cost of living for working-class and poor people. On remote islands and Indigenous lands across the globe, wealthy (predominantly) white Americans have created tourist communities and enclaves that gentrify native lands and price out nationalized residents all in the name of capturing their "laissez-faire" dreams. These practices are rooted in a crude individualism that sees freedom as being all about personal excess. This doesn't create a fabric of freedom. Freedom and exploitation are enemies. Freedom and hoarding are mutually exclusive. Freedom and excess are not bedfellows. Freedom cannot exist in a world where these injustices remain.

2. Freedom is not absolute, but it is complementary.

Something that was hard for me to learn was that freedom may never be absolute. I've noticed this with my students as well. A certain disappointment sets in when I teach them about Jacobs and her freedom in the attic. When I tell them that freedom isn't clear, evident, or easy, they often ask me, "So, do you not believe in freedom? Will we ever get there?" I have to explain to them that I am hopeful. I believe in the work of my ancestors and elders. I believe in myself and in my community. I believe in our capacity to do what is good and right.

I may always encounter a world that allows me freedom in some instances but not in others. As a Black queer woman aware of the histories of anti-Blackness and white supremacy that undergird this nation's sheer existence, I know that my freedom is predicated on the whims of the State, which is carceral in nature. This means that our nation is predicated on crime-and-punishment logics that are always seeking to mark people as insiders or outsiders, citizens or "others," and people who belong or people who should be annihilated. Under the carceral logics of the State that prioritize surveillance and policing to manage public movement and access, freedom has typically been elusive, especially for people like me. But as long as I have enough food to eat and water to drink; a place to sleep and have a private life; access to the healthcare I need to prevent medical catastrophes; a healthy outdoor environment that doesn't threaten me with chemical toxins; resources for education and mental health support; and protection from racial, gender, and other systemic discrimination and terror, I should be discernably free.

As a Black queer feminist who fundamentally believes that none of us is free until all of us are free, it is incumbent upon me to want this for everyone, whether I like them personally or not. Whether I believe they are deserving or not does not matter. It is my job to hold regard and respect for the experiences, traditions, and struggles of others.

3. Freedom is about collective imagination rather than institutional barriers.

In her book *We Do This 'Til We Free Us,* abolitionist and organizer Mariame Kaba explains that an abolition politic stems from this practice of political imagination. She writes, "So an abolition politic insists that we imagine and organize beyond the constraints of the normal. . . . Our charge is to make imagining liberation under oppression completely thinkable, to really push ourselves to think beyond the normal in order for us to be able to address the root causes of people's suffering."[15] Abolition, in this context, refers to the end of prisons and the Prison Industrial Complex. I'll discuss this in more detail in a later chapter but, for now, it should be taken as an effort to eradicate not only the prisons themselves but also the punitive ideas and logics that many public citizens hold about "criminals" and "deviants." Many of these ideas are inherently anti-Black, anti-poor, ableist, transphobic, and anti-immigrant. The above quote from Kaba's book lies at the heart of modern abolition movements: the idea that we are in a crisis of imagination. It has been our lack of imagination that has hampered our ability to get free all along. To this end, Kaba suggests that what is possible may have never existed before. It may have been deemed impossible, out of this world, or too extravagant for our present society. Later, Kaba talks about her reflections on the words of Patrisse Cullors, one of the co-founders of the Movement for Black Lives, who once explained that even the carceral system was once just someone's imagination. Prisons and police had to be imagined before they could become real. Kaba frequently comments that everything worth doing is done in community. This extends to the ways in which we envision freer futures for ourselves and for generations to come.

The point was that we are limited only by what we imagine is possible for ourselves. When we abolitionists envision a future world, we envision it *outside* of the systems of disprivilege, corporal punishment, and anti-Blackness that have already shaped American society and much of the known world. We envision a world that has not been created yet. It's just in our imagination.

If we can imagine a system that is inherently unfree, we can certainly imagine otherwise.

4. We deserve freedom without suffering.

Tell me how I made it over Lord, God, Lord . . .
I'm gonna walk the streets of gold
It's the homeland of the soul

Epic and iconic gospel singer Mahalia Jackson sang the song above, "How I Got Over." The song is about getting to Heaven after a life full of striving and struggling to run the Christian race. While I always loved this song and so many like it growing up, I always wondered why the only rest and reward we ever really talked about as Christians came after such a grueling life. Getting "over" to the other side never included instructions about how to live on *this side* without it being just an awful and tenuous journey. Songs told me I would fall down and get back up again; they told me that rest would come in the morning but only after wailing and crying; they told me that I essentially had to endure an entire lifetime of pain before rest. So, I took those lessons to heart. I learned how to suffer. I learned well. Like so many of my comrades and community members, I sang the same hymns in church and expected my life here on earth to be full of turmoil and strife.

Many of my earliest lessons about freedom were about suffering. The message was that Black people were made to struggle their whole lives. I was socialized into believing that struggling was inherently associated with being Black. I learned these lessons so well that I punished myself when I felt joy. When I was able to have more food in my fridge because my mother's tax return had come in or when I was able to buy

a pair of expensive sneakers, I felt guilty that I wasn't perpetually suffering like my peers and family members. I watched
movies where every story about Black people was one of
trauma, slavery, violence, and death. And, growing up in Oakland in the 1990s, I encountered police surveillance in my
neighborhood and at school, reminding me that I was an outsider, a "deviant." Taken together, my notion of freedom was
predicated on the strife I endured each day. They were two
sides of the same coin. In many ways, my hardships seemed
like a prerequisite for a freedom I could only dream of. Like I
had to serve my time before I could actualize the freedom and
joy on the other side.

As I grew older, I internalized this idea of Black suffering
and lack of freedom. I felt guilty when I wasn't embodying
the broken-down nature that I had been encouraged to per-
sonify. When I met white college students and co-workers,
they were suspicious of my happiness. Was I lazy? Not working hard enough? Flippant? Arrogant? Whiteness frequently
sought a justification for my ability to find solace in myself. I'll
never forget the times I was badgered because I chuckled to
myself. "What's so funny, Jennifer?" they'd ask. Every facial
expression—positive, negative, or in-between—was read as an
invitation for white curiosity and questioning.

Because Blackness is so frequently read as violent and criminal, white people are on high alert no matter the countenance
of Black people they encounter. This is why, when Black people display public joy, whiteness is so threatened by it. We have
seen this in recent years, for example, when fifteen-year-old
Dajerria Becton was tackled by police officer Eric Casebolt
and thrown to the ground, with him thrusting his knees into

her back and neck, at a neighborhood pool party in McKinney, Texas, for a "disturbance."[16] Or when, in my own hometown, a white woman called the police on a Black family for using a charcoal grill at Lake Merritt, a public body of water frequented by many of Oakland's residents. She accused the family of "trespassing."[17] Public joy, for Black people, is always met with great distrust and suspicion. Sometimes even by other Black people.

Now I understand that there is no price to pay for freedom. I realize now that the logics that underlie that ethos are white supremacist and anti-Black in their origins. In my pursuit of freedom now, I center my own joy. My hope is that all Black people embrace joy as they continue to struggle for freedom.

CHAPTER 2

Ida B. Wells Taught Me Radical Truth-Telling

I was taught that the search for truth and the search for justice are not incompatible and are, in fact, essential.

—*Gwen Ifill*

To tell the truth is to become beautiful, to begin to love yourself, value yourself. And that's political, in its most profound way.

—*June Jordan*

Growing up, I remember hearing the phrase "the truth will set you free." Folks would mutter it at church. Elders would cleverly drop the saying when a cousin or friend was hiding some indiscretion or secret. I always thought this was a cliché saying, meant for children who were prone to lying. As such, I paired it with other sayings I frequently heard from the same people—in particular, one about skeletons in the closet that would one day come to light. This was another one of the many lessons I heard from adults about how lies would somehow always bubble to the surface no matter how much we tried to hide or suppress them. My overactive, childlike imagination meant that I was always anticipating skeletons falling out of my closet doors and onto the floor, clattering loudly and startling onlookers.

It was clear from the way they talked that these grown-ups were speaking from experience. As though a bone or two had popped out of their closets unexpectedly at some point, leaving them exposed and vulnerable. Rather than focusing on just telling the truth from the beginning, these adults emphasized the risks of telling lies and how they would haunt us. According to these narratives, lies were ugly, dark, dirty, and dangerous. Lies kept us complacent, immovable, paralyzed in our own fear and shame. For my elders and community members, telling the truth was about personal absolution, about untethering oneself from the burdens of hiding. But there was a certain necessity to keeping the skeletons at bay; lying was a mode of survival. It was a way to shield parts of themselves from the public world so that they could have some peace and solace in private. In many ways, then, telling the truth was just another route to a form of self-reliance and self-authenticity that eluded so many Black people. I didn't understand any of this yet, but I sensed it. The grown-ups around me never talked directly about the fear, the risk, the threats, and the ways that some of us would be punished for truths that weren't even ours in the first place. They never told me that some truths could get you killed, ostracized, excommunicated, or rebuked. They didn't say that the truth could also be used against you, to demean and diminish you. I imagine they never told me these things because some of these lessons were unspeakable. They were shared only in whispers between the elders who had seen and heard the truth.

I learned the risks and rewards of truth-telling from one of our greatest journalists and Black feminists: Ida B. Wells. Wells knew what it meant to tell the truth, even when that truth came at great peril and threat to her own life. Wells told the truth at a moment when doing so meant that one would be met with mob violence and unbridled white supremacist terror.

Wells was born in Holly Springs, Mississippi, in 1862. Slavery was still the law of the land at the time. She experienced great tragedy at sixteen years old when her parents and a sibling died of yellow fever, and she became a teacher to help care for her remaining five siblings. By the time Wells was twenty-five, she had moved to Memphis, Tennessee, and begun writing about lynchings of Black Americans in the South for the Black newspaper *Free Speech and Headlight,* which she co-owned. Her fight against anti-Blackness, racial threats, and the violence of white mobs had already become a centerpiece of her life. Though Wells had already gone through a great deal of turmoil, it was her experiences in Tennessee that shifted the focus of her life's work.

On March 9, 1892, Thomas Moss, Calvin McDowell, and Will Stewart were lynched by a white mob. These three Black men were prominent, active members of the Black community in Memphis and were co-owners of the People's Grocery.[1] The three men had long known about a white man named William Barrett, who owned a competing grocery store adjacent to their own. Apparently, Barrett felt threatened by their thriving business and employed intimidation tactics against Moss, McDowell, and Stewart in an effort to get them to close down their store. They wouldn't relent. After drumming up false evidence against

Black Americans in the neighborhood, insinuating that they were planning to start a war against white Americans, Barrett went to the People's Grocery with reinforcements, including plainclothes officers. After defending their store, Stewart, Moss, and McDowell were systematically targeted, hunted, and lynched. Not only were they killed, but their bodies were also maimed, dismembered, and left to rot on a public road where other Black Americans could view them. It was calculated and gruesome.

The lynching deeply impacted Wells, who knew Moss personally. Following the murders, Wells began documenting and reporting in great detail the macabre mob violence Black Americans were being subjected to all over the country, but especially in the South. Her pamphlet *Southern Horrors: Lynch Law in All Its Phases* (1892) stands as a singular archive of the accusations, court proceedings, and outcomes that faced Black Americans during this period of overt, state-sanctioned white terror.

As Wells began documenting lynchings across the American South, she noted that many of these cases were not properly reported by police, rarely proceeded through the court systems in accordance with codified law, and—just as important— were reported on by only a few newspapers across the country. Black people were targeted by lynch mobs for reasons as thin as making eye contact with a white person on the street or, in the case of Emmett Till, a decade after Wells passed, being falsely accused of making advances toward a white woman. Wells made it clear that the press was complicit in this violence, too. The white press frequently wrote about Black victims of lynch mobs, who were typically Black men accused of raping white women, as if they were inherently guilty. "Fried Over a Slow Fire," "Fixed for a Barbecue," and "The Assault on Woman Avenged" are just a few headlines that newspapers ran on the topic of lynching.[2] They sensationalized the brutality and murders like they were the opening act of a dramatic play rather than the horrible deaths of actual people. They, too, hid the truth from the public.

Wells wrote under the pen name "Iola" to protect herself and her identity, and she had a simple goal: to expose "the threadbare lie that Negro men rape white women."[3] This phrase comes from an editorial she published in the *Free Speech*. At one point, while Wells was away in New York on vacation, the *Free Speech* was ransacked by a white mob. Members of the mob threatened to lynch the owners of the publication and the writer of the editorial. Wells wrote, "Mr. Fleming, the business manager and owning a half interest [in] the *Free Speech,* had to leave town to escape the mob, and was afterwards ordered not to return; letters and telegrams sent me in New York where I was spending my vacation advised me that bodily harm awaited my return."[4] The mob threatened Flemings with castration, while "a former owner of the paper, Reverend Taylor Nightingale, had been pistol-whipped and forced to recant the words of the May 1892 editorial that had detonated the violent response in Memphis."[5] As a result of the violence, Wells lost her newspaper and had to start her life anew.

Reflecting on the experience, Wells wrote:

> Since my business has been destroyed and I am an exile from home because of that editorial, the issue

has been forced, and as the writer of it I feel that the race and the public generally should have a statement of the facts as they exist. They will serve at the same time as a defense for the Afro-American Sampsons who suffer themselves to be betrayed by white Delilahs.[6]

Rather than cower, hide, or turn tail, Wells used this experience—an effort to silence her—as fuel for her lifelong campaign against lynching. She began documenting lynching after lynching after lynching with great fervor, detailing the cruel and barbaric treatment that Black men, women, and children experienced at the hands of white mobs. This work didn't make Wells a popular woman. She wasn't rebuked only by white Americans in Memphis; she was also maligned by other Black civil rights activists.

The National Association for the Advancement of Colored People (NAACP) was founded by W.E.B. Du Bois, Archibald Grimke, and Mary Church Terrell, along with dozens of white progressives, in February 1909.[7] By that time, Du Bois had emerged as one of the most prominent Black intellectuals and activists of the era. He became the first Black American to earn a PhD from Harvard University in 1895. Grimke was born a slave and was a revered orator and writer on behalf of Black rights. As Angela Davis explains in her book *Women, Race & Class,* Terrell, though born to slaves, enjoyed familial wealth after her father received a considerable inheritance from his slave-master father. Terrell was one of the first Black women in the country to earn a college degree, attending Oberlin College. She became the first Black woman appointed to the board of education in Washington, D.C., and was the head of the National Association of Colored Women in 1896. While Terrell was deeply respected by other Black elites and academics, Wells was a fierce critic of Terrell's because she believed Terrell had worked to exclude her from the National Association of Colored Women's Club in Chicago. Wells believed that her campaign against lynching posed a threat to Terrell, who had built a very public career opposing racism and violence against Black Americans. Their ideological disagreements stemmed from differences between their political approaches. Where Terrell believed that Black people should engage in traditional methods of racial uplift (more in line with the expectations of high society), Wells advocated for direct action and grassroots confrontations. The two women's rivalry spanned decades and represents one of the many ways that Wells was often located outside of the mainstream Black intellectualism and activism of her time.

Du Bois had built a name for himself after leading the Niagara Movement, an elite Black activist organization that comprised lawyers, intellectuals, activists, and businesspeople, from 1905 to 1910.[8] The organization laid the groundwork for the NAACP in its strategic approach to calling out discrimination and anti-Blackness. Their approach typically involved litigation and formally challenging discriminatory laws so that they might be overturned nationally. They were committed to establishing Black Americans as equal citizens following the passage of the Thirteenth, Fourteenth, and Fifteenth Amendments. While these laws codified the rights and liberties of

Black Americans, they were not enforced equitably across the country, as history has since shown us. Jim Crow laws, Black Codes, and other policies kept Black Americans from accessing their full citizenship, their right to vote, and their right to due process in the early decades after the Civil War.

When Wells arrived at the founding conference for the NAACP at New York City's Charity Hall on May 31, 1909, she was not met with a warm welcome.[9] Over three hundred advocates for Black liberation were present, and many were not supportive of Wells's radical approach to lynching activism. They saw her campaign against lynching as too challenging to the status quo because of her gender—women were expected to be demure and reserved; Wells was neither—and the fight against lynching was extremely dangerous due to the growing numbers of Ku Klux Klan members and white mob–led pogroms targeting Black communities across the country. For many liberal whites and even Black Americans at the time, Wells's work operated outside of the elite and intellectual spheres of Frederick Douglass, Booker T. Washington, and W.E.B. Du Bois. Many feared that her demands for Black self-reliance, community defense, and boycotts of racist businesses might incite race wars and white retribution. At times, she was criticized for stirring up a "spirit of strife."[10] Wells was not interested in the performance of mythmaking and lying about the realities facing Black Americans. She was courageous in the face of violence and potential harm, and her courage encapsulated what it meant to be afraid and choose to do the right thing anyway.

Despite her unpopularity among her peers and contemporaries, Wells pushed ahead. She argued that the NAACP needed an investigative journalism arm to continue the work of researching—and spreading the truth of—the violence that Black Americans were encountering across the country. She presented statistical data supporting her claims. As the conference came to a close, the attendees began working to define a Committee of Forty, which would be the governing body of the NAACP at its inception. Wells had spoken with Du Bois and considered herself a shoo-in for the committee. Even though she was one of the more "militant" Black Americans in attendance, her work had been critical in shaping the discussion so far. In 1909, Wells was disappointed when the governing body of the NAACP was announced: Du Bois, the only Black member of the selection subcommittee, read the names of the Founding Forty, and she was not one of them.

In the decades since, many have debated over why Wells was denied this critical appointment, despite all she'd accomplished on behalf of Black Americans as an investigative journalist. Many have suggested that conservative Booker T. Washington supporters felt that Wells was an extremist who would make it harder for the organization to appeal to moderate whites. There were also concerns that Wells's working-class background and strident personality might not bode well in well-to-do, upper-middle-class activist settings. The fact that she was a Black woman who moved in all-Black spaces gave Wells a demeanor that the respectable Black leadership worried would embarrass them in front of white women. Regardless of their impetus, Wells's comrades abandoned her politically when they felt her truth-telling was no longer tenable for their political aims. When Du Bois offered Wells a chance to have her name added back to the roster of the Founding Forty, Wells declined.

Wells's experiences with white mobs, the white press, and fellow Black activists and intellectuals make it clear how truth-telling for Black women frequently places them in positions of precarity. For Wells, truth-telling made her the target of wanton violence. It undermined her critical and incomparable contributions to what we know today about lynching. For so many of us, Wells's example has been a guiding light, especially concerning the true lived experiences of Black women in the United States. She created not only a path but a rubric for what it means to speak truth to power even when the pressure from our peers, and society more broadly, asks us to remain in the closet with our skeletons.

For many Black women in the United States, our truths have always been watered down, erased, and ignored. The truth about Black women's pain, traumas, scholarly contributions, and central role in political life has long been treated as background noise. Wells highlights this fact when she discusses the ways in which Black women and girls were frequently left out of conversations about lynching in the United States, as if the crime didn't irrevocably shape their lives. After discussing the brutal lynching of a Black man named Ephraim Grizzard, who was accused of raping a white woman, Wells writes, "The 'honor' of grown women who were glad enough to be supported by the Grizzard boys and Ed Coy, as long as the liaison was not known, needed protection; they were white."[11] Even as Black men were centered in stories of lynching and white violence, white assailants remained protected when they inflicted sexual and physical harm on Black women and girls. Wells notes, "A white man was in the same jail for raping eight-year-old Maggie Reese, an Afro-American girl. He was not harmed. . . . The outrage upon helpless childhood needed no avenging in this case; she was black."[12] For Wells, there was a clear difference in the treatment and value assigned to white versus Black women. What's more, Black children were just as susceptible to sexual violence and murder as adults. There were no protections for Black people; Black women and girls were not excluded from this reality.

The "threadbare lie" that was frequently used as a justification for the hunting and murdering of Black men became a veil of secrecy for Black women, too. In many ways, the lie that Black men raped white women diminished the significance of Black women's roles in the Black community. It also put forth the idea that white women were the primary targets of rape and sexual violence even as Black women were being regularly surveilled and targeted by white men as they worked in white homes as domestic servants. Much like the lies regarding Black women's sexual lasciviousness during slavery that sought to absolve white slave owners of the guilt and shame of rape, the veil of secrecy over free Black women's lives established a status quo wherein Black women's lived experiences were backgrounded in all aspects of civic society, rendering them essentially invisible. Historian Darlene Clark Hine describes Black women's efforts to cloak their inner selves as a "culture of dissemblance."[13] This culture, she explains, stems from Black women's position at the intersections of race, class, gender, and regional variation. Many Black women had to adhere to secrecy about their experiences with racism, sexism, and sexual intimidation not by choice, but as a way to protect their inner selves. She writes, "The dynamics of dissemblance involved creating the appearance of disclosure, or openness about themselves and their feelings, while remaining an enigma. Only with secrecy, thus achieving a self-imposed invisibility, could ordinary Black women accrue the psychic space and harness the resources needed to hold their own in the often one-sided and mismatched resistance struggle."[14] Here, Hine suggests that some secrets are necessary for resistance. She sets forth that, for Black women, keeping community secrets, secrets that protect kin and comrades, is inherently different from keeping the secrets of oppressive forces that would rather Black people not survive. This form of secrecy is critical to the preservation of Black community-building and insulation from the potential harms of anti-Black violence.

As Wells models, for many Black women, standing fully upright in our truth increases our visibility. It leaves us exposed to the anti-Blackness and misogynoir that threatens our freedom and liberty, let alone our personal lives. The culture of dissemblance is a coping mechanism that Black women have often had to employ to protect ourselves from a world that has sought only to use us up, never to pour into us. Dissemblance is about resistance against a system that objectifies and commodifies Black women. It is a reaction to a world that says we are nothing more than our bodies, our limbs, and the labor we produce. In the case of Wells, she experienced the culture of dissemblance not only in her efforts to expose the ravages of lynching, but also while working to challenge Black leaders to radically act in opposition to the mistreatment of Black people all over the country. In many ways, Wells had to maintain degrees of secrecy in her own objectives, strategies, and activism because she was frequently unsupported and maligned even by those who should have been her greatest supporters.

Dissemblance is so important because it maintains a secretive element that is integral in creating space for Black women to build movements and resistance. It provides Black women with a form of cover to shield us from the potential violence and harm that would likely befall us. This is because Black women take on immense risk when we choose to speak, write, and champion the truth despite a societal commitment to misremembering, watering down, and whitewashing history. These risks are only amplified when they are displayed in public and witnessed by people who hold negative ideas about Black women's veracity, worth, and virtue. When examined over time, it becomes clear that Black women continue to confront the true nature of this society despite the risks to themselves.

The Truth About Western Medicine's Violence Against Black Women

One of the most sinister "secrets" I learned in my adulthood about Black women's experiences in the United States was concerned with their treatment in hospitals and medical institutions. For example, modern gynecology was built on the lie that Black women don't feel pain. J. Marion Sims, sometimes called the "father of modern gynecology," developed the speculum and many gynecological procedures by performing violent, brutal surgeries on enslaved Black women. These procedures were typically performed without anesthesia. Sims opened his first women's hospital in 1855. While many of the women he violated were largely forgotten, Sims was memorialized in statues and textbooks across generations.[15] It has taken well over a century for us to both recognize and interrogate the ways that Sims's violence against enslaved Black women undergirds the advances he contributed to Western medicine. What's more, the harm he enacted on Black communities was disguised in favor of a whitewashed legacy. Only recently have truth-tellers in social movement organizations succeeded in starting national conversations about Sims through social media and other mobilization techniques. For example, in the ongoing debate about the removal of Confederate statues across the country that has been occurring since at least 2017, young Black activists have staged demonstrations where they wear hospital gowns covered in blood below their torsos to depict the sexual and physical violence of medical experimentation on Black women's bodies.[16] These activists were protesting the brutality of memorializing a man who pioneered vaginal surgeries by maiming enslaved Black women. That this secret history was obfuscated—and selectively memorialized—by white Americans speaks to the kind of public misremembering that Wells fought against in her lifetime.

Even after slavery ended in America, Black women were still subjected to violence in their professional and private lives. Black women were often relegated to working in the homes of the very same white people who previously enslaved them and their comrades. In the North, well-to-do white Americans employed Black women as domestic workers in a strictly hierarchical system. During this period, Black women were subjected to all manner of intimidation, sexual violence, and coercion. They were often caught between trying to make money to support their families and facing the racism and violence of their white employers. These are the same women who were wives, mothers, sisters, daughters, and community members in the post-Reconstruction era between 1877 and the 1940s: They witnessed and experienced the state-sanctioned mob terror that Wells immortalized. Their struggles to survive despite that inhumanity and ruthlessness laid the groundwork for future battles in the Black liberation struggle.

In recent years, Black women have told this horrifying story. Leaders like Aislinn Pulley of the Chicago Torture Justice Center, an organization born of radical protest and challenges to the State, set the example for how we can tell the stories of violence, harm, and erasure of Black pain despite the systems that work to obscure those truths.[17] Filmmakers Ashley O'Shay and Morgan Johnson, producers of the film *Unapologetic,* have helped to show the ways in which young social movement organizers risk their lives and livelihoods to challenge the police state.[18] By confronting the public shame and historical erasure that masks so much of our archival knowledge, these young women activists, writers, and scholars have taken up the mantle Wells placed before us.

Civil Rights, Critical Race Theory, and White Misremembering

Following the legal and cultural gains of the Civil Rights Movement, a reactionary wave of campaigns to label Black people as criminals, drug addicts, and lazy moochers birthed the devastating War on Crime and the War on Drugs. The War on Crime was declared by President Lyndon B. Johnson in 1965, while the War on Drugs became a government initiative, led by President Richard Nixon, in 1971. These joint initiatives laid the groundwork for a cultural shift in the present day toward the hyper-surveillance and pacification of Black communities, which increased prison populations through disproportionate arrests and broke down the structure of Black families and communities. These national policies resulted in a pendulum-like shift toward conservative politics and Evangelical ideologies that prefer "colorblindness" and post-racial agendas to confronting the effects of the past three or so centuries of targeted anti-Blackness and violence. In chapter ten, I discuss the specific ways that policing in this moment irrevocably shaped Black lives.

Now, in a time when surges in conservatism around the globe have resulted in increases of anti-Black, anti-Asian, anti-immigrant, and anti-refugee sentiment and violence, I reflect on the ways that Wells's work has set the benchmark for revealing the truths that many would like to keep hidden. What's more, her work provides a model for exposing the systematic misremembering of history (and the present). Wells, like many Black revolutionaries and radical feminists, laid the foundation for a set of politics rooted in challenging the status quo and dismantling the existing anti-Black institutions at its core. The contemporary battles over how we metabolize and remember history, whether those struggles be over Confederate monuments and other racist landmarks, history textbooks and their accounting for slavery, or the Ivory Tower in whitening and watering down white supremacist violence in the United States, can all be analyzed through the framework of truth that Wells offers us.

For example, in summer 2021, a year after George Floyd was murdered by Minneapolis police and mass protests erupted around the world in response, a new war sparked on the right: the fight against critical race theory (CRT).[19] The term comes from scholars like race theorist Derrick Bell and Black feminist Kimberlé Crenshaw who, as early as the 1970s and '80s, coined the legalistic term to describe the study of institutional racism and systemic violence that stems from white supremacy. The term itself is just meant to denote the ways that race is an inescapable aspect of United States culture and institutional development. CRT as a method of analysis is rooted in facing history and taking full account of the ways that race shapes and impacts society today. The battle against CRT stemmed from conservative pushback against local school boards for teaching K–12 students about the impacts of race in society. Much of the consternation about this curriculum has emerged alongside opposition to the Movement for Black Lives. The sentiment is essentially that children and youth do not need to learn about the violence of race in the United States because it can change their opinions of white people. Some parents felt that these lessons, coupled with the ongoing protests around the globe, were upsetting their children or exposing them to a history that would unfairly alter their vision of the wholesomeness of the United States and its institutions.

These opposing forces on the ideological right were successful in getting the White House involved in their suppression of the truth. In September 2020, President Trump issued a memo calling CRT "divisive, false, and demeaning propaganda" that "is contrary to all we stand for as Americans and should have no place in the federal government."[20] The concern was heightened after the international focus on Floyd's death brought conversations about race, policing, inequality, and systemic racism to the kitchen tables and living room televisions of people all over the country. Conservative activists and parents have accused school districts of indoctrinating children, using CRT as a catchall term for any and all education related to gender, race, and even LGBTQIA+ issues.[21] In the months and years since these initial concerns were raised, states like Oklahoma, Idaho, Iowa, Texas, and Tennessee have banned the teaching of CRT.[22] These efforts to suppress history and misremember the truth are not random, nor are they just about children's textbooks and history curricula. They are deeply rooted in the propensity of white supremacy to retell and rewrite the world around itself so that others cannot hold institutions and individuals accountable for the harm that they cause and benefit from. Unfortunately, the battle against CRT is yet another extension of the history-remaking lies that Wells fought during her lifetime. Black feminists, educators, activists, and writers continue to struggle against the intentional misremembering of history today.

As an educator who centers the experiences of Black, queer,

trans, disabled, poor, and working-class people (and as a person who has experienced life in each of these areas), the attacks on critical race theory have been particularly discomforting. First, for many Black educators, especially those of us who are queer, these attacks remind us that many people in civic society remain unconcerned about our day-to-day lives or the ways in which systemic oppression shapes our livelihoods. The posturing against CRT and the truth of race in the United States reinforces what we already know about this country: that many white and heteronormative Americans would prefer not to engage in conversations, learning, or any confrontations that might hold them accountable for the fact that so many are forced to live in a state of secondary citizenship. On paper, we have the trappings of full citizens. However, in reality, we make less money from our jobs, experience more harassment from police, are less likely to have access to adequate health care, and are at greater risk for a host of detectable diseases that ail our communities. Second, attacks on CRT have put many educators at risk of losing their jobs or being prosecuted simply for telling the truth. The violence of being required to hide the truths of this country's oppressive history (and present) under the threat of legal action rings authoritarian and seems antithetical to this country's obsession with liberty and justice. Moreover, it is emblematic of the ways that the State works to punish and criminalize anyone who challenges white supremacy. Third, times like these reveal the very real threats to the safety and well-being of Black women who dare to tell the truth. Wells recorded and shared her experiences of being exiled from her home and run off from her publication after exposing the violence of lynching. In this moment of the twenty-four-hour news cycle and constant access to social media, Black women in online spaces are subjected to the same threats of violence, isolation, and harassment that Wells decried in her lifetime. In 2020, attacks on women journalists increased dramatically and included ad hominem aggression directed at the women themselves rather than at the content they produce.[23] These attacks have frequently escalated to include doxxing, the process of releasing personal information online, to put these women at risk of physical harm in their own communities or at their jobs.[24] Black women throughout history have been arrested, beaten, and killed for choosing to tell the truth about the country we live in. The consequences of truth-telling are very real, very tangible, and, in many cases, very life-threatening.

Black Women Journalists and the Risks of Truth-Telling Today

Black women rarely enter the archives and annals of history. Our experiences are often lost to time, long forgotten, or intentionally erased. One example is the story of Henrietta Lacks, whose cells were taken without her consent or knowledge when she visited Johns Hopkins Hospital in 1951, complaining of vaginal bleeding. Lacks was a mother of five and was suffering from an aggressive case of cervical cancer. Doctors biopsied her cells and found that, unlike other people's cells, which died quickly, Lacks's cells reproduced every twenty-four hours. This became a major medical discovery. Lacks passed away at thirty-one years old. Now her cells are called "HeLa" cells, which underlie much of medical science today.[25] Yet Lacks has only recently been acknowledged as the source of these critical, lifesaving advances in medicine. The film *The Immortal Life of Henrietta Lacks* tells this story through the eyes of her daughter Deborah Lacks, a journalist (played by Oprah Winfrey).[26]

Black women's exclusion from the archives, both intellectually and narratively, has undermined the historical contexts and conditions within which Black women have long struggled. Thus, it becomes the burden of Black women to reclaim and tell our stories, even when no one wants to listen. Accordingly, it makes sense why Black Feminism and the work of anti-racism has always been closely tethered to journalism and truth-telling. If journalism is, at its core, public truth-telling, it is a critical route for vulnerable people to reach and seek justice. Visibility, shining a bright light on events that have previously been obscured, has historically been a tool (among many) to confirm the veracity of our lives and experiences. As such, it is clear that Black women in the public eye continue to take up the cause of truth-telling despite the consequences. Many of those women continue in the journalistic tradition of Wells as a means to directly publish and champion the truth in news media. Yet Black women journalists today, such as Gwen Ifill, Oprah Winfrey, and Yamiche Alcindor, have ventured to speak about their specific experiences at the multiple margins of identity. They are examples of women who, like Wells, have been systematically targeted by white Americans, mainstream media, and other vigilante aggressors to dissuade them from speaking their truths.

Over the course of her long career, Ifill interviewed count-less politicians, including sitting presidents and presidents-elect. In 2004, during a televised debate, she asked Republican Vice President Dick Cheney and Democratic vice presidential candidate John Edwards about the AIDS epidemic and its disparately harmful impact on Black women in the United States.[27] In 2004, 27 percent of new cases of HIV were in women. Black women made up the majority of those cases.[28] In 2018, of the approximately seven thousand women who newly contracted HIV, four thousand were Black. That's 57 percent of overall new cases. Ifill's question was clearly discerning. This was during a time when George W. Bush's administration was passing tax reforms and other policies that were negatively impacting Black communities, but most pundits and journalists were focused on the aftermath of 9/11 and America's wars abroad. As Mary Curtis later wrote about Ifill's question, "They had forgotten those particular Americans, but Ifill remembered. And on a national stage, in a world preoccupied with a terrorist threat, her clearly spoken, well-researched words cut to the heart of the matter. That was Gwen Ifill. Among her many talents was artfully demanding truth from power."[29] It was Ifill who suggested that it was the government's responsibility to do something about the AIDS epidemic among Black women, who, she noted, were thirteen times more likely to contract the disease than other women. Ifill was more than a journalist. Like Wells, she was a Black woman rabble-rouser who was courageous even when it posed a risk to her career. Sherrilyn Ifill, Gwen Ifill's cousin, wrote in 2016 that "Gwen's real legacy lies in the values she displayed every day in her work—dedication to the truth, to civil discourse, to professionalism, and to human dignity—values our angry and divided nation needs today more than ever."[30]

Television show host and producer Oprah Winfrey delivered an iconic speech at the Golden Globe Awards in 2018 as she became the first Black woman to receive the Cecil B. DeMille Award. In the speech, Winfrey talked about the Black women in the United States who endure abuse and assault. She named Recy Taylor, who was brutally raped in 1944 by six white men in Alabama. Winfrey explained that Taylor's experience was shared with the NAACP and that Taylor had lived until she was ninety-seven years old. "She lived, as we all have lived, too many years in a culture broken by brutally powerful men. And for too long, women have not been heard or believed if they dared to speak their truth to the power of those men. But their time is up. Their time is up. Their time is up," she said to applause. She also mentioned the critical role of the "insatiable dedication to uncovering the absolute truth that keeps us from turning a blind eye to corruption and to injustice." She continued, saying that she values "the press more than ever before, as we try to navigate these complicated times. Which brings me to this: What I know for sure is that speaking your truth is the most powerful tool we all have."[31] In January 2018, Janell Hobson wrote about Oprah Winfrey for the African American Intellectual History Society blog *Black Perspectives*. She wrote that Winfrey "made the personal a global experience, expertly linking the struggles for a free press to pursue truth with women telling their own truths and being believed."[32]

Some of the attacks on Black women journalists and truthtellers are more clearly political. For example, Yamiche Alcindor, a *PBS NewsHour* correspondent, was repeatedly attacked by President Trump during his time in the White House. When she asked him about his handling of the global COVID-19 pandemic in March 2020, instead of simply answering her question, Trump called her "mean" and "threatening."[33] Specifically, he said, "Look, let me tell you something. Be nice. Don't be threatening. Be nice." On other occasions, Trump had cast Black women reporters' questions as "stupid," "racist," and "rude," so his response was unsurprising. But it still put Alcindor at risk for attacks from conservative bloggers, Trump supporters, and onlookers who shared negative sentiments toward Black people, especially women. Alcindor, like Ifill and Winfrey, was working to expose the inequalities many people were experiencing as a result of Trump's handling of the COVID crisis. It was her efforts to reveal the true nature of the disease and its impacts on citizens across the country that left her vulnerable to the attacks from the White House. It's important to note that Alcindor was inspired to enter journalism when she learned about the murder of fourteen-year-old Emmett Till in 1955. Till was killed after a white woman falsely accused him of whistling at her. "I wanted to be a professional witness," Alcindor says. "I wanted to be someone who was bringing the hard truth to America, who was forcing the country to look at the flaws of these promises that we make to treat every man and woman equally and how we don't live up to that a lot of times."[34]

Gwen Ifill, Oprah Winfrey, and Yamiche Alcindor, among so many other Black women writers and journalists today, represent the tradition that Wells set forth in her work. More important, they embody the types of personal and bodily risks that Black women take up when working on behalf of Black people and revealing the truths of white supremacist violence. What is most disappointing about this reality is that, as time passes on, the targeting of Black women truth-tellers has only become normalized and expected. In many ways, Black women's work to lay bare the harms Black people endure at the hands of the State is hazardous and inherently dangerous due to this normalization.

Telling the truth should not be radical. However, we live in a society that centers whiteness as a normative and faultless identity; prefers heterosexual coupling to all other forms of romantic companionship; positions men as inherently more valuable than women, femmes, and nonbinary people; and relies on invisible markets, which are inherently racist, to extract labor from poor people while the wealthiest among us hoard life-sustaining resources. This is what Black Feminists mean when they describe our status quo subsistence as being located in a white supremacist heteropatriarchal capitalistic society. It is the primary reason why so many Black Feminists argue that we must fearlessly tell the full story of our experiences at multiple margins of identity. In a hegemonic society such as this, we frequently confront the mythmaking mechanisms that help to perpetuate notions of American exceptionalism. In the process, these myth-creating systems also erase and rewrite the real, lived experiences of Black people and other vulnerable populations. This is the reason why the truth is so powerful and disruptive in a society like ours: because, for generations, those in power have rewritten and overwritten history so that they are always the victors and heroes. They have made Confederate soldiers into brave warriors fighting against tyranny, and they've turned genocidal murderers and criminals into hapless explorers and adventurers who stumbled upon the already-occupied lands they named "America." Not only have white supremacist ideas dominated our conceptions of what is worthy of being considered "our" history, but they have also shaped and influenced what we record, retell, and teach new generations.

Telling the truth is about much more than honesty and transparency. It is about cataloging and remembering ourselves. It is about creating an anthology and language to translate and interpret contemporary events. Telling the truth is about believing in the ability of those who come after us to do what is right. As Black women, we have often been so afraid of what might happen when our truths are discovered or potentially used against us. At times, we are scared to death. But telling the truth is about self-love. Telling our truths frees us from the shackles of other people's expectations. Telling the truth about the ways that we love, the ways that we desire, the ways that our bodies move and grow, and about what we want for ourselves—that's how we liberate ourselves and our communities.

Telling Our Own Truths

I struggled to write a chapter about truth-telling. I didn't feel prepared or experienced enough. For most of my life, I didn't tell the truth. At least not the whole truth. I didn't tell the truth about my gender or my sexuality. I didn't tell the truth about my desires. I hid them all away because I was ashamed of myself. I was afraid of what might happen if people knew who I was—like, *really* knew. I had seen how other Black people were punished when they bent their wrists too much or banged the tambourine at church too femininely (whatever that means). I noticed how other young Black girls were called "hos" or "fast" when they expressed the normal desires of adolescence. As their bodies developed naturally, these criticisms usually got even worse. They socialized young women into silence. Over the course of my girlhood and early adulthood, I was frequently rewarded for comporting myself to fit the expectations of others rather than embracing the natural and instinctual ways of being that emanated from my inner self. I came to realize that sitting at the nexus of Blackness, girlhood, queerness, disability, and working-class life would often mean that I wouldn't be allowed to walk in all of my truths simultaneously and that I would usually have to find the ones that made others most comfortable.

These implicit norms kept me silent about a whole host of truths I knew about myself. Though I knew I liked girls as early as third grade, I made sure to tuck that away in my closet with all my other skeletons. I had already seen the way people talked about my uncles and other gay people at church. They whispered, made eyes, and questioned the validity of such relationships. In high school, when I failed at heterosexual dating and looked awkward every prom season as I tried to assimilate into norms not made for my body, I chalked up my unconvincing behavior to nerves and anxiety. I hoped I would get better at lying eventually and that the skeletons would fit in the closet a little more neatly. But I never did, and they never did, either. Instead, I learned more about myself—that I was not only queer but also polyamorous and genderqueer. I didn't have words for any of this at the time, but I knew that I didn't agree with monogamy and I didn't always feel like a girl. Sometimes, I felt like no gender at all.

Holding my truths away from public sight taught me a lot about myself and the world around me. I began to understand that people would reward me for not ruffling feathers, for adhering to the status quo, and for moving in alignment with the general mores and expectations of others around me. I learned that stuffing my closet full of secrets would grant me a certain freedom of movement in public that, while inauthentic, felt like being "normal." And, even though that normalcy was a lie (as all normalcy is), it would sometimes clothe me like a warm blanket in winter. It would cloak me in a form of safety and calmness that I desired and even liked.

In response, I pretended to be stronger on the outside than I felt on the inside. I put on a face that emoted agency and power even when I felt unanchored and powerless. On the street, I tried to look more masculine to give the impression that I was unassailable, untouchable, and unmovable. In classrooms, I overprepared and overemoted so that no one would think I was unintelligent or could belittle my knowledge. At work, I tried my hardest to be "professional." I straightened my hair and dressed in preppy clothes that I couldn't afford and that were often uncomfortable. Then I would go and cry in the bathroom or my car at least once per day. Contorting myself felt like the most vulgar and violent chore. It was only worsened by the fact that I was doing it to myself. I felt such immense pressure to be "normal" by avoiding my Blackness, queerness, and gender questioning in public that I started to avoid those parts of me everywhere. I figured that it was less challenging and risky to simply cope in these ways than to always be the unpopular one in the room, the troublemaker, the shit-starter, or the instigator.

Sadly (and maybe fortunately), I learned that holding my truths in this way would always leave me disconnected from my true self and, therefore, disconnected from my people and my community. I figured out that the truth connects us to memory and to our ancestors. It connects us to community and to loved ones who, like us, are searching for parts of themselves that have been long lost. It is a bridge across which we can rediscover pieces of ourselves that were stolen, denied, and neglected. But for Black Americans, truth-telling has always been fraught because the nature of subordination, oppression, and exploitation is to erase truth and overwrite the past. They set forth a present that meets up with a status quo meant to delimit our identities and deny us full access to ourselves. In contrast, truth-telling is a process of self-reflection, unlearning, facing shame, and engaging with the unknown parts of ourselves.

Because of the stories I had been told or seen on television about my inherent inability to feel fullness or to experience real pain, I gaslit myself. Those stories were only reinforced when I witnessed other Black women around me coping in the same ways. Many were in unhappy marriages with men who were chauvinists and womanizers. Some wanted to pursue other careers and take on more political responsibility but were often discouraged by folks around them who diminished their potential. Others pursued their dreams only to be punished by people in their community for thinking they were "all that" or "too good" for the neighborhood anymore. I internalized all of these messages, whether they were explicitly stated or not. They made clear to me that my race, gender, class, and sexual orientation made me someone "other." They marked my body as inherently deviant and criminal. These messages taught me stigma and shame well before I knew those words. Eventually, I sometimes became the voice in my own head telling me stories that made me an extra in the stage play of my life. I stopped being my own main character. At times, my limited truth-telling was a reaction to my perception that violence would soon meet me if my truths were exposed. At other moments, I told partial truths about myself to protect the tender spots and hide the vulnerable places from predators. I learned how to participate in the culture of dissemblance before I grew into a woman. It was necessary to survive adolescence.

Because of the instinctual nature of these exercises in "untruth-telling," I've had to come back to myself and to my truths time and time again. I've had to check in with myself about what is true about me today. Who am I right now? What are my philosophical commitments at this very moment? How do I make clear who I am and what I stand for in every room I enter? What am I willing to lose for this freedom? Through therapy, community accountability, and a deep love for my ancestors, spirits, and self, I have grown to realize that the concern was never about the bones cooped up in my closet or falling out. The concern was about having to encounter rejection from a world that already wanted people like me to be invisible, unheard, and irrelevant before they knew about even half of my so-called skeletons.

The skeletons weren't indiscretions. They weren't acts

against humanity. They were truths about my identity and my struggle against white heteropatriarchal capitalism. Hiding them in my closet was akin to Wells calling herself "Iola" to shield herself from the violence that would certainly befall her if white supremacists were to discover her true identity. For Black women throughout history, truth-telling has been one of the most challenging and fraught acts. While the rewards are immeasurable, it does not eradicate the unrelenting isolation, exclusion, discrimination, and violence so many of us confront just for fully embracing our identities, communities, and lives.

Without knowing, embracing, and believing the truth about ourselves, our histories, and our present conditions, we leave our stories to be written by mythmakers and fairy-tale writers. In every society, the political actors who have control of the narrative and the archive are often the oppressors. Black Feminists associate this form of historical deceit with the culture of domination rooted in white supremacy. In her book *Sisters of the Yam: Black Women and Self-Recovery,* bell hooks writes, "White supremacy has always relied upon a structure of deceit to perpetuate degrading stereotypes, myths that Black people were inferior, more 'animalistic.'"[35] Essentially, hooks notes that lies about Black Americans have been foundational to re-producing the anti-Black status quo. This status quo allows for the realities of the United States' violence to proceed without real accountability. When we avoid the difficult truths about slavery, racial injustice, state-sanctioned violence, mass incarceration, policing, and the like, we fail to confront the ugliest parts of ourselves and our histories. We set ourselves up to make the same mistakes over and over again. And we do injustice to ourselves and others.

It took me lying about my sexuality and struggling with my gender (even into my midthirties) before I understood what it really means for the truth to "set you free." After my father passed away in 2014, I felt a new freedom that emboldened me to begin exploring what my queer life might look like. After years of comporting myself to fit white middle-class standards to collect a paycheck and to fit into heteronormative society (the collection of social norms that make heterosexual coupling the status quo and all other forms of coupling "other"), I was tired of hating the parts of myself that wouldn't simply assimilate and become "normal." Instead, I began to systematically give up on whiteness, straightness, and normalness before I really understood how to find the truth I was meant to tell. While I didn't have the words, I searched for other queer people with whom I could find respite. I built safe spaces among other polyamorous people who were focused on a Black liberation ethic. And I took my time in telling my truth to the world. Yet it was hardest to tell my truth to myself. It took so much from me to tell my truth that sometimes I felt like everything had been stripped away.

Telling the truth is not just about freeing ourselves from the weights that press down on us. It isn't just about shining a light on those things that lurk in the dark. Telling the truth is about vulnerability, intimacy, showing up for ourselves and our comrades, and accountability to those we hold dear. Truth-telling opens up new sites of tenderness. It makes the sensitive places that we've left hidden under hurt, grief, and past trauma softer. Truth-telling frees us. But even more than that, it has the potential to radicalize us.

For many Black women, telling the truth about ourselves is

a tangential practice of history-making and history-living. We reclaim ourselves from one world while writing another wherein we exist as our full selves rather than as the pieces left for us. "Well-behaved women rarely make history" because women are *expected* to be well behaved. They are expected to align themselves with the status quo, becoming machinations of the larger processes and systems that often discriminate against them. It is when women, especially Black women, intentionally disrupt that expectation by living more fully in their identities, moving away from traditional notions of femininity, and protesting the limitations set on our intellects and bodies that we open up the world for a new way of being. This site of contention is also a site of social and political opportunity to reimagine the world as a place where our experiences and lives are centered and respected. I imagine that's what Wells intended when she forcefully and persistently demanded that the truth of lynching be public record and that those lives stolen by white supremacy be honored and esteemed.

How do we, Black women, protect ourselves from this cycle? How do we find ways to insulate ourselves from a process that disbelieves us and forces us to bear witness to the horrors of our own exploitation? The answer is community. Writing this book is just one example of that work to resist the erasure of our stories and experiences. Telling our own stories, stories of solidarity with our kin and comrades, illustrates how our communities are often our first sites of refuge and vulnerability in a world committed to misunderstanding us. Joining in community with others who recognize, regard, and honor the fullness of Black women's lives (the good and the bad) is a form of truth-telling. It is a way to see the truth in others and to honor the truths we hold about ourselves. Making space for Black women to stand fully upright, relieving us from having to hunch ourselves over and shrink into rooms that were never built for us, that is how we fight. But most important, that is how we survive.

CHAPTER 3

Zora Neale Hurston Taught Me About the Reclamation of Our Labor

In search of my mother's garden, I found my own.
—*Alice Walker*

If you are silent about your pain, they'll kill you and say you enjoyed it.
—*Zora Neale Hurston*

Growing up, I never understood what it meant to truly labor for something that mattered to me. I knew a specific form of "labor" as a verb, a thing that people with uteruses did to bring new life into the world. Labor was an invisible process that many Black women in my community went through after months and months of carrying a baby in their belly. They would go into the hospital and then *boom,* a baby would be snuggled in their arms. As I got older, I learned that the process was much more complex—and much more painful—than that. It involved invasive medical procedures and was often riddled with a great deal of risk to these people's bodies. But they did it anyway because they believed in the future. And, clearly, they believed in something greater than themselves.

Labor, as I understood it, was about newness, blessings, miracles, and the promise of bringing forth a future filled with possibility. It was about meeting the ends of our imaginations with courage and stepping forward into the unknown with hope and excitement. Labor was meant to push us toward a new way of living, healing us and growing us by necessity. Even though I didn't want to have any children of my own, I held a deep respect for the process of laboring for others and giving one's life and body to do so. The sacrifice seemed like a worthy endeavor. But, in witnessing the experiences of my foremothers and community members, I saw that Black women's labor was not always regarded in the ways it should be. What's more, Black women would often labor in silence, out of the public eye, and in ways that were frequently overlooked or ignored. It was at eleven years old, when I first picked up Hurston's work, that I learned that Black women would always be seen as "de mule uh de world."[1] Through her writing, I began to see the complex ways that Black women's love, lives, and livelihoods have been critical sites of identity-making and personal struggle.

Finding Zora Neale Hurston, Reclaiming Her Labor

Hurston was an American author, anthropologist, and folklorist who lived in New York City during the Harlem Renaissance. She emerged as a part of a Black cultural class that defined a generation, and she would go on to become one of the most important Black Feminist authors of the twentieth century. Though Hurston published alongside prolific writers like Langston Hughes, Countee Cullen, and James Weldon

Johnson, her work was undervalued during her time. While many of her contemporaries, like Alain Locke, lauded her work, her use of African American dialect drew both praise and critique.[2] Some criticized her rendering of Black life, with the most vocal critic being Richard Wright, who accused Hurston of "cynically perpetuating a minstrel tradition meant to make white audiences laugh."[3] Many of her critics felt that her illustrations of Black people were simple, backward, and diminishing. Hurston was writing what she knew. A proud Black girl from the "Negro town" of Notasulga, Alabama, Hurston wrote of her hometown as the site of the "the first attempt at organized self-government on the part of Negroes in America."[4] Hurston's embrace of this rich Southern heritage would show up in her novels and lace the pages of her stories. Unfortunately, her books later went out of print for decades, and she struggled to feed herself on her meager income.[5] Because she was written out of the Black American canon, few knew of her legacy and her literary work until years after she passed away in 1960.

Hurston's posthumous celebrity is largely due to the heroic efforts of Alice Walker, one of her contemporaries. Walker never met Hurston, but she was compelled to go and search for her after discovering her writing and feeling tethered to the beautiful stories about Black people.[6]

In 1973, Walker went through considerable effort to locate Zora Neale Hurston's unmarked grave. Hurston was so financially unstable at the time of her death that members of her community had to come together to raise money for her funeral and burial. Her family didn't attend, as they were estranged. Walker asked inhabitants of Hurston's hometown to guide her through the community, claiming to be Hurston's niece, seeking a burial place that could only be found through word of mouth. Soon enough, Walker learned the location of the cemetery, the Garden of Heavenly Rest. What she found there surprised her: "As far as I could see there is nothing but bushes and weeds, some as tall as my waist."[7] The burial grounds spanned over an acre of land and looked "more like an abandoned field."[8]

Hopeless, swimming through the weeds, trying to use worn stones as landmarks, Walker yelled, "Zora! I'm here. Are you?"[9] As she called out, Walker stepped backward. Her foot sank deep into a hole. The six-foot-long rectangle was precisely where the map placed Hurston's grave. It was a moment of reclamation. "There are times—and finding Zora Hurston's grave was one of them—when normal responses of grief, horror, and so on, do not make sense because they bear no real relation to the depth of the emotion one feels," Walker writes.[10] "It was impossible for me to cry when I saw the field full of weeds where Zora is . . . because there is a point at which even grief feels absurd."[11]

Who will resurrect Black women's legacies but other Black women? This question seems to have haunted Hurston as well. Her writing foretold a day when she might meet defeat. And yet she never intended to go without a fight. Looking back on her life, Hurston wrote in her autobiography, "I have been in Sorrow's kitchen and licked out all the pots."[12] Later she wrote:

> What I had to swallow in the kitchen has not made me want to low-rate the human race, nor any whole sections of it. I take no refuge from myself in bitterness. To me, bitterness is the under-arm odor of wishful weakness. It is the graceless acknowledge-

ment of defeat. I have no urge to make any conces-
sions like that to the world as yet. I might be like
that some day, but I doubt it.[13]

These are the words of a woman who fought tirelessly to bring
her writing into the world against a tide of people who believed
her to be out of her depth, underprepared, and unrespectable.
She confronted her forced obscurity with courage, grit, and
sheer will. She labored and toiled despite opposition from people
who intentionally misunderstood her, including her own kin
and comrades. Hurston's political and artistic project was about
depicting the fullness of Black life, not just the elites or well-
to-do Black folk who were palatable to white Americans. Those
descriptions didn't reflect the variety of Black experiences she
had grown up with in Black, rural Alabama. Yet, this is part of
the work. The nonlinearity of Black liberation efforts means
that there are never any guarantees that we will share ideological commitments, beliefs, approaches, or concerns. This is especially true where it concerns Black women, who were often
opposed by Black men who were against formalizing a gender
analysis within Black movements because they believed it might
detract from the more general work of Black struggle. For Black
Feminists like Hurston, the fraught nature of laboring on behalf
of people who might reject her was a central part of the battle.

Finding My Foremothers, Reclaiming Their Labor

I walked through the massive cemetery, searching for her
gravestone. I knew she was there. I had no idea where, but I

felt her spirit. The spring air was crisp and light. The clouds looked like wisps of cotton candy that had been gently pulled away from their tubing. The sun shining on the grass gave the illusion that this was a place that had never seen hurt. Birds fluttering in trees overhead, butterflies flitting about, and a few visitors quietly shuffling through the campus were about all the movement I could see. I had stopped by the visitors' center on my drive in to get a map of the area. In the top right corner I could see her name: *Clara Mae Logan.*

Gravestone after gravestone, paver after paver, I hiked through the hilly cemetery, searching for a grandmother whose memorial had happened on a freezing day many winters before. I was only seventeen when my grandma Clara died, and I hadn't understood how or why such a loving and gentle woman was no longer in my life. Within that overwhelming sense of loss, I felt pieces of me retract and fall away. My grandma Clara had always been so kind and soft with me. She'd let me be a child. She'd seen innocence in me that many others hadn't. I'd treasured her.

Despite all of this, my relationship with Grandma Clara had been complicated: For most of my childhood, I thought that she was my father's biological mother. No one told me otherwise, and their close, special relationship had exhibited precisely the type of mother-son bond I hoped to one day have if I ever raised a boy. But one day, when I was eleven, my mom received a call from my dad with some news.

"Your grandmother passed away," she told me after she got off the phone.
"Grandma Clara?" I replied, tears welling up in my eyes.

"No." She looked back at me, puzzled. "Your father's real
    mom. Christine."
"Who is Christine?" I asked.
"You know who Christine is," my mom scolded before mak-
    ing eye contact with me. "Oh, no one ever told you?"
I shook my head. My eyes began to fill with tears for a differ-
    ent reason.
My mother softened her gaze and hugged me.
"Hold on," she said.

She stepped away as I began crying for a grandmother I didn't
know and never would. She returned with a photo album and
showed me pictures of a woman with my cheekbones, the same
slanted eyes I saw every morning in the mirror, and the brown
and yellow undertones in her skin that I had, the ones that
made me three shades darker every summer. This woman belonged to me. There was no doubt about it. There was even a
picture of Christine holding me as a baby. She knew about me
for eleven years, even as I had no idea that we belonged to each
other.

I found out that day that Clara was my great-aunt. She
adopted my father when he was a small child. Neither my father nor my mother had ever shared this with me, likely due to
the shame it invoked for my father: He was the only one of
Christine's seven children to be given away, and he clearly always harbored something against her for giving him up. At
eleven, I didn't have the maturity or language to process my
feelings, but I know now that I felt betrayed. I felt betrayed
because I was not told who my real grandmother was. I felt
betrayed that everyone knew the secret but me. I felt betrayed

that she had met me as a baby and chosen to stay out of my life anyway. And I felt equally betrayed by the suggestion that somehow my grandma Clara wasn't my real grandmother. She was the woman who had taught me to roller-set my hair and spent hours giggling with me while we watched old TV shows and read Terry McMillan books that were inappropriate for my age. Grandma Clara was the one who called me on every birthday and holiday. She was the one I took for granted, as grandchildren often do.

After learning this family secret, I never asked my grandma Clara about Christine. The shame had been effectively passed on to me. I hid my feelings of anger toward my parents for hiding something so critical to my existence. I swallowed down the hurt when my cousins talked about all the fun they had with their "Grandma Christine," going school shopping and just hanging out. I tuned out everyone's familiar stories of Christine because I had none. I suppressed the parts of me that felt rejected, disposed of, and isolated by my own kin. Instead, I just searched for my grandmother in Clara. *She* was real.

At the cemetery, I struggled with my guilt. I was in my early twenties, had gone off to college, gotten married, had a child, and started a life without ever coming back to visit my grandmother. It felt like I had betrayed her, too. It had been seven years since that gloomy morning when my grandma's body was lowered into that grave. My father's face had been so cold and stoic that he had looked like a statue erected in that cemetery.

How could I have let so much time pass? How could I not have shown up for the one who had shown up for me? Feeling like a wayward granddaughter, caught up in a world so far from my grandmother and so committed to forgetting her, I trudged through the grass and weeds, sobbing. My partner walked with me, my firstborn child in tow.

Then, out of nowhere, we found her. Viny growths like taut rubber bands stretched across her quaint and understated gravestone. Next to it was the gravestone for Clara's husband, John Logan, a man who'd died before I was born but whom I understood to be the love of her life. I ripped away the foliage, leaned over the grave, and cried from the deepest parts of me. Tears fell on the stone, changing it from a light slate gray to a deep near-black. Little circles appeared on the gravestone, bringing life to the cold surface that had not been touched for years. Through my tears, all I could utter was "I'm sorry."

I've since tried to recover information about Clara, craving knowledge of her and the life she lived. My father recently passed away, and I realized that my children and I were her last living descendants. I searched through the few family records I had on hand, given to me by my stepmother as a sort of inheritance from my dad's passing. There was nearly nothing there. A few pictures here and there. A few letters.

Growing up, I had learned about how hard it was for Black Americans to hold on to the memories and details of their pasts due to intergenerational trauma, slavery, and the anti-Blackness that had permeated every institution in the United States. I had seen commercials on television for Ancestry.com and 23andMe.com promising would-be customers that they could trace your lineage back generations. I was always tempted to join in with the waves of Americans who were trusting these private organizations with their genetic information. I wanted to know who my people were, where they came from, what connections to the continent of Africa I had, and how my people had zigzagged across such a treacherous landscape for so many centuries.

For many Black Americans, tracing our histories back beyond a few generations is nearly impossible. This is an intentional byproduct of anti-Blackness and the history of racial discrimination that brought Black folks into the United States as chattel rather than humans. For many Black Americans whose ancestors and elders were forcefully removed from their indigenous communities, tracing heritage remains a site of tenderness and trauma. It is a gaping wound that reminds us that we once belonged not to ourselves, but to others. For me, this manifested in bouts of tears and anguish every so often when I struggled to put the pieces together.

Feeling like I needed to find more traces of Clara than the meager archive I'd inherited, I took to the Internet, searching for any information about this woman who had been a real and present force in my life. I searched for her name, her last city of residence, and any details I knew of her life. But I couldn't find her there, either. I didn't know where to find her obituary in my father's possessions. I searched and searched and searched again. Looking for her, and for me. Feeling hopeless, I called the cemetery, hoping that they had something to identify her. At this point, I was starting to feel like I had failed my grandmother again. I was starting to feel guilty that this woman, who had had such a deep impact on my childhood, was fading both from my memory and from the material world in ways that I couldn't control. Crying, I called my mom and told her about my fruitless search, and expressed feelings of shame for having never been able to catalog her life or record a detailed history of her experiences as a young Black woman living in California during the Civil Rights Movement. I felt a deep guilt for having so few pictures of her, and none of us together.

"I think I still have a copy of the obituary," my mom said to me.
A wave of relief swept over my body.
"Wow, can you take a picture for me and send it to me?" I exhaled. She agreed.

That was something, something more than I had. And it would have to suffice for the time being.

Finding Myself, Reclaiming My Labor

I was sitting at my desk on a warm summer afternoon at Disneyland. It was my first job out of college. I was twenty-three years old, five months pregnant (a fact I had only recently shared with my employer and colleagues), and a newly minted first-gen college grad. Working at Disneyland as a Workload Staffing Analyst was the job of my dreams. I was the only person in the department with an engineering degree and one of the only college-educated people on the team. I was also the youngest, one of few women of color, and someone who had been hired from the "outside." This meant I didn't get my start working in the theme parks or some other funneling position to build my way up to a salaried job. I was chasing after my American Dream.

On this particular afternoon, I felt what seemed like a looming migraine. I was used to pushing through migraines at work because being a respectable, company-friendly woman meant that I couldn't present myself as fallible, imperfect, or human. But this pain was different. It throbbed so deeply that it made me hold my breath. It hurt to think. The room felt so bright I could barely keep my eyes open. Every time I peered at the ceiling or the windows, I could feel the rays of light hitting the back of my skull. Holding my head up felt like balancing a bag of bricks on my neck. I could tell that something was very wrong, and I was afraid.

I tried to keep working, plucking away at emails, building spreadsheets, and setting up meetings to manage what was our busiest time of year. I was also keenly aware of my mostly white colleagues watching me, whether overtly or not, from their desks in our open working space. I was so afraid that if I was perceived as not working hard enough, or not giving my job my best effort, then I would be punished. (I would later learn that this feeling wasn't just paranoia on my part: Some of my co-workers were tasked by our bosses to "keep an eye" on me—the new, young, college-educated Black girl.) Despite my efforts, I could no longer bear the pain, nor keep my head and neck upright. I laid my head down on my keyboard.

"You okay over there?" a co-worker asked. She was a white woman who had long made it clear that she did not like me. Not only that, but she had also personally put me in awkward and uncomfortable situations, once discussing my marriage at work and inviting me into a conversation about gender and sexuality in front of our entire team.

"No, I don't think so. I think I need to go home," I whispered.

Talking was incredibly difficult, and the sound in the office (though relatively quiet) was only making the throbbing worse. Soon, the pain started to go down my spine. I started to feel nauseous. I swallowed hard, stood up, and walked about twenty feet to my manager's office. I alerted her that I would be leaving. "Okay," she responded drily, an unimpressed and quizzical expression on her face. I gathered my things and headed to the tram, which provided the short rides we used to get from the offices at the amusement park to our designated parking area. I held my eyes closed and bit my teeth down hard to counter the pressure on my skull. The sunny Orange County afternoon was too much for my sensitive eyes. When I tried to stand up and walk to my car, my legs felt heavy, as though I was wearing ankle weights and wet shoes.

I made it to my car, crying from the pain and also the fear of being alone. The idea of driving seemed impossible to me, so I lay down in the passenger seat, opened my eyes just wide enough to see the screen of my phone, and called my partner, Daren. "I can't walk or drive. It hurts so bad," was all I managed to say. He asked me where I was. I slurred my words as I described the parking area to him. Then I lost consciousness.

Miraculously, Daren was able to retrieve me from the parking lot. He drove me to the emergency room. After moving through a few holding rooms and writhing in pain on floors and gurneys, I was admitted to the hospital. The hospital staff worried that my spinal fluid was too low, and that I was at risk of losing my limbs—or possibly even my life. Several spinal taps later, I was told that I had contracted E. coli meningitis, a disease so contagious that staff and family members were required to wear hazmat suits when they were in my room. Because I was pregnant and had an underlying heart condition, the hospital staff was especially concerned that I might not recover fully. Worse yet, they worried that the narcotics I had to take to manage my pain might have permanent developmental effects on the baby developing in my womb. I had already had one miscarriage less than six months prior—a tragedy that still loomed large for me and my partner. I was terrified about losing another baby. Luckily, we had already passed the twenty-week mark, so the baby's core organs and brain matter were fully developed. Doctors made sure to tell me that, if I had come in even a few days earlier, they would have suggested that I terminate the pregnancy.

I was in the hospital for over a week. I couldn't walk or eat for much of it. I was eventually moved to a room without hazmat suit requirements so that folks could visit me. When I was finally released, I went home with a tube in my arm to inject nutrients, saline, and medicine. It took a full month for me to return to work. I was so anxious to return that I talked about it for weeks, worried that people would judge me for having been away so long. This is the violence of misogynoir and the extraction of labor from Black women. In moments when we should be healing, caring for ourselves and our communities, and releasing ourselves from responsibility for outsiders, we still frequently feel compelled to show up and prove to others that we are fully capable and productive. We betray ourselves out of fear that we will be punished for being human. We behave like superheroes because we don't know any other way to be.

The first day I returned to work, I walked to my desk and said hello, and a white co-worker said, "Wow, you're back.

Can you give me meningitis so I can be off for a month?" He stuck out his arm, exposing his wrist as if he were asking me to infect him. This is the same co-worker who joked about how I like fried chicken and watermelon because I'm a "stereotype." I held back tears.

"I almost died," I said to him incredulously. "I almost lost my child."

"Well, I just mean I would love some time off, too," he replied and turned back toward our shared computer. My team knew I was returning to work that day, but there was nowhere for me to sit.

The oddest thing about my male co-worker's constant plucking at me was that he was a very openly gay man. He frequently joked about the "Black woman inside" his body as if it were a compliment to me that he thought all his sassiness, his witty nature, and his Z-shaped snapping ability came from Black women. While I was very early on in my queer journey, I recognized the visceral feeling that erupted in my gut every time he mentioned his inner Blackness as an homage to a people he was not in community with and had little to no political interests in protecting. This was my first exposure to the fragility of white gay male solidarity. It took years for me to learn that my experience with my co-worker was just a small, somewhat insignificant example of the ways white gay men have long overlooked and overshadowed the work of queer Black women.

Likely the most prominent and enduring example of Black queer and trans women's erasure is Marsha P. Johnson and the overlooked labor of Black trans and queer women at the Stonewall Inn on June 28, 1969.[14] It was a Black butch lesbian and drag king named Stormé DeLarverie who ignited the confrontation between police and onlookers when she allegedly punched police who were arresting her.[15] Johnson is frequently credited with throwing the first brick that set the inevitable dust-up in motion.[16] In the hours that followed, Johnson and fellow organizer Sylvia Rivera protested the arrests and the raid on the Stonewall Inn. Police tear-gassed and beat protestors, many of whom were trans women, as the crowd continued to grow. Many white gay men were finally seeing this as their struggle.

It was on the one-year anniversary of the Stonewall Rebellion that the first Pride Parade commenced on June 28, 1970.[17] Over the years, Pride has been reduced to a performance of white gay male visibility without proper acknowledgment of the ways that Black trans and lesbian women were central to its existence and creation. While LGBTQIA+ activists are working against this tide today, it remains challenging to be in solidarity with white gay men whose whiteness and maleness often operate in tandem to privilege them over all other trans and queer people.

What's deeply concerning about Johnson's short life and her relationship to the gay rights movement is that I, personally, didn't even learn her name until I was nearly thirty years old. So much of her life and legacy has been erased and whitewashed that even the conditions of her death remain unknown. Johnson, like Hurston, was nearly eradicated from the annals of history but for Black trans women like Founding Executive Director of the Marsha P. Johnson Institute,[18] Elle Moxley,[19] who have fought diligently to ensure her name, her movement work, and her legacy remain prominent in the archives. Johnson finally got her obituary in *The New York Times* in 2018, more than twenty-five years after her death.[20]

Over the next few weeks, my co-workers repeatedly reminded me about how hard it was to cover for me during "my time away." They framed my near-death experience more like a vacation in the Bahamas than four terrifying weeks of me fighting for my life and the life of my unborn child. Soon after, the colleague who disliked me was given an award for all her work while I was recuperating. The man who had jokingly asked me to infect him on my first day back had nominated her, and my manager strongly advocated the nomination. My manager called me ungrateful for not being more excited about what they did "for me" while I was hospitalized. I felt like I was being gaslit and abused.

Still, I stayed there for five more years, and I endured a number of other overt aggressions regarding my race and gender. From unwanted and invasive comments about my body and hair to the subtle racist conversations I encountered about Black people being "lazy," I felt as though I was under constant assault. My time at Disney dovetailed with major political crises like the fight for fair wages, marriage equality in California, the creation of affordable healthcare, and the beginnings of the Occupy movement challenging the wage gap in the United States. I walked in on conversations between older white co-workers who were upset about how Black, gay, and poor people were demanding rights that they hadn't earned. There were ongoing comments about our Spanish-speaking employees, and their accents were frequently mimicked behind their backs.

I inevitably became complicit in upholding these systems. Every conversation I witnessed while quietly keeping my head down made me a participant in a culture of exploitation and bigotry that was harming me, too. Because I couldn't afford to lose my job, I became so afraid of ruffling feathers that I just swallowed it. As a disabled person in the era of "pre-existing conditions," I had already gone through the turmoil of being uninsured between college and my first job. That was when I miscarried my first pregnancy. My insurance provider required that I fill out form after form after form detailing specifically when I began to miscarry, what exactly happened, when I fully "passed" the fetus, and when I alerted insurance. I knew that leaving a job with reliable healthcare while I was pregnant, disabled, managing a heart condition, and not independently wealthy could be a financial catastrophe for my family.

So, I kept working. I waited for promotions that would never come. I watched people get awards that I would never be nominated for. I got review after review that focused on my personal character rather than on my job performance. I finally learned that labor wasn't always about creating something new: For me, it was sometimes about languishing day after day in plain sight, but being invisible nonetheless.

My time at Disneyland ruined my fantasy of the American Dream in many ways. It exposed me to overt racism and workplace exclusion that reminded me that no matter how I contorted myself to fit the ideals and social mores of white people,

I could never fully assimilate. The frequent comments about my hairstyles, clothing choices, and "accent" (even though I was born only six hours north of Anaheim) made me feel like an outsider and an alien. I had permanently straightened my hair for this job, taken out piercings, covered up tattoos, and watered down the Blackest parts of my identity for a company I had idolized, only to find out that it was a nexus of anti-Blackness and misogyny.

It also illustrated for me that the capitalistic fairy tales about working hard and assimilating into white ways of being will always, and I mean always, leave Black women exposed and unprotected. In my five years there, no one stood up to defend or protect me from racist and sexist comments. My work was stolen so many times that I started hiding my projects on personal thumb drives so that I could always keep them on my physical body. I was so demoralized by the dismissiveness regarding the constant discrimination I faced that I slumped into a depression and isolated myself at work. The pain of rejection stung every day I stepped into the office. I felt foolish for thinking that I, a Black girl with an engineering degree and a dream, would be treated as their equal.

Finally, my career at Disney taught me not to rely on the logic of white institutions to define me or my worth. I started my job feeling a sense of pride at the fact that I had secured such an elite position right out of college. I relied on the fringe benefits of the job, like free entry at the parks and discounts at expensive restaurants, to reassure me that the assaults I received on my personhood each day weren't having a significant impact on my emotional wellness and health. I placed more emphasis on what I was getting from my job materially (not in the form of equal wages because I wasn't receiving those) than I did on loving my own humanity and identity. These were hard lessons in my early twenties. I realized while working there that I was also behind the stage pulling the strings, the same strings that were pulling me.

It took me struggling through years of this to realize that there were other, freer ways of being. It took me laboring in both hypervisibility and invisibility to understand that my time, body, and energy are absolutely mine. When the world was telling me that Black women belong to men, employers, communities, children, institutions, and consumers, it was in the works of women like Hurston and Walker that I learned what it meant to take myself back from a system that never served me in the first place.

Finding Us All, Reclaiming Ourselves

Hurston's years of obscurity remind us that Black women's contributions to American life—especially in entertainment, politics, and business—are too often lost to history, whether by intention or circumstance. This is not happenstance. It is one of the many vestiges of slavery that remembers Black women as possessions, pack mules, units of labor—objects to be utilized by others. But as I grew older and watched my mother, my grandmothers, and the elder women in my community labor to keep their homes, labor to put food on the table, labor to ensure their children were cared for, and labor to protect themselves from a difficult world that persecuted them for being Black, women, and poor, I learned that labor holds so many other meanings.

Black women's labor was often unseen, underpaid, undocumented, and erased from much of mainstream society. The labor of my foremothers, elders, and othermothers (women and community members who frequently acted as caretakers for children they did not birth themselves) often happened at the expense of their rest and against a larger narrative that they were less feminine and less deserving of respect for doing that very work. This all stemmed from stereotypes coming directly out of enslavement.

The Mammy figure, which was one of the most sustained and insidious stereotypes, depicted Black women as asexual maids and house mothers who were so concerned with taking care of white children that they neglected their own. This racist caricature of enslaved Black people migrated off of plantation lands and became associated with Black women who were working as domestic laborers in white households during and after Reconstruction. While many of these workers were young and building families of their own, their experiences as women were frequently undervalued compared to those of white women. For a large part of America's formative years as a nation, an especially passive, idealized vision of white womanhood—the "angels in the home"—was the norm against which all women were measured, and Black women were given infinitely less space to participate in these traditional forms of feminine identity. These tropes and dynamics have persisted into the contemporary moment.

Black women's labor has long been essential to supporting

white life, yet it is frequently exploited, extracted, and left depleted. The process of co-opting, using, and objectifying Black women based on the labor they provide is a central feature of our culture. It is one of the ways that people convince themselves it's okay for Black women to be paid less for equal work, supported less for the domestic labor they contribute in households and communities, and recognized less for the leadership they provide in social movements and other community-based initiatives. Black women are often masculinized, deemed more "manly," and essentially left out of conversations regarding "mainstream" feminist movements.[21] Black women's inherent existence precluded them from embodying womanhood and femininity in ways that aligned with dominant standards and social mores. These standards were not accessible to Black women not only because we are Black but also because of the unique conditions facing Black people in the United States. As Michele Wallace explains in her book *Black Macho and the Myth of the Superwoman,* Black women "lived in a dangerous environment, the black community, which did not protect its girl children, and beyond that the United States of America, which viewed black women as beasts of burden and sex toys."[22]

In some ways, this process is connected to the American Dream, the social norm and fantasy that centers a white nuclear heterosexual marriage, two and a half children, and a picket fence. For Black people, this was the razzle-dazzle fantasy I saw depicted on popular shows like *Family Matters* and *The Fresh Prince of Bel-Air.* I'll never forget the episode of *Family Matters* in which Harriet, the tough-talking Black mom and wife of a respectable Black police officer named Carl, took the day off because her family had started taking her for granted. The family was completely inept without her. They couldn't find their own clothing or feed themselves. Harriet was so integral to the household that they literally could not function without relying on her. Yet they couldn't even say "thank you" after begging her to coddle them through their issues and hold their hands through simple tasks. While the household was typically depicted as the ideal, heteronormative Black American Dream, Harriet's experience appeared to be conditional upon the ways that her husband, children, and extended family valued her presence and her work. The show's critique of the ways in which women are frequently exploited for labor in their own homes was refreshing, but it still only told half of the story. It never touched on the ways that Harriet's treatment was also affected by race, nor did it discuss the privileges the Winslows had because they were a heterosexual-passing, middle-class couple.

I eventually figured out that the American Dream was never about dreaming but about mythmaking: It was like a bedtime story for children that masked the hard reality of the world, designed to make them believe in happy endings. What's worse, I was growing to comprehend that these myths weren't even concocted for me. They were written for white children who were privileged enough to be protected from the truth. This fantasy was established and handed down by white Americans convinced of their inherent goodness. These same white people drafted laws and held positions in national leadership that granted them the ability to shape policy and institutional change. The American Dream is merely a reflection of white Americans' experiences with capitalism. The centering of white Americans' social and political experiences in our society constitutes a form of power wherein white people may absolve themselves of guilt for their privilege and remain complicit in systemic racism, intentionally or otherwise. This was clear for me during my time at Disney, a place where they purported to care about people of color, children, and families but overworked and underpaid cast members to the point that they were burnt out and forced to take more shifts just to feed themselves. Meanwhile, the extremely wealthy white executives leading the organization used nepotism and in-house networks to get their kids cushy summer jobs and backstage opportunities with celebrities. Because white Americans have been so committed to the fantasy of their own inherent perfection, there has rarely been space in that imaginary world for the proper recognition and affirmation of Black women's laboring bodies and the exploitation they endure just to survive.

We still see today how Black women's labor continues to be exploited for profit without any consideration for how that exploitation affects Black women's lives and livelihoods. While childbirth remains a beautiful and sacred experience, it has become increasingly associated with medical risk and potential death for Black women. According to the Centers for Disease Control and Prevention, Black women in the United States have the highest rates of death during childbirth when compared to other racial groups.[23] Black women with college degrees are more likely to suffer pregnancy-related complications than white women with high school diplomas.[24] Many social movement organizers and community advocates have been spotlighting this fact in recent years to draw public attention to the risks of childbearing for Black women. Even celebrities have shared how their experiences with childbirth highlight the disparities between the treatment of Black birthing bodies and that of other groups. Serena Williams, arguably the greatest tennis player of all time, suffered from blood clots after delivering her daughter, Olympia.[25] When she started struggling to breathe, she asked the medical staff at Los Angeles's Cedars-Sinai Medical Center for a CT scan and a heparin drip. Initially, nurses and doctors didn't listen to her, even as she explained to them that she had a history of blood clots. Instead, they recommended a Doppler ultrasound, which does not detect blood clots. Her condition worsened. Eventually, they listened, discovered several small blood clots in her lungs, and began administering heparin. That day, Williams had to save her own life. She is a megastar who can advocate for herself in the face of opposition. However, other Black women have died in hospitals after doctors left them in agony, dismissed or downplayed their pain, ignored their symptoms, and overlooked opportunities to keep them alive.

Black women are also frequently exploited in their jobs. It is universally understood that Black women are over-represented in low-paying jobs and are underpaid for the same amount of work as other employees. They earn sixty-two cents to every dollar that the average white man earns in the same period.[26] In 2021, Black Women's Equal Pay Day was on August 3. This means it took more than seven additional months for the average Black woman to earn the twelve-month salary that a relative non-Hispanic white man earned in 2020.[27] During the COVID-19 crisis, Black women in essential roles—like food service jobs, medical support, education, and childcare—were called upon to respond to the needs of Americans all over the country, but they continue to be underpaid even in those positions.[28] In these conditions, Black women laborers are socialized to work harder with fewer days off to earn less money. They take more jobs to support their families. They push their mental states and bodies to the limit. And, often, they make themselves physically sick trying to remain productive in an anti-Black, misogynistic world that doesn't reward them equitably. Along with the stereotypes of Black womanhood, the American Dream socializes Black women into heteronormative coupling and the idea that truly "making it" means getting married to a cisgender heterosexual man, buying a home in suburbia, and raising a family, even when that dream has disparately negative effects on their longevity. But as Black women chase that dream, they are met with structural and systemic barriers meant to eradicate Blackness itself.

These phenomena connect deeply to the work of social justice and activism, as Black women are frequently the creators of movements in addition to being laborers who provide for their communities and families. For example, Black Lives Matter was started by three Black women who had long found their community in social movements. Alicia Garza tweeted the phrase "Black Lives Matter" in 2013 after the jury in the George Zimmerman case found him not guilty. Seeing this message from her comrade, Patrisse Cullors replied with the hashtag "#BLACKLIVESMATTER." Ayọ (formerly known as Opal) Tometi would join with her comrades to co-lead the organization, and this simple phrase became the rallying cry and moniker for a burgeoning and long-standing movement that would expand beyond the confines of Twitter timelines and into the homes and lexicons of people all over the world. Black women have long been behind social movements, and many of the ones in this book—like Ella Baker, Fannie Lou Hamer, and Angela Davis—have rarely had their work fully recognized or their leadership affirmed in public media and discourse. Even as these Black women have placed their bodies under immense risk in the name of Black liberation, they have struggled to receive acknowledgment for their efforts. This creates an undue burden on Black women that is rarely recognized or paid for adequately.

Even as societal expectations of Black women remain disproportionately high and rarely come with equitable remuneration, it is the duty of those seeking to do anti-racist work to ensure that they do not engage in actions that are exploitative or co-optive of Black women.

CHAPTER 4

Ella Baker Taught Me Why We Should Listen to Young People

We have a powerful potential in our youth, and we must have the courage to change old ideas and practices so that we may direct their power toward good ends.

—*Mary McLeod Bethune*

All of these young people have some kind of potential in them. And if we don't invest in them as a nation, regardless of where they come from or what color they are, if we don't invest in them, we lose.

—*Michelle Obama*

The Negro must quit looking for a savior, and work to save himself.

—*Ella Baker*[1]

The most powerful person in the struggle of the 1960s was Miss Ella Baker, not Martin Luther King.

—*Stokely Carmichael*

We had just under an acre of land in upstate New York, what many of our friends lovingly called our "forest," where we bumped into more deer on the average day than stray dogs and cats. My children were running in our backyard, blowing bubbles at one another, and we were planting collard greens, cabbage, green peppers, tomatoes, kale, strawberries, and mint. It was our first year building an outdoor garden.

My thirteen-year-old son was a reluctant participant, pouring water over the vegetable starters and dropping in more soil when asked. My nine-year-old daughter wanted to assemble the seeds and fertilizer. Anything to get as dirty as possible. It was my seven-year-old who seemed the most curious. "What's that, Mommy?" and "Why do we have to put that stuff in there?" he asked. I explained how the raised gardens needed light, food, and water to give nutrients to the plants to help them grow. I showed him how we added lime and plant food so that the soil was prepared to mimic the real dirt in our backyard. He seemed satisfied with my answer. I smiled at him, and he smiled back, as he always does. We both returned to planting.

I couldn't stop staring at my children, wondering at the ways they moved about the back patio, joyful and carefree. I lived vicariously through them for a bit that day. It was a moment to be childlike, messy, and capricious without consequence. I don't really remember being seven years old. I remember flashes here and there, uncomfortable church stockings and dress shoes and maybe a cute glance from my best friend on the playground. But being a child and enjoying childlike things seemed like the business that others tended to do. I also don't remember ever really feeling the sense of safety and protection that I try to make sure my children feel. Instead, I remember a childhood full of uncertainty and exposures. Exposures to violence, sexualization, harm, and vulnerability. I remember pushing through childhood and young adulthood in spaces and places that reminded me that being Black, perceived as a girl, and poor would open me up to all manner of indecency and impropriety. I remember being scared and, often, alone. Not only that, I remember feeling as though I had no control over my life and what I might encounter each day. Being Black and poor in my city meant I wasn't afforded the innocence and protection of childhood when I set foot outside of the house.

There's one particular experience from my high school years that speaks to those exposures, though there are countless that I could recall. The Bay Area streets were always cool on weekday evenings. My jean jacket was the only thing that protected me from the wind. I was homeless for the second time in my seventeen years. This time, it wasn't my mom who had put me out. It was my dad. He said I was coming home from school too late, so he started fastening the chain lock on the apartment door to keep me out. Sometimes, he would talk to me through the three-inch crack in the door, yelling at me and accusing me of sleeping with boys. After a few weeks of being intermittently locked out, I brought my older cousin and my best friend over to help me pack up some things. I would rather couch surf than get locked out randomly. I spent hours on the AC Transit and BART, moving between the homes of friends and family who would house me. The bus and rapid train system had kept me moving all over the Bay Area since I got my first bus ticket in junior high school.

I had been sitting at the unassuming bus stop for about ten minutes when a young man joined me on the bench. He was wearing nondescript clothing, just a T-shirt and jeans, and was mostly unremarkable, so I didn't pay him much attention. He started fiddling with his pockets, I assumed to grab a cigarette, so I slid farther away on the bench in case the smoke blew in my direction. As a rule, I avoided eye contact with men, so I looked to my right, down what people in Hayward refer to as "Mission Boulevard." Having grown up in Oakland, I knew it as East 14th—a street I had once lived a few blocks north of. It wasn't a safe area. It wasn't an area with many white people, either. But it was a neighborhood rich with culture. East 14th and High Street, the cross-street that took me home, were virtually in the center of Oakland. Living in this epicenter meant that I could get anywhere in "The Town" in roughly thirty minutes or less. It offered access to amazing food from all over the world—Filipino, Chinese, Mexican, and Ethiopian. East 14th was a place where I felt like I knew what was coming, what to expect. In Hayward, people were new and different. And they weren't Black. I felt less safe there, like I was constantly being watched rather than being welcomed. Because so few people looked like me, I found myself frequently nervous and anxious about interacting with strangers in this peculiar new land.

At this point, I realized that the man at the end of the bench was staring at me. He was looking directly at my face. I glanced over and saw that he was masturbating. I made a face of utter disgust, but by that point in my life I was already used to strange men touching themselves, making unwanted advances, and violating my privacy in public. I'd seen men on buses and BART trains touching themselves or asking to perform sex acts on girls walking by. Sometimes, they would yell out the details of what they wanted to do to our bodies in large crowds where everyone could laugh and look at us. It raised my anxiety every time. Though I was only seventeen years old, being in public, riding buses, hopping in taxis, catching trains— and now, being homeless—meant a lot of unwanted interactions. Sometimes, to drop off a college application, I would jump into a stranger's car, hoping they were just a nice person rather than a violent predator. I would ride in cars with strange men in the dead of night because the bus line had stopped and my parents weren't speaking to me. Once, a young white man drove me up a long, tall hill away from my destination. I asked him to drive me back and he refused. He took me to a house and tried to get me to go inside, where he said he had friends. I told him I'd seen his face and that I would fight and scream. Thankfully, he got scared and took me back to where he found me.

The man on the bench was grinning at me now.

"What the fuck?" I yelled as I jumped up off the bench. I snarled again, reasserting my disgust.

I stood at the end of the curb until the bus arrived. I made sure to never look back at the man, who scurried off as the bus stopped. On the bus, I did my best to erase his creepy grin from my mind, but I could still see it; I will probably always be able to see it, if not in my memories, then certainly in my nightmares. Being a homeless queer teen in Oakland meant that I was frequently in these scenarios, with no protection.

Just a few months after the incident at the bus stop, I was a freshman at an elite, predominantly white university in Southern California. Some of my classmates drove cars that I had never seen before with foreign names I couldn't even pronounce. They shopped at stores I had never heard of for clothing I had never seen anyone in my community wear. I went there to escape a hometown where I had never truly felt safe, believing the promise that getting out and going to college was the one way out for people like me. I was convinced that with a heart condition that wouldn't allow me to use my disabled body to earn a living in sports, I would have to use my brain to prove to a jury of countless white people and white-owned institutions that I was valuable enough.

I was waiting at another bus stop, this time in front of a bustling grocery store, with two huge suitcases in hand. I had been dragging my clearance-rack suitcases with me from Richmond, California, where my mom lived with her newest husband. It was Christmas break of my first year, and I had been kicked out of my home again. My mother's husband was tired of me being there on my visit, so, rather than leave us both in misery, I packed up, switched my flights, and came back to campus over a week early. When I got off the bus and looked toward campus, I remember feeling hopeful and optimistic about my future, despite my recent personal turmoil. In the distance I could see Fluor Tower, my dorm, the only home I had left.

Houselessness meant living out of suitcases that were often so overfull that the handles broke or buckled when the bags were lifted from the ground. The suitcases were stuffed with what was left of my childhood. I was carrying trinkets I made at art camp in Massachusetts, blankets I slept with when I was still potty training, and picture books I salvaged lest my mom and her husband throw all my belongings in the trash. That was when they changed the locks on me. These objects were the last of the things that made me *me*. Ceramic bowls I threw in pottery class last summer with the nickname "Jen Jen" etched into the bases. Trophies from my track meets and basketball championships. Little ribbons that reminded me that I won something before this sequence of catastrophic losses. I was carrying the last few things that had survived on the corner of my little tucked-away Oakland street, carrying my whole life with me—anything I could find that reminded me of home, of myself.

Standing on the busy street, I breathed the Los Angeles desert air deeply into my lungs. It smelled like Mexican food, smog, and dryness. It reminded me that I was in a foreign place, alone. Again. I bent my knees, hunched my shoulders, awkwardly grabbed the side straps to my suitcases, and pulled the bags behind me. The sidewalk was bumpy, and the suitcases, their rickety wheels no match for the uneven pavement, fell over. Embarrassed, lonely, I realized that I had so far to walk before I would arrive at my dorm. I put my right hand over my chest to check my heartbeat. It was probably ineffective, but it was the only method I had to monitor my heart rate and be intentional about the strain I put on my disabled body.

Satisfied that my heart was doing okay with the level of intensity this journey required, I got back to it and slowly made my way to campus.

When I finally got to the dorms, everything was locked. So, I pressed the button on the security panel at the parking garage.

"Hi, can someone let me into Fluor Tower?" I asked when the officer answered the line.

"Did you get locked out or something?" he asked.

"No, I am back early from Christmas break. I have nowhere else to go," I told him.

"Hold on," he said after a short pause. I felt that this was a pause someone would call "pregnant." "Someone will come over and let you in. Just make sure you have your student ID."

"Thank you so much," I sighed, relieved that the journey would end now. Even though the home I knew was gone, I would have opportunities to find myself somewhere else. I didn't tell the officer that my mother had put me out and my father wouldn't speak to me. I didn't tell him that I had no money and no way to feed myself. I just told him "thank you."

I think frequently about that moment and how that security officer had no idea how he affected me that day. Maybe it wasn't really him that affected me, but the feeling of being welcomed somewhere—of a door opening for me rather than being locked in my face. As I journeyed farther and farther from Oakland over the following years, I found many places where I was welcomed in and treated with this kindness. The journey led me to a PhD program and, later, to teach young people who looked, lived, and languished like me. My experiences at the margins of race, gender, class, and sexuality grew to become central components of my political ethics and commitments.

It was my first year as a tenure-track professor at an elite, private, predominantly white university. I was lucky to be teaching Black Feminist Politics to a class of mostly Black, Latinx, queer, first-generation, poor, and working-class students. Many of them were juniors and seniors who were very active socially and politically on campus. These young people were truly amazing. During the fall of my first year, students began organizing in response to ongoing racial aggressions on campus. Fraternity parties, swastikas displayed in parking structures, and discrimination from campus public safety officers had created an environment where marginalized students felt ostracized and targeted on campus. In response, they mounted a campaign to demand that their university provide Black, Latinx, Indigenous, Asian, queer, poor, and first-gen students equal access to education. This included more access to campus mental health facilities, recreational spaces for students of color, funding and support for students from targeted communities, and financial support for on-campus resources like printing and laundry services. The movement had escalated into a sit-in that turned into a lock-in. Students were stuck on campus for weeks as they attempted to negotiate with campus officials.

On one such evening, we were in a three-tiered lecture room on campus. It was late and we had been debating with campus administrators over the students' demands for days. The students were initially locked in; campus security officers wouldn't let them have visitors, food, or exit privileges after they staged a sit-in. Then the administration started sending threatening letters to their parents. The ordeal left these Black, Latinx, Asian, and Indigenous students in precarity. Many of them were worried that they wouldn't be allowed to graduate just a few months later.

"Dr. Jenn, we need your help. Will you help us?" they told me late on that Tuesday evening after we had negotiated with the university. Here they were, with more courage than I ever remembered having, asking me for help. I felt honored but also afraid. I wasn't young anymore. I didn't know what mattered to young people. But I wanted to serve. I wanted to stand in the gap that was so familiar to me. I wanted to protect them in the ways that no one protected me. So, we sat in front of people with tailored suits and stern faces, and we demanded justice. We yelled. We cried. We stormed out. We cursed. We pleaded with an institution more concerned about its reputation than its students. We demanded that they acknowledge that the university was complicit in white supremacy. We demanded that they tell the truth about what they did to the students at the sit-in. As we witnessed them, the students taught us—their advisors—about grace, patience, and vulnerability as they bared their traumas to an institution that stared directly through them to the fine print on its legal documents. It was heartbreaking to watch. Yet, it was also astoundingly beautiful to witness these young people in community with one another, seeking to build an alternative future for themselves. A future not limited by the visions of anti-Black institutions but expansive enough to usher in new generations of Black, Brown, trans, queer, poor, working-class, immigrant, and disabled students in places where they would typically be rejected.

This was a full-circle moment for me. It was not only a reminder that I was no longer "young." It was a reminder that I once was and that, when I was young, I was quite powerful. More powerful than I thought I was. Maybe it was my being alone that hid that truth from me. As young people at the margins of identity, we are most vulnerable to the fraught nature of race, gender, class, and sexuality. Our firsthand experiences with education systems that support the school-to-prison pipeline and with economic insecurity rooted in political failure often leave us ill-protected and unsafe when social and environmental crises occur. For young Americans, especially young Black Americans, these times are riddled with uncertainty.

In many ways, my own experiences at these margins led me to teaching and social organizing specifically related to Black women and young Americans. The young people I have trained in Chicago and the college students I have nurtured over the years are adults now. Some have gone on to become academics, pursuing doctoral and legal degrees. Others are organizers and activists working at think tanks, social movement organizations, and nonprofit funding agencies all over the country. I often marvel at their Instagram feeds, which show them traveling to places like Cuba, Senegal, and Palestine to seek solutions to the problems they've witnessed both at home and abroad. I have watched them live through an entire global COVID-19 crisis. Schools closed. Restaurants stopped seating people. Businesses shut down. Job applications piled up. Grad schools stopped taking applications.

My own children have grown. My three Black children, who have found joy, safety, and solace at home, are experiencing a sort of vulnerability that I cannot fathom. Just like my college students and just like me when I was younger, my children face economic, social, and political precariousness every day. They do so without the knowledge that everything will be okay. They do so as social safety nets are being ripped away and replaced with high-end interest rates, reverse mortgages, and low-paying jobs with little to no benefits.

The young people I serve and the children I am raising are living through a moment I will never truly understand. While I was a child once, I have already had my journey. I am safe now. Or at least as safe as I can be in a white heteropatriarchal capitalistic society. The safety I experience now is a privilege and a responsibility. It compels me to show up for young Black people in the ways that I needed most. And, because I hold intimate knowledge of what it means to be young and vulnerable in the United States, I also hold insight regarding the experiences of those young people who are too often abandoned, thrown away, ignored, and disregarded.

This is why youth-led movements are so critical. They are born out of struggle and strife and come from a place of true vulnerability and insight. They are authentic, rebellious, and real. Young people are full of imagination and energy, and they still believe they can change the world. This is why young people are so critical in imagining what a truly just world should look like. For centuries, Black freedom fighters have struggled against anti-Blackness, colonialism, and white supremacy through movement work. Many of the leaders of the Civil Rights Movement were twenty-somethings who were struggling to build families, start careers, and obtain an education. Martin Luther King, Jr., was only twenty-six years old when he became pastor of Dexter Baptist Church in Montgomery, Alabama.[2] This thrust him into the limelight of political leadership before he was even thirty years old. Young Black folks in their twenties and thirties have been critical in providing the intellectual, emotional, and physical energy needed to launch and sustain mass movements for global liberation. Ella Baker knew this, and she made sure to use her labor to nurture, aid, and encourage these young movement leaders.

Ella Josephine Baker was born in Norfolk, Virginia, on December 13, 1903. Her grandparents on both sides had been slaves. Baker grew up in a family and community that was deeply committed to serving those less fortunate than themselves. She took this message with her into the movements and organizations she served during her long career as a freedom fighter. After graduating from Shaw University in 1927, she moved straight into national organizing. Eventually, she became the national field secretary for the NAACP, but once there, she was disheartened by the lack of grassroots leadership and organizing.

So, in 1957, Baker moved on to help Martin Luther King, Jr., found the Southern Christian Leadership Conference (SCLC), where Baker utilized her skills and training to bring together groups of people in the name of Black liberation. The organization was an offshoot of the Montgomery Improvement Association,[3] which was instrumental in launching the 381-day Montgomery Bus Boycott to end segregation on public buses and throughout the South.[4] Many people fail to consider how complicated it was and how much strategizing it took to orchestrate a mass bus boycott in the 1950s and '60s without social media platforms like Twitter and Facebook to help mobilize participants. These movement workers created networked communities and an internal carpooling system to ensure that everyone in the community still made it to work and school without ever setting foot on public transit. Because of the massive success of the bus boycott, the SCLC was catapulted into the national limelight as a protest organization.

Another byproduct of this incredible success was the propensity for onlookers to focus on the young, charismatic King without fully acknowledging the many organizers and freedom fighters who worked with him. Baker and openly gay organizer Bayard Rustin were critical facilitators of the Civil Rights Movement, holding down the fort behind the scenes even as Martin Luther King, Jr., grew to be the public face of Black civil rights. King was the president of the SCLC from its founding until his assassination in 1968. During that time, Baker became disillusioned with some of the mainstream efforts to secure Black liberation because she did not believe that they were taking full account of the experiences of young Black Americans, who were facing increasingly hostile and dangerous conditions created by the State and by racist organizations like the Ku Klux Klan. She believed that young Black people had the power, knowledge, and expertise to lead their own movements and make lasting political change in the United States. In April 1960, Baker helped establish the Student Nonviolent Coordinating Committee (SNCC), one of the first movements led by Black students and young people in the United States.

It was at a meeting of the SCLC that Baker made sure to include the voices of John Lewis (who would later become a member of Congress), Marion Barry, and Diane Nash. Barry went on to become SNCC's first chairman. Lewis later led

SNCC. Nash was critical to developing strategy for the organization. This student leadership conference at Baker's alma mater, Shaw University, was SNCC's seeding moment. SNCC was a radical organization that gained notoriety due to the risky, life-threatening sit-ins and Freedom Rides they facilitated in direct action against discriminatory laws, voter suppression, and the vestiges of legal segregation.[5] SNCC also organized Freedom Schools, places for volunteer teachers to center the educational and political needs of young Black Mississippians.[6] These "schools" were a part of a SNCC program that utilized the vast experience, education, and knowledge of the hundreds of volunteers seeking to support the organization. The Freedom Schools were designed to work against the discriminatory and unequal schooling in Mississippi and provide Black students with a place to explore their experiences openly and in community. These young people were not only educated using a curriculum meant to supplement the deeply inequitable teaching models held over from the segregated school systems in the South, but they were also encouraged to join movements. By the mid-1960s, SNCC activists were changing the landscape of political organizing in the United States and mobilizing a whole new generation of Black radicals.

For Baker, it was important that young people lead their own movements on their own terms without that work being co-opted, diminished, or taken over by older activists and organizers who "bear the scars of the battle, the frustrations and the disillusionment that come when the prophetic leader turns out to have heavy feet of clay."[7] Baker emphasized "group-centered leadership," as opposed to the charismatic leader approach (like that of the SCLC and Martin Luther King, Jr.), which she saw as neither sustainable nor equitable. The latter did not fully represent the voices, concerns, and experiences of young Black people, who were most intimately affected by the conditions of anti-Black racism, white supremacy, and institutional inequality at lunch counters, on college campuses, in public squares, on buses, and at water fountains all over the country. As Baker once said, "Martin didn't make the movement, the movement made Martin."[8] According to Baker, group-centered movements that were led by young people were the only movements that would truly lead to liberation for all people. Starting at age twenty, activist and organizer Julian Bond was the communications director for SNCC from 1960 to 1965. Bond went on to join the Georgia House of Representatives, become an esteemed scholar of government and history, and chair the NAACP. Bond recalls Baker telling other young organizers in SNCC that "Strong people don't need strong leaders."[9] Strong people can do strong things all on their own.

As a part of her political ethos and praxes, Baker believed that it was the job of older activists and leaders to protect young organizers. She said that many communities in the South "have not provided adequate experience for young Negroes to assume initiative and think and act independently," thus amplifying "the need for guarding the student movement against well-meaning, but nevertheless unhealthy, over-protectiveness."[10] Baker critiqued older movement makers who condescended to young activists who were formulating their own models of participatory democracy. She believed that young people's experiences were primary sites of political action and strategy that older organizers were often too distant from to understand or recognize. Baker embodied this belief in her own movement work. She was rarely center stage. There are few recordings of her public speeches or talks. Instead of drawing attention to herself, Baker worked diligently to ensure that the work was centered. Her efforts shifted movement strategizing away from traditional, patriarchal models that failed to hold space for the full freedom of Black people.

Baker's vision for organizing has endured into the twenty-first century. Her efforts to decenter charismatic men have made space for women, gender-nonconforming people, and queer and trans folks to take the lead in grassroots movements rather than wait for someone to come and save us. Today's movements have been primarily led by young Black Americans whose proximity to the State through the carceral system, hyper-surveillance of Black communities, and increasing inequality between racial communities has put them in constant danger. One prominent example is the Hands Up United organization in Ferguson, Missouri, which was created shortly after Michael Brown was killed.[11] Local organizers, activists, musicians, and community members recognized the need for systemic change with respect to police violence in the city, so they stepped up. One of the organization's founders, twenty-nine-year-old Darren Seals, was found shot and burned in his car two years after Brown was killed.[12]

Many onlookers and outsiders have noted that these movements seem leaderless. Because so many in the public are accustomed to social movements with charismatic male leaders like Martin Luther King, Jr., Malcolm X, and Kwame Ture (also known as Stokely Carmichael), they frequently struggle with the Movement for Black Lives emerging with a focus on the people. This focus allows for the people most directly affected by local and regional issues to build the strategies for how to solve them. Historian Barbara Ransby refers to this movement model as "radical democracy in action."[13]

Over her five decades of organizing, Ella Baker earned the nickname "Fundi," a Swahili word meaning "a person who teaches a craft to the next generation."[14] She was a giant among giants, though she chose to remain out of public sight. I frequently reflect on the fact that Baker died in 1986 on her eighty-third birthday. Unlike many of the Black Feminist foremothers and teachers in this book, she lived well into her golden years. I sometimes wonder if it was partly due to her refusal to be centered and targeted in her work that she was able to preserve so much of her energy, life, and breath. In this way, too, Baker was a model for how Black women teachers, organizers, and fighters can move in their purpose while holding space for their own humanity simultaneously.

Confronting the Ghosts from Our Youth as We Build Our Abolitionist Futures

It is impossible to write about the voices and power of young people without acknowledging the centrality and significance of the Internet. When I was in high school, we were embarking on a technological revolution that was beginning to put smartphones in our pockets, bringing the world to the tips of our fingers. I was in college when Facebook launched, first as an exclusive social media platform only accessible for college students with a ".edu" email address. Quickly, the platform expanded, causing more passive platforms like Myspace to become obsolete. By the 2010s, social media was a primary data and information source for most people across generations. But platforms like Twitter were starting to become sites not just for entertainment and media consumption. Young Black, Brown, queer and trans, disabled, and immigrant folks were realizing that these platforms could connect us not only to other individuals but to other communities in collective struggle.

Probably the best example of Twitter becoming a primary site of mobilization for emerging movements was after the killing of Trayvon Martin by street vigilante George Zimmerman in February 2012. Because social media had already been helpful in holding governments accountable across the globe, most notably during the Arab Spring, many young activists in the United States were already aware of the potential power that sites like Twitter afforded them. After Trayvon Martin was killed, Twitter circulation of the events coming out of Sanford, Florida, amplified the story and helped draw national attention to the fact that Zimmerman had not yet been taken into custody.[15] As local news reports from the *Miami Herald* and the *Orlando Sentinel* struggled to reach a national audience, Twitter activists put pressure on local authorities to take action. These efforts led to the creation of the Movement for Black Lives. Following the police killing of Michael Brown in August 2014, Twitter again became a primary site for political mobilization for young Black people. As the Ferguson Police Department worked to suppress information about Brown's murder, Twitter users relied on one another for up-to-theminute updates and breaking news. Heat maps of the tweets about Ferguson, Mike Brown, and the phrase "Hands up!," which became synonymous with protests against Brown's killing, showed that these events transcended the boundaries of local politics.[16] It was the coordinated and intentional efforts of young Black organizers on the ground in Ferguson that pushed past the artificial limitations of our localized concerns to make "Black lives matter" an international claim.[17] Young Black Americans effectively shifted the media narrative about Ferguson to refer to the moment as an "uprising" rather than a "protest." They used both their wisdom from prior political moments and their savvy with media to frame a story, direction, and orientation for the movement, which was only successful because they had a finger on the pulse of our gravest issues.

Young people, especially young Black Americans, have leveraged social media and encrypted-messaging apps like WhatsApp and Signal to cloak their strategies and tactics from police surveillance while mounting mass-scale, global liberation campaigns from Paterson, New Jersey, to Palestine. This is precisely the type of social change that Baker knew young people were capable of. Not only did she know it, Baker believed it was incumbent upon all of us to nurture and uplift this work.

In my transition from young person to graduate student to professor, I have been lucky enough to maintain close ties to young Black movement makers, activists, and scholars. As a researcher of policing and racial trauma in the United States, I have spoken with hundreds of young Black Americans across the United States in cities like Boston, Philadelphia, Baltimore,

Chicago, New York, Atlanta, Houston, Los Angeles, and Oakland. In these conversations, young Black people have shared with me the unique experiences they've had at the intersections of race, gender, and class. Overwhelmingly, the young Black Americans I have spoken to believe that we are moving toward a radical political revolution, one that they will lead. When I asked them what we should credit with this resurgence of political activism, they said that social media has played a significant and irreplaceable role in the development of today's movements. Many of them suggested that they themselves would've been disconnected from movements and the work of their comrades had they been without social media and Internet access. For this generation of young people, the ability to connect with people who share their identities, experiences, and concerns has only strengthened their claims for both liberation and solidarity.

These conversations and the intensity with which these radical dreams have been shared with me remind me of the vulnerability and capaciousness of my own youth. As an educator, I reflect often on the ways that teaching draws out the memories, traumas, and vulnerabilities I once experienced myself. When developing a curriculum, I consider not only how my students' experiences will be foregrounded in my classroom, but also how my own interactions and past lives might bubble to the surface each week. In graduate school, when I was formulating my pedagogical and philosophical commitments, I confronted many moments that challenged me to step back into the shoes of my high school self. The girl who felt abandoned, alone, and excluded. On one such day in Chicago, I remember the sun was blazing on my back. It had to be at least ninety degrees outside and extremely humid. My clothes had been stuck to my skin since the moment I left the house. The air smelled wet and the trees were rumbling with cicada songs. I had been driving around the Hyde Park campus for at least thirty minutes looking for a parking space. It was summer and there was construction everywhere near campus.

During the summers, I was working with Chicago Public Schools to offer supplemental training in civic engagement. My students learned basic statistical and policy reporting techniques so that they could identify social issues in their communities and schools that administrators and local officials should resolve. The work was strenuous and, at times, felt overwhelming. But I was always proud when students began connecting the theoretical precepts of the course to their own experiences with racism, anti-Blackness, educational inequality, environmental discrimination, and food insecurity. This particular day, I had a trunk full of laptops I had been transporting for my students. My students, some of whom were as young as thirteen years old, were full of light and hope even though they often faced instability and precarity in their day-to-day lives. They had a deep love for their communities and families. They loved their city and they truly believed in making Chicago a better place. I was still a graduate student, working through my summers to help pay to send my two youngest kids to Montessori school. In many ways, I felt galaxies away from these young people despite having grown up just like them.

I finally found a parking spot, but it was three blocks away from the building where I taught each day. Because of my heart condition, I knew not to carry anything over fifteen pounds per the doctor's instructions, but I wanted to deliver the laptops. They were stored in white mail delivery bins, which were beat up and flimsy, showing the wear and tear of sitting on a college campus for an extended period of time. I started piling items in my arms, balancing bags full of snacks and writing materials for the students, too. I grabbed the laptops and lifted them from my knees. The weight combined with the sun made it feel like I was literally carrying a ton of bricks. About halfway down the block, I put the pile of supplies down on the ground to catch my breath. I couldn't help but remember that day in Los Angeles when my suitcases buckled and shame lay on my back like the Chicago heat. I felt those same tears well up in the back of my throat.

I took my time getting to the building, but by the time I got there, I was sweating profusely. I looked up and saw the handicap ramp to enter my building. The journey was coming to an end. At the bottom of the ramp, I deconstructed the pile of snacks, notebooks, and laptops into smaller, more manageable sections. I delivered the first to the door. Then, just as I had with my suitcases over a decade before, I hunched over, hoisted up the laptops, took a few paces, and delivered the container. Two more times, and I was done.

For a second, I was a freshman in college again. Alone and embarrassed. But the feeling passed: I had overcome this trial before, and I was heartened when I closed my eyes and reflected on how far I had come and how my community had risen up to meet me. Instead of feeling sad, I felt resolute, accomplished, whole. I realized that with every step 'up that ramp I was walking toward a purpose that had been written for me well before my life ended up in trash bags on the street.

I was moving in alignment with a vision for my life that had been ordained, sketched out by foremothers like Baker who knew that the work of teaching and listening to young Black people would have the power to move me out of my despair and into a place of hopefulness for the future. And because I was called to teach a new generation of Black radicals, scholars, and activists, I knew that I belonged here.

Like Baker, we older Black educators, activists, and organizers have a unique and critical position in stitching together movement moments. We, having experienced the struggle and survived it, are called to provide scaffolding for the freedom dreams of our future movement leaders. We are the connection between movements of yesterday and those of tomorrow. Like I noted in reference to Harriet Jacobs's struggle for freedom, it is in these moments that the struggle seems most precarious. It might even seem unattainable for young people who are starting out. For those of us who believe in freedom, though, we have a birthright in the movement. Even after we've grown away from the violence and traumas that brought us to the struggle, we must return to envelop those who remain in it.

CHAPTER 5

Fannie Lou Hamer Taught Me to Be (Un)respectable

Nobody's free until everybody's free.

—*Fannie Lou Hamer*

I'll never forget the first time I heard Lauryn Hill's outro to her live album released in 2002. It was an MTV Unplugged special that she performed with a thin band and her guitar. In the video, Lauryn is sitting on a stool, slightly slouched over the mic, wearing her signature cap over a headscarf. Her big dangly gold hoops swing next to her perfect chocolatey skin. She has just performed "The Conquering Lion" with her voice cracking and a tear on her cheek. After finishing the song, she says this about the ways that her privacy has been disregarded and disrespected over the years:

> Everybody's going through the same stuff, same issues, it's just a bunch of repression. And I'm saying, man, life is too—is too valuable, man, for us to sit here in these boxes all repressed, you know? Afraid to admit what we're really going through.[1]

She talks about having her children and the ways that people have used her life experiences as ammunition to shame her. She tells the audience that she has essentially leaned into all the stories that people have told about her. Instead of trying to be someone she's not, trying to comport herself to fit the standards and expectations of others, she chooses to step fully into being "crazy" if that means she gets to be free.

Later, Lauryn talks about how people think she's "crazy" and "deranged."[2] She says that she is at peace, but that she's sticking to the story that she's not well. At first blush, the words sound a little weird. You can't tell if she's joking or if she's serious. The commentary feels sad but also unburdened. It only makes sense in the context of Lauryn Hill's life. She is a Black woman who hit stardom unexpectedly, and who had a baby out of wedlock that people shamed her for. Critics told her she wouldn't have a career anymore if she kept her child (a fact she has spoken about at length and documented in her song "To Zion" on the album *The Miseducation of Lauryn Hill*). Hill has publicly dealt with mental health issues, messy breakups, and financial woes that have become fodder for tabloid media and fans alike. In 2013, Hill was jailed for three months on tax evasion charges in New Jersey. This became headline news and further accelerated public criticism of her life and career. In that context, her comments make sense. She was tired. She was tired of having to perform both on and offstage, tired of people expecting her to be perfect.

I wish I had heard it when I was a child. I wish I was able to internalize this level of not giving a fuck. When I was growing up, I was raised by church mothers, community members, and men to understand my female body as the property and terrain of the larger community around me. Specifically, I learned that my style of dress; way of speaking; orientation to boys and, later, men; and my choices in romantic partners should take up a great deal of my time and energy. Not only that, I was taught to present myself in ways that would appeal to boys and men despite my deep attraction to other girls and women. Whether by television shows or by the homophobic comments I overheard adults making, I was taught to suppress my homosexuality, my gender fluidity, and any aspect of my personhood that might not appeal to potential suitors. As early as age eight, I had started feeling attraction to other girls. At eleven years old, I told my mom I wanted to be a boy. She immediately dismissed me. I didn't have words for my feelings about my gender and desires, but I knew they weren't allowed. It wasn't just men and boys who pressured me into these beliefs. Women and other girls also reinforced the idea that we, as women, were the property of others. That we didn't truly belong to ourselves. That we were simply moving through the world waiting to be chosen.

Pressed hair.
Stockings.
Long skirt.
Dress with a slip.
No makeup.
Legs crossed.
Speaking softly.
Apologizing.
Accentuating my breasts.
Rolling up my dress.

Flirting.

Apologizing again.

I learned the language of my gender and I learned it well. I became fluent in obedience and shrinking. I became an expert at hiding myself, at only showing the parts that would garner favor, prestige, or male attention. My elongated body, which reached the height of five foot ten by the time I was nine years old, gave the impression that I was much older than I was. By twelve years old, I was well over six feet tall. My training in my assumed gender and in compulsory heterosexuality meant that I was fending off the advances of my friends' dads, deacons at church, catcallers on the streets, and men and boys in nearly every public space I entered. And, rather than being taught to rebuff them, I was told that their harassment was a compliment and that the unwanted attention was a good thing. I stayed on top of my training. I ironed my dresses. I hand-washed my stockings. I overprocessed my hair with chemicals. I paid too much for acrylic nails that curved long and shiny. I got asymmetrical haircuts because singers like Monica and Salt from Salt-N-Pepa wore them. I chased an image of woman-hood that I thought would be mine if I just kept at it. If I just kept practicing, I would get good at it. Maybe I would stop liking women. Maybe I would stop feeling shame about the fact that I didn't even know if I was actually a girl or not.

I didn't know any of this at the time, but the "craziness" Lauryn Hill was talking about was the same container for womanhood that left me feeling obligated to engage in robotic domestic practices and hyperfeminine behaviors before I was even old enough to drive. I didn't know that women were typically deemed "crazy" when they did anything that ran counter to the heteronormative expectations for their bodies. For Black women, going "crazy" was rarely about medical diagnoses but about labeling independence, autonomy, and personal ambition as out of step with the submissive images of womanhood and femininity that centered white women. According to this paradigm—a holdover from the Victoria era—women should be seen and not heard.

Respectability, then, was all about modeling forms of femininity and identity that neither upset the status quo nor disrupted misogynistic ideas about women's aptitude—or perceived lack thereof—for leadership and sovereignty. For many Black people, respectability has required that we code-switch in public or change the tones and dialects with which we speak so that white Americans feel more comfortable. It has been the underlying force behind, for instance, corporate rules banning Black American hairstyles like dreadlocks and braids. Respectability requires everyone in society to move in alignment with white cisheteropatriarchy even when it is impossible. Conversely, embracing unrespectability by being queer, masculine, loud, tattooed, or unfeminine was a social risk as well as a political one. It drew attention. But by stepping outside of people's expectations, I eventually learned that it was never really my humanity that people were valuing in the first place. It was their projections onto my body—their myths, fantasies, and dreams—that they were valuing all along. In seeking their respect, I was diminishing myself.

Unfortunately, white women have long benefited from the ways that the politics of respectability centers whiteness as the norm and white women as the pinnacle of beauty, domestic ability, and femininity. Even in the struggle for the right to vote, white women showed that their gender solidarity would always be conditioned by racism. For example, prominent suffragists Elizabeth Cady Stanton and Susan B. Anthony distanced themselves from abolitionist efforts after the Fifteenth Amendment was passed, giving Black men the right to vote before white women.[3] The idea that so many Black people would have access to the vote before these middle-class, high-society white women enraged them. After the Nineteenth Amendment passed in 1920, Black women remained disenfranchised.[4] To build solidarity between Northern and Southern white women, Black women were frequently left out of critical campaigns for the vote.

Even movements for racial justice have to bend to respectability, which often means assimilating into whiteness or getting as close to it as possible. When Claudette Colvin was passed over as the face of the Montgomery Bus Boycott in favor of Rosa Parks, it was for a host of reasons related to respectability politics. Colvin refused to give up her seat on a Montgomery bus a whole nine months prior to Rosa Parks. But Colvin was only fifteen years old, darker skinned, and young, and shortly after her arrest, she became pregnant. According to Colvin, Rosa Parks's "skin texture was the kind that people associate with the middle class."[5] After her experience, Colvin was shunned by some in her own community. Colvin's experience depicts the ways that colorism, or the preference for lighter skin tones within communities of color, holds a host of political implications. This preference is rooted in the perceived primacy of whiteness and the anti-Black narratives that position Black Americans at the lowest position in a mythical racial hierarchy.

Few political leaders in our history have embodied what it means to be unrespectable. It's hard to be elected to public office or treated as a viable leader without aligning with social norms. However, Fannie Lou Hamer (also known as Fannie Lou Townsend) embraced unrespectability, and she advocated for politics that centered those who fell outside of these normative boundaries. Hamer was born on October 6, 1917, in the Mississippi Delta. Growing up as a young girl in Ruleville, Mississippi, Hamer believed that she should work to serve and support other Black Mississippians. She was the child of sharecroppers, a class of folk who were expected to keep their heads down and mouths shut. As a poor child with nineteen siblings, Hamer was not expected to read or write, or even speak, for that matter. She often had little food and no shoes. In those days, sharecroppers were paid fifty dollars for every child they bore—a carryover from slavery that put a price on Black women's reproduction and commodified the labor of Black children and families. The Townsend family would often pick cotton for plantation owners who, just a few decades earlier, would have been their slave masters. Instead of slavery, sharecroppers were pushed into a system of indentured servitude with plantation owners. As Kay Mills writes, "Most sharecroppers lacked the education to keep records of what they had borrowed and what they were owed after giving the landowner half the crop."[6] This meant that plantation owners could manipulate Black sharecroppers into working for much less than they were due, and they could do so without any fear of reprisal.

And sharecropping was grueling work. Whole families labored to pick cotton and till the soil without any real confirmation that their labor would be compensated or their homes protected. The anti-Black, predatory actions of white American property owners shaped Hamer's entire life and, eventually, her activism.

Hamer's politics, like Hurston's and Baker's, were informed by her childhood and adolescent experiences. In her work, she often spoke about the overt disregard she experienced as a child: She was poor, she was darker skinned, she wasn't thin, and she did not comport herself to fit traditional ideas about femininity. Hamer was ignited by the politics of her mother and father growing up. Prior to her official entry into activism and organizing, she was concerned about the attacks on voting rights for Black Americans.[7] In the late 1950s and early 1960s, Mississippi and neighboring states, like Arkansas and Alabama, were hotbeds for racial division and contestations. It was in 1961 that Freedom Riders across the American South were met with violent confrontations from police officers and white mobs along their routes.[8]

It was also in 1961 that Hamer was forcibly sterilized after going to a Sunflower County hospital for a minor surgery to remove a tumor. Many at the time called the procedure a "Mississippi appendectomy," a process by which doctors and medical staff would take away Black women's ability to reproduce without their consent.[9]

This experience ignited Hamer's quest for justice for Black people. Mills writes that Hamer was "touched with sorrow, about her lack of control over her own life."[10] Hamer had lost two pregnancies to stillbirths and was raising two adopted daughters. But she still had plans to have children of her own until the Sunflower County hospital chose to sterilize her with no notice or acknowledgment. These sterilizations of Black women, which were an issue that would become a national crisis in the following decade, were not happenstance. They were a systematic method of controlling Black reproduction and exerting power over Black people's bodies. Moreover, they were another way that white people (and the institutions that privileged them) marked Black people as subclass citizens who were inhuman and unworthy of respect and dignity.

After this awful experience, Hamer dedicated herself to fighting for Black voting rights. In summer 1962, Hamer became an organizer with SNCC and led seventeen volunteers to register to vote in a Mississippi courthouse.[11] The group was harassed as they ventured home and charged a one-hundred-dollar fine by police because their bus was "too yellow." That night, Hamer was fired from her job and forced to leave her home because she had joined the movement to support Black voting rights. Much of the property she and her husband had acquired was confiscated, and they were forced to leave. This was one of the many points in Hamer's life when the intersections of her Blackness, gender, and class status situated her at the nexus of white supremacist and state-sanctioned violence.

Hamer's political style was verbose, confrontational, and direct. She was notorious for speaking in plain terms about the treatment she received as a voting rights organizer in the South. In 1963, she said, "I can tell you what it is like to suffer for things that are essential in order for one to survive throughout these economical and social changes. So many times as a child, I have gone hungry and now as an adult, I'm still hungry."[12] For Hamer, the right to vote was about securing the right to humanity. It was about becoming a "first-class citizen" after so many generations of being disregarded and disrespected. Hamer's passion for political freedom and economic justice for Black people grew. She understood how vicious and savage whites in Mississippi had been to her comrades, and she was seemingly fearless in confronting these institutions and citizens about their anti-Blackness.

Hamer was a rich orator who often spoke about the macabre violence facing Black Americans in the South as they struggled for the vote. In 1964, while delivering a speech alongside Malcolm X, Hamer said, "My name is Fannie Lou Hamer and I exist at 626 East Lafayette Street in Ruleville, Mississippi. The reason I say 'exist' [is] because we're excluded from everything in Mississippi but the tombs and the graves. That's why it is called that instead of the 'land of the free and the home of the brave.' It's called in Mississippi 'the land of the tree and the home of the grave.' "[13] In this speech, she described how several Black women had been shot in Ruleville during a voting registration drive. Later, several protestors were arrested and intimidated by police officers for traveling to encourage Black people to obtain and secure their right to vote. These experiences laid bare the very real stakes of anti-Black racism in this political moment. Hamer was able to articulate not just the systemic variables that made it hard for Black people to "exist" in her home state of Mississippi, but also how the State frequently entered the lives and livelihoods of Black Americans in intimate ways. Hamer had endured so much violence in her lifetime, violence that she encountered because she believed Black people deserved equal citizenship. In this speech, Hamer retold the gruesome story of how she was beaten while in police custody. The white police officers ordered two Black prisoners to beat Hamer until they were each exhausted. Then, the officer pulled up her dress and continued to beat her, hitting her in the head. Hamer recounted how she screamed in agony as she endured the blows. She was given no medical attention. Hamer later found that the beating damaged blood vessels behind her eye. This sexualized violence, meant to humiliate Hamer and degrade her body, is just one example of the ways that unrespectable people often suffer from targeted forms of harm meant to violate them both physically and emotionally. The overt disregard for their humanity and their rights as citizens reflects a lack of compassion and empathy for people deemed disposable and insignificant. This is the goal of a white supremacist social order: to mark Black bodies as useless while simultaneously exploiting them for labor, culture, and energy.

These experiences didn't keep Hamer from holding the government accountable. When she implored the United States government to assist her in responding to her experiences, they stalled, explaining that it would take time to redress her grievances. Hamer was not amused, nor was she pacified. In response, she told the audience, "For three hundred years, we've given them time. And I've been tired so long, now I am sick and tired of being sick and tired, and we want a change."[14] This is likely one of Hamer's most iconic phrases, but people should consider that it was born out of a deep despair over the state of justice in the United States. For Hamer, the treatment of Black people in Mississippi was an indication that *no one* was truly free. If she and her comrades could be beaten and killed through extrajudicial violence simply because they were Black, if doctors could sterilize her without her consent, and if police officers could arrest them, fine them, and assist in stealing their land, it meant that the promises of the Thirteenth, Fourteenth, and Fifteenth Amendments were never truly fulfilled. These Reconstruction Amendments told Black Americans that they were no longer enslaved, had a right to due process under the law, and had been granted the right to vote, respectively.[15] However, in actuality, Hamer experienced forms of re-enslavement on the plantation as a sharecropper, had her rights erased by doctors and officers, and still struggled to register Black Americans for the vote. While white women were granted the right to vote in 1920, it wasn't until the Voting Rights Act of 1965—an act meant to enforce the promise of the Fifteenth Amendment—that Black Americans fully gained access to the vote. Hamer understood that, while the Constitution was the law of the land, being Black, unrespectable, and poor signaled the execution of a hidden set of rules and policies that were detrimental to Black Americans all over the country. She closed out the speech by telling the audience, "You are not free in Harlem. The people are not free in Chicago, because I've been there, too. They are not free in Philadelphia, because I've been there, too. And when you get it over with all the way around, some of the places is a Mississippi in disguise."[16]

Hamer was critically important to civil rights and justice work because she shifted the focus away from the mainstream ideas about Black respectability and traditional notions of citizenship that predominated the church-led movements of the time. Instead, she declared that "nobody's free until everybody's free."[17] Her focus was on the least of us rather than the most respectable of us. It became an organizing principle, model, and declaration for young people seeking to situate themselves within larger, more established movement work. Hamer's efforts to cast light on the unique plights and concerns of Black Mississippians became a beacon to shine an even brighter light on the injustices that Black people all over the country were enduring.

Hamer died on March 14, 1977, at only fifty-nine years old. She suffered from heart failure, which was brought on by diabetes, hypertension, and cancer.[18] I can't help but think that the struggles and violence she endured at the hands of the State were responsible for her passing so early.

Blackness and the Role of Respectability Politics

The concept of respectability is usually framed as a negative thing. It has been used to ostracize Black working-class and poor people like Fannie Lou Hamer and exclude them from full citizenship and access to life-sustaining resources. Respectability has also been used to justify extrajudicial violence against Black people at the hands of police authorities and citizen vigilantes. Respectability is a natural byproduct of anti-Blackness and white supremacy. In a system that prioritizes and centers one way of being, it is only logical that all others will be organized and policed to measure up to the default category. Respectability itself is not violent or harmful if individuals are able to consent to it as a way of embodying their own identities. However, the culture surrounding respectability, a culture that marshals the military-like components of the State to eliminate outsiders, is rooted in terror, as is clear in the life of Hamer. The State frequently used the notion that her life didn't matter to enact all manner of violence against her. She withstood that violence until the day she died.

For many Black people, respectability is also a means of survival in a white-leaning world. For those people, respectability—the ability to comport oneself to a set of generally acceptable social norms and behaviors that are usually tethered to whiteness, middle-class status, and heteronormativity—is how they determine their self-respect. Self-respect, then, is regulated by the gaze of others and by the ability to measure up to a set of standards that exist outside of one's true identity. For most people, determining respectability is a process of assessment and judgment. They evaluate people's hairstyles, clothes, speech, and other social cues to decide whether or not someone deserves their respect. This process almost always excludes Black people, immigrants, trans and queer folks, disabled folks, fat people, women with multiple children (especially if those children are suspected to have different fathers), drug users, the chronically ill, those with mental disabilities, and anyone else deemed "other." These exclusions are not accidental. Rather, they are an intentional way that systems of oppression control ideas about who qualifies as an "insider"—someone who deserves the benefits of tax policy, state benefits, and protections—and who is considered an "outsider"—someone who deserves nothing more than the trash heap.

Black Feminist historian Evelyn Brooks Higginbotham is often credited with coining the phrase "the politics of respectability."[19] In her analysis of Black church women's activism in the late nineteenth and early twentieth centuries, she says that this process "emphasized reform of individual behavior and attitudes both as a goal in itself and as a strategy for reform of the entire structural system of American race relations."[20] She explains that for many Black people during this era, respectability was a tactic to reshape the terrain of anti-Black racism. It was a tool, among many, to show white Americans that Black people actually were due the respect of citizenship. Respectability politics were an effort to situate Black people within a larger community of American social mores that had frequently excluded them. This was imperative for Black people who were working through multiple ways to achieve Black liberation. But there is an ugly side to respectability, too.

When Black people are able to signal to the larger world that they are respectable, upstanding citizens who can assimilate (or at least attempt to assimilate), they are often granted proximity to whiteness in ways that feel like inclusion. This might mean getting a job (like Clarence Thomas in the U.S. Supreme Court) or gaining fame for one's opinions (like Candace Owens). Sometimes, they are taken in by white people and white-led institutions that regularly harm Black people. Frequently, those Black assimilators mistake this performative and conditional inclusion for freedom. However, as I write in chapter one, freedom cannot rest on exclusion and oppression. If we learned nothing from Hamer, we learned that unrespectable folks are worthy of humanity and deserving of kindness. No matter their class or station. No matter where they come from. No matter the languages they speak or the disabilities they carry in their bodies. All people are deserving of respect.

Respectability politics show up in today's movements in a number of critical ways. The most prominent and relevant example of this issue is Black leaders such as Al Sharpton and Jesse Jackson, who often place themselves in public-facing positions, typically in community with white Americans who are able to distance themselves from the conditions of vulnerability that many Black Americans face. It was in 2014 that young people overtook Al Sharpton's efforts to put on a show of respectability, staging a march in response to the Movement for Black Lives's efforts to continue to draw attention to police violence against Black Americans. Sharpton has often dismissed the feedback from young activists who believe his closeness to political campaigns and news media has decentered his focus on the communities most affected by this problem.[21] (Note how this mirrors the critiques Ella Baker leveled at experienced activists and organizers who condescended to and disrespected the work of young Black organizers in the 1960s and '70s.) By spurning young activists, respectable, patriarchal movement leaders like Sharpton reproduce hierarchies that fail to take into account those who are most vulnerable to harm. Moreover, he ends up taking two steps forward only to take three steps back, a phenomenon Black folk simply refer to as "hustling backwards."

In August 2020, Jesse Jackson made a public comment about the "looting" in Chicago after weeks of protests following the police-sanctioned murders of Breonna Taylor and George Floyd and the ongoing police violence against Black Americans in Chicago. Jackson posted on Twitter, "This act of pillaging, robbing & looting in Chicago was humiliating, embarrassing & morally wrong. It must not be associated with our quest for social justice and equality. #DrKing, #MedgarEvers & #JohnLewis, our martyrs, cry together in shame. #StopTheViolence #SaveTheChildren."[22] Many organizers saw this comment as an attempt to shame young Black people for their righteous discontent and to use respectability tactics as a mechanism to control their behaviors. What's worse, organizers have maintained that Jackson has nothing to do with the movement that he has made public comments about.[23]

For many respectable Black people, especially those from older generations rooted in Christianity and the narratives of the nuclear household, justice doesn't include mass protests, burning down police precincts, flipping cop cars, and blockading streetways to the local lululemon. It looks like piecemeal, step-by-step, time-consuming requests for a seat at the table. This is not to say that previous generations were not ready to fight for radical political change. Rather, it is to suggest that there are always multiple perspectives on how to get free. Historically, leaders like Booker T. Washington have represented the respectable ethics in many Black communities that are primarily concerned with reform rather than radical change. Washington is best known for his "Cast down your buckets" speech,[24] which implored Black Americans to make the best of their situations no matter the conditions they faced. It was an articulation of American individualism and bootstraps logic that says that if you just work hard enough, you can overcome anything. We now know this logic is fallacious, as it fails to account for the ways that systems and institutions actively work to make Black people's lives more difficult, no matter how hard they work or how sturdy their bootstraps might be. More generally, while there have long been advocates in Black communities for violent confrontations with the State, there have likewise been strong proponents of nonviolence because Black people, like any other group, contain multitudes. So, when new generations of young Black people step out of these constraints and demand to be heard, regardless of their background, education, place of origin, immigration status, wealth, or emotional state, many people (including Black people) recoil from their concerns, becoming unresponsive and unreceptive to their demands. For respectable Black Americans, it isn't what young organizers and activists are saying but how they are saying it that matters. This is one of the primary issues with respectability politics.

Respectability shows up in other insidious ways as well. In recent years, since police violence against Black Americans has become more nationally acknowledged and smartphones have captured these moments in living color, respectability politics have even been wielded against deceased Black Americans posthumously. One such example of this emerged in 2014 after eighteen-year-old Michael Brown was murdered by now-former Officer Darren Wilson in Ferguson, Missouri. Brown was crossing the street with friends after leaving a local store. After an altercation, Wilson shot Brown at least six times, twice in the head.[25] Wilson claimed that he was afraid of Brown, whom he described as a "demon" during his grand jury testimony.[26] Brown's body was left in the middle of the street for hours as his community languished, watching officers mill around him. After Brown's murder, *The New York Times* ran a retrospective of Michael Brown's life where they referred to the teenager as "no angel."[27] The article detailed Brown's interpersonal altercations with neighbors, accused him of alcohol and drug use, and suggested that he was stealing cigars just before he was killed. *The New York Times* faced immense backlash after publishing such an insensitive article at a time when so many Black communities were actively grieving yet another police killing of a young Black American.[28] The focus on Brown's behavior before his murder was a tactic of the mainstream white media to justify violence against Black people: If he was "no angel," the logic suggests, then perhaps his extrajudicial murder wasn't so bad after all. It implied that, for Brown's life to matter, he needed to be perfect. Rather than chalking up any of his rambunctious behaviors to the fact that he was a high schooler finding his way, they judged secondhand stories about his life just days after his murder to decenter the police brutality that resulted in his death. In that process, they reinforced respectable notions of identity that unfairly punish Black people for merely existing while rewarding white Americans for their unearned privilege.

These messages suggest that Black people should first prove themselves respectable before they are heard and regarded, even in death. It means that, before our concerns are acknowledged at all, they must be packaged up and sugarcoated in such a way as to make white people comfortable. That usually means that Black people must be pristine, blemish-free angels who have never smoked marijuana, flipped anyone the middle finger, or taken a picture of themselves making a hand gesture that looks like they are shooting a pistol. Otherwise, that same picture or instance might be used to summarize their entire existence. It might be used to criminalize them. Or, worse, to justify violence against them. That's the message behind Sharpton's and Jackson's chastisement of young Black organizers for their method of protest. And it becomes weaponized against young people like Michael Brown (and so many other young Black people who have been killed by police) when they interact with police authorities. My point here is: The stakes of respectability politics are extremely high. And it is only through coalitions, community-building, and solidarity with other Black people that we can combat the divisive nature of compulsory respectability.

Respectability is inherently anti-Black and continues to treat whiteness, heteronormativity, and middle-class experiences as an ideal. Moreover, respectability is an unattainable objective for many Black women because it is rooted in the ownership and sexualization of Black women's bodies that stems directly from chattel bondage. Rather than allowing Black women to fully embody themselves in ways that honor their experiences, respectability limits how we can express sexuality (otherwise we might be deemed "fast-tailed"), how we engage in labor (otherwise we might be deemed "lazy"), and how we express emotion (otherwise we might be deemed "angry"). For many Black women, self-identification is a very complicated thing. It is so mediated by the outside world that we often consider the perspectives of others even when naming ourselves. We frequently oscillate between courage and fear when making proclamations about how we will comport ourselves in public. We are afraid of stepping outside of boundaries and potentially exposing ourselves to physical violence, isolation, rebuke, or simply shame for being something other than what others want us to be. For many straight women, these fears are heightened because of narratives that unrespectable women may not be appealing to men, may not be marriageable, or may not be suitable mothers. As Black women get older, if they remain

unmarried, they are labeled as sexually promiscuous, irrespon-
sible, and unethical. Not only that, but news articles[29] and governmental documents like the 1965 Moynihan Report[30]
continue to paint unwed Black mothers as the problem in
Black communities. This "study" of Black families was rooted
in anti-Blackness and centered the social standards and expectations of white middle-class families. Because so many Black
families are non-traditional and non-nuclear, the report labeled them as broken and dangerous to future Black generations. The deeply flawed Moynihan Report has been so
enduring in its indictment of Black mothers and its assertion
that Black families suffer from a "culture of poverty" that we
still discuss its impact today, more than fifty years after its initial publication.[31] Respectability is an all-encompassing, lifelong process that shapes our very existence from womb to
tomb.

These historical frameworks of respectability continue to
shape the present. They induce fear and anxiety for many
Black women daily. For many of us, fear has kept us alive.
Fear has been the very thing that kept us "on the straight and
narrow." It has kept us out of potentially dangerous situations
and away from potential threats. As I describe in chapter two,
in which I discuss truth and the "culture of dissemblance,"
many Black women have come to realize that sharing our true
identities in public puts us at risk for discrimination, persecution, and violence. So, rather than revealing ourselves in all
spaces and places, especially the parts of us deemed unrespectable, we have developed tools to expose only pieces of ourselves
at work and among community outsiders so that we will be
protected. But that very same fear also keeps us from reaching

136   *Black Women Taught Us*

too high or moving too far from home. It keeps us from dreaming too big or thinking too much of ourselves.

In many ways, the work of respectability politics is done not only to protect us and to reinforce the norms of white heteropatriarchal society, but also to preserve a status quo where Black women are subordinate to white people and men of all stripes. That's why Fannie Lou Hamer's lessons have been so critical for us to bring into the present day. Hamer was keenly aware of the ways that respectability and white supremacy worked together to marginalize Black people in the United States. It was only through standing fully upright in our unrespectability, speaking clearly and frankly about our experiences, and demanding that we all be seen as human that we might actually get free.

One thing that has given me immense hope as I have aged is watching the ways that every generation pulls further and further away from the respectability standards of the generation preceding it. According to recent surveys, Gen Z (those born between 1997 and 2012) constitutes the queerest generation in history, with more than 15 percent of polled respondents identifying as queer or transgender. This rate is a drastic increase from prior years, but it is also another data point along the trend line of each generation reporting more comfort with identifying in this way.[32] There was a time when declaring I'm queer would have resulted in a choir of gasps and pearl grabs. Now, in the 2020s, I am among many people who have the access and ability to choose otherwise. To choose to be who I am on my own terms and to also demand that my various interlocking identities be honored, respected, and valued.

Feminist Cathy Cohen says in one of the most seminal queer theoretical texts ever written:

For many of us, the label "queer" symbolizes an acknowledgment that through our existence and everyday survival we embody sustained and multi-sited resistance to systems (based on dominant constructions of race and gender) that seek to normalize our sexuality, exploit our labor, and constrain our visibility. At the intersection of oppression and resistance lies the radical potential of queerness to challenge and bring together all those deemed marginal and all those committed to liberatory politics.[33]

Here, Cohen suggests that maybe many more of us are queer than we think. She asks us to consider that maybe those of us who fall outside of normative boundaries sexually (not just because of who we love but because of how we love and who we are) are all queer in some way. The welfare queens, the punks, the trans folks, and the other non-normative Black people whose life choices have been maligned, targeted, and persecuted by the State—maybe we are all just a little queer. If, as Cohen declares, espousing a set of queer politics is truly about resistance to being erased, radicalizing our futures, and pushing back against the normalization of gender, sexuality, and identity, then we, as Black people, have the opportunity to see ourselves as a broader, more connected community when we free ourselves of the weight of respectability. When we come to realize that Blackness and queerness are wrapped up together because, to whiteness, Black people have always been and will always be different, unassimilable, outside, and excluded, we will have the ability to tap into the radical potential of our own politics.

CHAPTER 6

Shirley Chisholm Taught Me to Hold Whiteness Accountable

Coachella, thanks for allowing me to be the first Black woman to headline. Ain't that 'bout a bitch?

—*Beyoncé*

If they don't give you a seat at the table, bring a folding chair.

—*Shirley Chisholm*

It's a cold morning in Los Angeles, so I snuggle down into my USC hoodie, getting cozy in my awkward one-sided desk. It's an American history class, and my professor, a frail-looking cartoon character of an old white man, is pacing in front of a packed lecture hall. The audience is mostly white, but speckled with a few Black, Latinx, and Asian faces. We make eye contact with one another. Sometimes we give each other a nod, an acknowledgment that we are here. We exist. It's a predominantly white, elite university in one of the Blackest, most diverse parts of Los Angeles. I selected this university because it allowed me to stay in my home state of California. I was close enough to my hometown to not feel homesick but far away enough to feel grown up.

"If white people had a culture, what would it be?" the professor asked. His scraggly white beard crinkled as he curled his lips to form the words. "If white people had a culture, it would be genocide."

Oh.

I shrink down even more in my seat, looking around the room to see if everyone else heard what I heard. I feel the blood rushing to my cheeks, but I don't know why I'm embarrassed. Maybe it's because I agree with him. Maybe it's because I feel some shame. Maybe it's because I was taught not to have these conversations in front of white people.

Some of the white students who were looking down at their phones look up, concern showing on their faces. I see one white male student shake his head as if he is upset.

Now that I see the white people are reacting, I feel a little empowered. The professor transforms into a hero, and I revel in what he's said. I have never heard anyone say these words before, especially not in front of "mixed company." I can't wait to get back to my dorm of all Black students to tell them about my class today. I know they aren't going to believe me.

Guns, rape, murder, taking lands that don't belong to them—my professor tells us that these are the most consistent parts of white culture. He tells us that the movie *American History X* is an accurate representation of the ways that white people pillage and steal.

The one white student who shook his head earlier puts on his backpack and leaves the class. He makes sure that the door makes a *WHAPPP!* sound as he leaves.

"This is a history class," the professor says nonchalantly, after the student leaves. "If you don't want to hear this stuff and learn about your own history, what are you doing here?"

A few days later, it's our weekly discussion period with my white cisgender male teaching assistant. He is average height, handsome, with dark hair and a non-commanding presence. I like him even though he seems insecure about teaching a class about the history of racial discrimination in the United States.

The white students who were completely silent in class two days ago are speaking today. With only two Black women in the class, they seem comfortable to express their concerns about what the professor shared this week.

"It's not just white people."

"What about the ways that Black people also use guns and cause crime?"

"Seriously, like our school is in the 'hood. I have to avoid certain neighborhoods because I don't want someone to bust a cap in my ass," the other Black girl says with a smirk.

The white students nod in agreement.

I see my teaching assistant make eye contact with me as he struggles with what to say next. The other white students look at me as if they are expecting me to agree with the other Black girl. I mean, I am also a Black girl, after all.

"Yeah, I just think that it's hella racist to talk about Black people this way when white people were the ones who created this entire problem in the first place," I say. The color leaves my teaching assistant's face. White students around the room scowl at me. A few of them nod their heads in agreement. The other Black girl in the room rolls her eyes. No one speaks to me after that. My teaching assistant changes the subject and we move on. I feel triumphant. I feel as though I have disrupted a current in the class and on a campus that prioritizes white students' feelings over my experiences. After my comment, I realize that I have been holding that sentiment in my body for months since moving to Los Angeles. I notice that there is a lightness in my body because I have shared my truth, a truth that, to me, matters.

Throughout college, there were multiple moments of truth-telling that weren't just about my own self-expression and the ways that my truths are rarely heralded and valued. Those moments were also about setting boundaries and standards with the people in my orbit. I made sure to take advantage of these moments, whether they were at school, at work, or on the street. For me, it was imperative that I articulate the stakes of people's actions to those whose ability to avoid the truth gave them permission to enact all manner of harm. In these moments, I knew that I would rarely be received well or willingly. These sorts of truths, truths about how other people's actions and choices affected me, were the ones people seemed to hate the most. But their inability to face reality was not my concern, nor was it my problem. I learned from my Black Feminist foremothers that holding white people to these standards and keeping them accountable wasn't a form of punishment. It was a way for us all to become free.

One of the greatest teachers on the importance of holding whiteness and (by extension) white people accountable was Shirley Chisholm. She was born Shirley Anita St. Hill on November 30, 1924, in Brooklyn, New York. She was the oldest of four daughters born to immigrant parents. Chisholm's father, Charles St. Hill, was a factory worker from Guyana. Her mother, Ruby Seale St. Hill, was a seamstress from Barbados.

As the St. Hills dealt with the financial insecurity of the Great Depression, Chisholm spent much of her childhood and adolescence being raised by her grandmother in Barbados.[1] Chisholm returned to the United States for much of her schooling. She graduated from Girls' High School in Brooklyn in 1942 and from Brooklyn College summa cum laude in 1946. When professors encouraged her to pursue a career in politics, she would tell them she faced the "double handicap" of being both Black and female.[2] But Chisholm would not only have an eventual role in politics, but also go on to become the first Black woman to run for president of the United States on one of the major two-party tickets.

Chisholm's positionality developed within her as a frustration with the status quo. Her experiences at the margins of Blackness, womanhood, and working-class status often made it harder for her to express her political beliefs and concerns without challenge.[3] In Chisholm's autobiography *Unbought and Unbossed,* she details the ways that her identity as a child of immigrants, a poor person, and a Black woman made her specifically threatening to the United States' electoral status quo. She wrote:

> I think blacks from the islands tend to have less fear of white people, and therefore less hatred of them. They can meet whites as equals; this is harder for American blacks, who tend to overreact by jumping from feeling that whites are superior to looking down on them as inferior. Both attitudes equally isolate them from the greater society in which eventually we all have to learn to live.[4]

Chisholm recognized her relationship to the islands as something that set her apart. While this quote might be misread as dismissive of Black Americans' responses to anti-Blackness and white racism, it is rather an exploration of the ways that our unique experiences under white supremacy shape our attitudes and responses to the systems of oppression we encounter. For Chisholm, her differences from many Black Americans were an asset despite how white people had made her feel about being a child of immigrants. For these reasons, Chisholm encouraged Black Americans to hold the government and white people (in general) accountable for the disproportionately detrimental conditions facing Black communities.

Today, when we talk about Hillary Clinton's run for the presidency or Kamala Harris's pathbreaking position as the first Black and Asian woman to be elected vice president of the United States, we have to first acknowledge that it was Shirley Chisholm who carved out that path for them to make their way to the White House.

Chisholm was never the subtle or quiet type. One of my favorite reminders of this fact is the story about how she would walk around her borough early in her political career with a bullhorn, often announcing herself in fluent Spanish. They called her "Fighting Shirley Chisholm."[5] Shirley fought all the way to the United States Congress.

When she noticed injustice or unequal treatment under the eyes of the law, she spoke up clearly and explicitly. In her autobiography, she details her concerns with a Congress that she believed was not truly listening to the needs of the people. Chisholm was doubtful that Congress members were equipped to address the needs of poor and working-class people. She writes, "The antipoverty programs were designed by white-middle-class intellectuals who had no experience of being poor, despised, and discriminated against."[6] For Chisholm, being situated at multiple margins of identity was critical to formulating legislation and programs that could adequately address the inequalities vulnerable people faced.

Chisholm was clear that this work would require an analysis of the racism and exclusionary ideas that underlie much of the political process. She comments, "Most of the poor were poor because they were labeled niggers or greasers or hillbillies or canucks or spics. They belonged to despised, powerless groups."[7] These groups of people, Chisholm recognized, were outside of the average congressperson's realm of political imagination. These were the unwanteds. They were the milk carton kids of the political arena: lost to history so much so that they became myth. These supposed deviants, misfits, and outsiders were frequently left out of the political process altogether.

Chisholm was keenly aware that Congress would typically work to uphold and maintain the status quo even when it set out to address the needs of the poor and marginalized. She writes, "The federal programs were intended to give the poor something tangible, quickly, and without alarming the middle class. Congress, in particular, did not want to cause any disruption of the political structure."[8] If Congress was working so hard not to disrupt the status quo, how would they truly address the needs of people whose concerns fell outside of the typical political structure? How would they extend resources and political insights to accommodate people they didn't even fully understand or account for?

In Black Feminist circles, we often refer to this tension as the dilemma of reformative justice versus radical or transformative justice. Reformative justice is primarily concerned with maintaining existing oppressive systems, leaving them intact for financial, social, or other reasons. Under this approach, solutions are usually tweaks or manipulations to existing models (whether those models have proven successful in the past or not). Reformist methods take the bit-by-bit approach to politics that frequently leaves marginalized people for last. Even when these piecemeal methods are proven unsuccessful, many citizens cleave to them because of a fear of radical change that might dismantle these systems wholesale.

But Fighting Shirley Chisholm was not in the business of creating more myths. What's more, she was not in the business of overlooking those who needed the interventions of the government most. Chisholm firmly believed that it was the duty of the U.S. government to work on behalf of those who were most vulnerable: women and minorities. She demonstrated this belief in a 1971 letter she penned on congressional letterhead to Congressman Don Edwards, chairman of the subcommittee responsible for conducting hearings on the Equal Rights Amendment (ERA). During this time, Chisholm was actively working to help pass the ERA, and she was concerned that groups of young women, those directly impacted by the outcomes of the ERA, were not being heard. She was also the only woman to be a founding member of the Congressional Black Caucus, another signal that she was willing to put herself in direct conversation and confrontation with potential opponents to women's rights so that she could wage her fight. Rather than following the red tape and bureaucracy of the legislative government, Chisholm went directly to the chairman of the subcommittee and asked that young women have the opportunity to testify.[9] Chisholm faced opposition from every side as she worked to pursue justice and fairness for Black folks and women of all stripes. It was a *New York Times* reporter who made sure to tell the world that he believed Chisholm was "not beautiful" and had a "scrawny" physique.[10] The reporter also commented on Chisholm's lisp, not acknowledging that she was likely fluent in more languages than he was.

It wasn't just white reporters who created obstacles for Chisholm. At times, it was other Black people and even women who failed to support Chisholm's 1972 run for the White House. Gloria Steinem, for instance, was a prominent supporter of George McGovern instead of Chisholm.[11] Steinem referred to McGovern as "the best white male candidate" in the race and was a part of the McGovern campaign's effort to court the women's vote.[12] Steinem noted that she supported both candidates (even though she had been actively campaigning for McGovern).[13] This was a deeply personal blow to Chisholm, as Steinem had long been a supporter of Chisholm's political career. At least two years earlier, Steinem had tried to convince Chisholm to run against Republican Senator Jacob Javits. Accordingly, many felt that Steinem abandoned Chisholm[14] (a fact that Steinem herself refuted much later).[15] Chisholm was working with Black men who she had hoped would support her presidential efforts. However, many of them were not willing to support Chisholm's campaign for fear that her politics were too oriented toward women, minorities, and building coalitions with groups that they did not want present in the political arena.[16] In her autobiography, Chisholm shares how the fight for justice for all people and against white racism radicalized her. She writes, " 'I am fighting,' I tell them. 'I know I'm here in Congress, part of the Establishment, but you can see that I haven't started to conform. I haven't sold out. I'm fighting within the system. There is no other place to fight.' "[17]

The self-proclaimed ex-moderate says she is a "militant," and that she understands that if racism is not abolished swiftly, the country will see "real, full-scale revolution."[18] For Chisholm, the fight was coming to a head. It was the moment when Black people were becoming fed up with the institutional racism and structural inequalities that had plagued their lives. She writes, "Black Americans today are serving that notice on white-oriented institutions. They are saying they are ready to do anything. . . . After enough time, we will be tired of talking."[19]

Black Mothers, Anti-Black Violence, and Holding the State Accountable

There is something particularly powerful about the ways that Black motherhood emboldens and empowers entire communities. Black women who mother must see themselves at the helm of the future of Black communities writ large so the stakes are just higher. As a mother of three free Black children, I have felt this sentiment myself.

For me, having children deeply shifted my commitments to Black liberation. While I had long believed in abolitionist principles and ethics, I hadn't been able to concretely formulate a systematic way of life to align my day-to-day choices with my beliefs. Truthfully, I could talk about it, but I couldn't always *be* about it in ways that I was proud of. It was when I had my first child at twenty-three years old that those feelings began to change. I started to see myself as uniquely situated to influence the next generation of Black activists, leaders, thinkers, and freedom fighters. I started investing myself in Black political issues and the global conversations about our communal Black struggle. I started linking my life choices and outcomes to others who looked like me. It wasn't theoretical anymore. It was about life and death.

As a mother of Black children in the United States, I have witnessed the violence against Black people with this duality. On one hand, I am a Black person myself, and I wake up every morning knowing that my race, gender, class, and sexuality all intersect in ways that orient me to power differently from people who do not share these characteristics. On the other hand, I am the guardian of fragile, new lives who trust me to protect them in the very same world that often scares me to my core. This is the deeply personal and political nature of raising Black children in an anti-Black state. And living this way in the face of increasing vigilante and police violence against Black people has meant that I am constantly reminded that not only am I not safe or protected, but my children aren't either.

When twelve-year-old Tamir Rice was killed in a neighborhood park in Cleveland, Ohio, by now-former police officer Timothy Loehmann, I was living in Chicago, Illinois, with my spouse and three children. My oldest son was only six years old. My daughter was just turning three, and my youngest child had just turned one. We were new to the Midwest and its history. The segregation we had experienced in Southern California was overt, highly visible. You could see it coming. In the Midwest, the anti-Blackness and racism was much more subtle. White people were still nice to you in public, but they called you a nigger when they got home. They would stand on blocks where you didn't belong, watching you drive through, just to make sure you left and didn't stop. They would make their neighborhoods so inaccessible, overpriced, unwelcoming, and distant that you wouldn't want to be around them anyway. I learned quickly that racism in the American Midwest is as common and as expected as apple pie and French fries.

Living in the Midwest, I remember being so fearful for my sons after Tamir Rice was murdered. The officer didn't even take a moment to step out of his car before drawing his service weapon and pulling the trigger. In reflecting on the ways that the State has the jurisdiction and power to enter our homes, I think about seven-year-old Aiyana Stanley-Jones. Trayvon Martin was killed for being tall, Black, and wearing a hoodie. Michael Brown was killed for crossing the street. Now, Tamir had been killed for playing with a BB gun in a local park. I knew that my children were no different from these Black children. I knew that there was nothing I could reasonably do to protect them from a world that snuffed out Black childhood so easily.

Anthropologist Christen Smith offers us a notion of "sequelae" to explain the connections between state-sanctioned Black death and Black motherhood. She explains that the State actively works to kill Black children and annihilate Black families to enact terror upon Black communities. Under this system, Black women are the true targets of carceral violence because the goal is to stop Black children from being born and nurtured. Black women, the people who are often birthing and rearing Black children, are terrorized and systematically oppressed not only for being both Black and women but also because they are mothers. This suggests that Black women are often under attack from the State in subtle and sometimes invisible ways. These attacks affect Black women's mental health and life expectancy because they are a form of daily terror specific to Black women's lives. Many medical and mental health scientists now refer to a phenomenon called the "weathering hypothesis," wherein it has been found that Black women's health begins to deteriorate earlier than that of other groups because of the constancy of racial oppression and discrimination.[20] For Black women, while we may continue to look young on the outside well into our sixties, these data suggest that the internal health of our reproductive systems and nervous systems might actually be impaired because of the conditions of the world around us.

To be clear, the terror enacted upon Black people by the State affects all genders of Black people. Black motherhood is not relegated to cisgender Black women with uteruses. Black motherhood includes all forms of mothering, which may come from extended family members and friends, community members, chosen family, and the like. Many queer and trans people mother Black children that they have not physically birthed. This definition could also be expanded to include community mentors and parental figures who do not necessarily raise children but whose roles in children's lives and in the community are pivotal. So, this is not to suggest that Black motherhood has a gender or phenotype. Rather, it is to suggest that the State is inherently against the nurturing of Black children and that the act of raising and protecting Black children is an act of revolution. This is why caring for Black children changes us. It makes us fight harder for redress. It pushes us to extend ourselves to ensure that those who come after us will have something better left over for them. It makes accountability that much more important.

This is where Chisholm's teachings become so valuable for us. Her boldness and her unwillingness to be bought or bossed give us courage to confront the systems of oppression that threaten our lives and livelihoods. Chisholm taught us that we cannot absolve these systems of their responsibility to serve us. She showed us that the debt would have to be fully accounted for and paid. Even though whiteness is constantly seeking to avoid a reckoning, we must tarry with the truth until it actually sets us free.

Perhaps the greatest embodiment of this concept is illustrated by Mamie Till-Mobley, the mother of fourteen-year-old Emmett Till. I discuss the conditions of Till's murder at length later when discussing anti-racism and Angela Davis. What is critical to know here is that, after Till's mangled and disfigured body was recovered from the very bottom of the Tallahatchie River in northern Mississippi, he was missing an eye (it had been gouged out), his teeth were missing, and he had been beaten beyond recognition. His once full and soft face was sunken in, bloated, and broken. Mamie decided, rather than hiding her son's body from the public, to leave Emmett's body completely exposed in an open casket at his memorial services. One of the saddest and most powerful images to emerge from this social moment is that of Till-Mobley, hunched over her son's casket at his services in South Chicago. She insisted on an open casket because, in her own words, "everybody needed to know what happened to Emmett Till."[21] Till-Mobley called top Black magazines and national newspapers to tell them what had happened to her son. Rather than hide the gruesome and disgusting violence that white supremacists had enacted upon her child, Till-Mobley opted for public accountability. Many argue that her efforts to tell the truth about the death of her son sparked the Civil Rights Movement.

Black mothers today have followed the example of Till-Mobley. After her son, Michael Brown, was killed on August 9, 2014, Lezley McSpadden explained that she would "never forgive" Darren Wilson for killing her son (as did many of the mothers of Black Americans slain at the hands of police officers). In 2015, a year after her son was killed, McSpadden told Al Jazeera, "He wouldn't even admit what he did was wrong. He wouldn't admit he had no reason to do what he did."[22] I remember having a deep respect and admiration for McSpadden at this moment. She was saying what all of us mothers of Black children felt. Both Till-Mobley and McSpadden show here what it means to fight like Chisholm fought: in public and meaningful ways. Not for performance, but to reveal the true nature of white supremacy and anti-Blackness in the United States.

Accountability is not about public performances of apologies or other symbolic displays of grief. Accountability is about harm acknowledgment, harm reduction, and healing justice. Acknowledging the harm means that we must first be able to tell the truth about what has transpired. Harm reduction refers to the process by which those truths are assessed to identify methods to eradicate or reduce the impacts they have on people who are vulnerable. And healing justice is about taking these lessons and centering the communities that have been harmed, allowing them the space, time, and efficacy to take the lead on solutions.

Chisholm's example shows us that accountability requires that we have the courage and wisdom to confront these systems head on. And when given the choice to elevate symbolism over sincerity, we have to choose the latter. Likewise, when Black women, namely Black mothers who have lost their children at the hands of the State, refuse to offer public forgiveness and retain their right not to forgive harms against them, they reject the efforts of the State to absolve itself of the indignities it sanctions against Black people. This act of righteous indignation is another way Black women retain their autonomy and authority over their own lives, regardless of how inconvenient it may be to those who seek to own their lives and choices. Moreover, it is another way that Black communities hold these systems to a higher standard.

As a Black Feminist scholar and organizer, I am pushed by Chisholm's example to reflect on my own confrontations with whiteness and with holding systems accountable for the ways anti-Blackness is frequently rewarded. I think often about my experiences in those predominantly white classrooms in undergrad. Because that was my first time being in such close proximity to white Americans on such a consistent basis, it is still very representative of my overall experiences with challenging whiteness and its effects on my life. I learned so much from those interactions that I likely would not have learned elsewhere. I learned that week in class what accountability for white people would look like. I learned that white people would frequently want absolution without accountability. They would expect forgiveness before offering an apology or even an acknowledgment. It would always be this negotiation, this process of give and take, this system of compromise. I learned that white people would never willingly stand upright in the truth about what their ancestry meant and how the long arc of racism, white supremacy, and anti-Blackness shapes every single part of our everyday lives.

These lessons became even more important to me after college when I entered corporate America, where I was one of only two Black women in my department, on my floor, and even in my building. I immediately recognized the ways that my white co-workers would and could make racist comments about my body without reprisal because that was just "how they are." They would openly share their opinions about my hairstyles, insinuate that I liked watermelon or fried chicken because I was Black, goad me into conversations about queer people, and roll their necks to mimic my style of speech. In response, I was told to simply let it go. To let it slide off of my back because they didn't mean anything by it. I will never forget sitting at work and listening to them practicing their "Blaccents," a way of speaking that mocks Black vernacular, because they had been watching Black Entertainment Television (BET).

Experiences like these socialized me out of a healthy relationship with myself and my boundaries. I remember when a white woman at work reached out and touched my braids because she had "never seen hair like that before." On the inside, I was mortified. My skin was screaming and crawling at the same time. But on the outside, I had already learned how to project calmness and a demure tone to white people even when they violated my space, made me deeply uncomfortable, and disregarded the rules that everyone else seemed protected by. It took my leaving corporate America to finally figure out how to set healthy boundaries with co-workers and to create safe distances at which to learn and labor alongside white people.

These harms against me were often enacted by white women who used their fascination with my body as an excuse to violate me. But even after leaving corporate America, I have found that white men have continued to be the ones who seem most indignant about their racism and violations of Black women's intellectual and personal boundaries. In my experience, they condescend to me, questioning how I know such big words in front of my co-workers and company executives. Sometimes, they chuckle after I make comments about my research, suggesting that it is trite or insignificant. In a broader sense, they sit on research panels and deny the work Black women submit because it is "me-search" rather than research, according to a fallacious narrative that Black women academics study only themselves. (Meanwhile, almost every scholar of Germany or Russia is a white man.) White men frequently act as gatekeepers to nearly every occupation, educational opportunity, or legal institution because they are overrepresented in all walks of life. And, because of this privilege, they are rarely held accountable for the ways they harm others. When they commit crimes or injustices, it is because they made a mistake, a forgivable mistake. Yet when we, Black women, respond to those injustices, we are deemed angry, aggressive, ruthless, and cruel. It is a vicious cycle perpetuated by misogynoir and patriarchy. Differential power structures in the United States (and glob-

ally) offer greater innocence and absolution to cisgender heterosexual white American men over all other groups. In the
case of Black Americans, we are frequently required to forgive
others while the State and other citizens regularly deny us forgiveness. This narrative highlights how Black women in particular are frequently expected to do the emotional labor of
forgiving even when there has been no justice, no restoration,
and no transformation.

Accountability is not a feeling, it's a practice. It is the practice of acknowledging previous harms, naming them, identifying those who enacted and facilitated the harm, and working
through methods and processes to prevent the harm from happening again. It requires the truth-telling that Wells taught us.
Even more than that, however, it requires that we use the systems and mechanisms at hand to adjudicate and exact the solutions to the harms that have been named. Accountability isn't
avoidance. It isn't enclosures, obscurity, obfuscation, and mis-
leading narratives. It isn't a string of dismissals. It isn't about
assigning blame for the sake of assigning blame. Rather, accountability is about naming harm for the sake of changing the
world. We practice accountability because the status quo is in-
sufficient. We practice accountability because doing nothing is
supporting and misremembering violence.

I mention boundaries so explicitly here because I have encountered far too many Black women who, for one reason or
another, do not have them. Some of the women scrawled across
these pages struggled with their boundaries. This is because
living under this anti-Black oppressive system systematizes
violations of our boundaries from such an early age that many
of us struggle to develop them later in life. It is impossible to

hold anyone, whether an individual or institution, accountable to anything without first knowing what our limits are. These theories of white absolution have created a culture wherein the only people whose boundaries matter are white people. They are only ones whose privacy is protected and honored. They are free to violate the privacy of everyone else not only inter-personally but also by leveraging the surveillance state, calling police on people they deem "sketchy," enacting laws that re-duce the mobility of people of color, and supporting efforts to take away protections for queer and trans youth and adults.

We can't hold anyone or any system accountable until we first get clear on what we deserve and who we are. We are nei-ther property nor playthings. We are neither beasts of burden nor caricatures for public fodder. We are worthy of care and protection. We are worthy of true justice, meaning not just the kind of justice that is meted out only after we die. We deserve systems and interactions that honor our fullness and reinforce our need for survival. This is the truth. To get about the busi-ness of holding white people and institutions accountable to that truth, we have to first believe it and honor it ourselves.

CHAPTER 7

Toni Morrison Taught Me That Black Women Are Powerful

It is the language that drinks blood, laps vulnerabilities, tucks its fascist boots under crinolines of respectability and patriotism as it moves relentlessly toward the bottom line and the bottomed-out mind. Sexist language, racist language, theistic language— all are typical of the policing languages of mastery, and cannot, do not permit new knowledge or encourage the mutual exchange of ideas.

—*Toni Morrison*

Sula, Denver, and Pecola met me at the foot of my bed each night. Smooshing down the mattress on my daybed, the weight of their stories put a dent in my resting place. They were little Black girls, like me, wayward, confused, misunderstood, and determined. When the sun went down and my mother tucked me in, they would pile into my twin-sized bed, telling me stories about their complicated lives. They'd whisper in sweet tones so they wouldn't wake my mother just a few steps down the hall. We'd giggle together, as little girls do, laughing through the painful parts. I'd curl up under my soft beige sherpa blanket with the satin trim, using the light from my bedroom window to accentuate their faces. Sometimes, I would grab a flashlight to track along with their words. My peach-colored walls glowed warm in the dim light, reminding us girls that we were in a safe and gentle place. Together.

Sula, a beautifully brown Black girl with thick lips and a proud grin, sat incredulously with her legs crossed. She was tense, shoulders taut and toes at a point. Her wool cloche hat resting snuggly against her pincurls, Sula wrapped her lips around every word like they were made of pure sugar. She talked with her hands, as big-spirited girls do. It was Sula who told me that Black girls aren't always cared for. This is especially so for Black girls who grow up and break the rules. The ones who go against what is expected of them. Those who rebel proudly. She tells me about the mistakes she made, but says that she is still proud of herself because at least she survived. "I'd rather be shunned for who I am than accepted for who I'm not," she whispered to me. Sula had been labeled by her community, ostracized, and excommunicated, becoming a scapegoat for the sins of The Bottom, a place ravaged by racism and white supremacy. But she was a convenient enemy. She knew that, and I could relate. I understood that feeling of being on the outside even when standing inside of the container made for us. I knew how it felt to feel alone even when people who looked like me were everywhere around me. Sula was sad, but it was in the background; I saw it in her eyes, but only because I had the same gaze. We both buried our sadness so that the world couldn't see it. We kept our true selves hidden away from people who might harm us, acting out on the surface what everyone thought we should be: good or bad. That was how we made it through.

Denver, with her curly, flowing hair, soft presence, and honey-complected skin, reminded me of my fairer-skinned cousins. She never raised her voice and her eyes always looked hopeful. It was Denver who told me about the ghosts in the walls, the ones who remind you that you can do more than you ever thought you could. The ghosts who remind you and your kin that sometimes, the world is a very ugly place that makes your people do ugly things. And even when we do ugly things, we are trying to capture our power, trying to reclaim ourselves from a world that doesn't want us, or only wants pieces of us. Her mother, Sethe, showed her that. "Mama doesn't always see it," she'd say. "Sometimes, the grief is too much, the despair is too heavy, and Mama gets overwhelmed." I understood that experience, too. It was mine as well. Denver's mom was haunted by the baby she had killed to save her from captivity. My mother was just haunted by being a Black single mother in a country that wanted people like her and, by extension, people like me to disappear. Mom would languish, sometimes in bouts of anger and sadness, as she tried to hold on to her sanity in a world that was driving her crazy. She'd cry at the foot of her bed, just as quietly as I whispered to Denver. Our house was the place where all of our survival techniques were honed and crafted. For Denver, it was Sweet Home, the place her mother was trying to turn into warmth and gentleness. For me, it was a small two-bedroom home in the center of Oakland where I spent most of my time either alone or sitting close by my mother's feet. I wanted nothing more than to be near her, even with all her ghosts. And the ghosts in our walls. The ones left by my dad and by her husbands. The ghosts that plagued my brother before he left. The ghosts that kept me up all night, afraid that, if I slept, they would badger me in my dreams. Sometimes they did. Denver beat the ghosts when she developed a community with her elders and foremothers. She beat the ghosts when she made connections with the women who loved her. There was a triumph and joy to Denver that made me feel like I could survive. She helped me to see myself in the future.

Pecola, with her deep, dark skin, coarse hair, and deeply sad eyes, sat with her head slightly bowed, her braided pigtails sticking out on either side of her round face. It was Pecola who told me about the pain of wanting something, praying for it, begging and asking God for it, only for it to never arrive. Pecola wanted blue eyes so that she could possess the beauty of the white world. Those piercing blue eyes that stared through her and never gave her solace. Instead, she got salt in her wounds, sexual abuse, ridicule from her community, and shame and guilt for being a girl in a place where girls weren't safe. Pecola and I would compare notes, swap prayers, and mull over our unrequited love. I'd stay up begging God for lighter skin, longer hair, and a curl pattern that bounced and flowed with the wind rather than standing straight up on my head. I sometimes asked God to make me smaller so that the boys wouldn't punch me like I was a boy, too. I asked for a softer voice, straighter feet, and femininity. I prayed and prayed and prayed, closing my eyes so tightly that they sometimes watered. The water turned to salty tears as I pressed my face into my pillow, knowing I would still be dark, nappy-headed, and ugly when I woke up. I sometimes cried myself to sleep. Pecola would pat my back. Encouraging me. She didn't have any answers or solutions. She just understood me. She understood the pain of being in a body that the world found ugly and how that ugliness seeped in everywhere, even into the tender and soft places. The sacred places. She couldn't tell me how to keep the pain or the ugly out. Pecola only knew how to be there for me through it. That was her power.

Morrison's characters, these little girls, rose up to meet me in a time in my life when I had not yet formed words, beliefs, and ideas about who I was and what I wanted to do with myself. Us four little girls would imagine together at the foot of my bed, wrapped up tightly in the covers, peering into the pages of the perfection Morrison had gifted us with. There was a power on these pages that I couldn't find anywhere else. The power to write me into the world even when that world wanted to write me out. There was a sense of inner knowing and outer recognition of being Black and of living Blackly without regard for a white world that would no doubt want to co-opt, water down, and erase our stories. Morrison created a new world with just words alone. She was a god. And she used her power to create and re-create us over and over and over again.

Toni Morrison was born Chloe Anthony Wofford on February 18, 1931, in Lorain, Ohio, a small Midwestern town that had a great deal of racial and ethnic diversity. Polish, Portuguese, Italian, Irish, and Black people lived in the same neighborhoods as white Americans. Lorain drew immigrants and laborers from all over, as there was a booming industrial labor market for freighters and shipyard and steel workers. As Morrison once said, Lorain was "neither plantation nor ghetto."[1] The advantage of growing up in the 1930s and '40s—despite the economic ravages of the Great Depression—in a place like that was that Morrison's Black experience and the stories she was called to write were nuanced and rife with the notion that Black people are complete and complex. Morrison still knew deeply what it meant to grow up Black in America. She understood anti-Black violence, which was frequently unprovoked and rooted in a prolonged hatred of people simply because they were the "other." Perhaps one of the most visceral ways that anti-Blackness and the violence of racism entered Morrison's life was when her landlord set her house on fire when she was a child.[2] Her parents were struggling to pay rent, which was just four dollars a month. The experience likely colored many of the stories and narratives Morrison created, as so many of her characters struggle in their own homes, which are riddled with fiery personal and familial battles, ghosts, and the ravages of intergenerational loss. Morrison never wanted these experiences to be watered down. Rather, the author, essayist, and editor spoke during her life (and wrote extensively in books like *Sula, Beloved,* and *The Bluest Eye*) about the ways that Black girls' and women's abilities to overcome seemingly insurmountable barriers are often consumed, romanticized, and commercialized. She did this not by centering the concerns and experiences of Black men or white women, but by making space for Black women and girls to tell their own stories. To show their own magic.

Because of her experiences in the Midwest, Morrison brought with her an expansive imagination about what Black people's lives meant and who they could be. There, she witnessed the daily strategies of survival that rural and working-class Black folk created without rubrics or scripts. She also acknowledged in her writing and her publishing work the importance of recognizing the experiences of Black people in Middle America. Morrison's connections to Black communities expanded as she continued her studies. After high school, she went on to Howard University and then Cornell University before arriving at the Mecca of American literature: New York City.[3] This was the beginning of Morrison's deep love affair with the written word and the northeastern chill of the United States.

One of the most important characteristics about Morrison was that she was committed to writing solely about Black people and their experiences. She even wrote about the traumas and violence that we are often encouraged to hide from public sight. Truthfully, I never knew what writing "Blackly" meant until I read Morrison. In the documentary *Toni Morrison: The Pieces I Am,* Morrison explains how she spent her entire career writing to decenter and ignore the white gaze. Even while critics discouraged her from her focus on Blackness, Morrison made an intentional decision to tell stories about Black people in their fullness against a current in literature to focus on white America. For her, this work was about eliminating the white gaze, the watchful eye of the community outsiders, and choosing her own "sovereignty" and "authority as a racialized person." The intention with which Morrison dismissed the white gaze in her stories created a new terrain for generations of Black writers and artists.

This work was not just about Blackness on its own. Morrison centered the stories and experiences of Black women and girls, many of whom were abused, traumatized, and harmed by people in their own communities. She did this to move away from the idea that Black girls were only interesting if cast against a white background. Morrison was against the notion that Black girls were "props" who were meant to complement the experiences of white Americans. Morrison called this the "master narrative." It was the concept that little white girls were the definition of beauty, that their rosy-colored cheeks, blond tendrils, and pale skin were the epitome of goodness and purity. This master narrative was precisely what Morrison disregarded and undermined in her writing and publishing work during her lifetime. In an interview with Charlie Rose on *PBS NewsHour* in 1993, Morrison said, "If you can only be tall because somebody is on their knees, then you have a serious problem. My feeling is that white people have a very, very serious problem. And they should start thinking about what they can do about it. Take me out of it."[4] This was the same year that Morrison won the Nobel Prize for Literature for her book *Beloved*.[5]

To be clear, however: Morrison was not handed her accolades in a leisurely fashion. Rather, it took her community of writers and supporters standing up for her work to garner the acknowledgment she truly deserved. After the book was denied the National Book Award, forty-eight Black writers and critics (including Maya Angelou and Amiri Baraka)[6] signed a statement in *The New York Times Book Review* bemoaning the fact that Morrison had not received a Pulitzer or a National Book Award for her work.[7] It was only then that Morrison was awarded the Pulitzer. Unlike women like Wells, Hurston, and Chisholm, Morrison was blessed in her lifetime to be consistently supported by her peers. If not for the protests of other prominent writers of all races and creeds, Morrison might not have won the Pulitzer. This is a rare occurrence for Black women whose work is rarely supported even by those who look like us. In fact, acclaimed poet June Jordan wrote the letter and statement in favor of Morrison receiving these accolades just a few months after activist and thinker James Baldwin passed away.[8] It was important to Jordan and those who supported the letter that Black thinkers be honored in their lifetimes rather than only posthumously. In the letter, they wrote, "What we have undertaken to do is to pay tribute to a great American writer in our midst while she is alive. I'm talking about before you're dead." It is important to note here how this support for Morrison stands in stark contrast to the typical erasure and oversight Black women experience regarding their labor. As I note with the experiences of pioneers like Zora Neale Hurston and Shirley Chisholm, it is very common for Black women's work and intellectual property to be co-opted, overlooked, and simply left out of the archive altogether. That Morrison was supported in this way underscores not only how critical her contributions have been to literary history, but also how powerful she has been in impelling others to foreground and preserve her vision. Morrison was such a force that she commanded such respect without even asking.

In her lifetime, Morrison published dozens of books, essays, compilations, and talks. But perhaps her most enduring influence on our culture and lives was her commitment to supporting and championing the work of other Black thinkers, scholars, and writers. While many people focus on Morrison's work as a writer, little is publicly shared about the ways that she worked behind the scenes as an editor to push forward the writing and ideas of a whole generation of Black writers. Morrison was an editor at Random House between 1967 and 1983.[9] She was the first Black editor in the company's history. In an overwhelmingly white and male-dominated industry, Morrison carved out space for Black life to shine brightly, publishing books by Gayl Jones, Angela Davis, Henry Dumas, Muhammad Ali, and many others. Morrison is to be credited for shifting the publishing industry and the way that stories are told. Many contemporary writers from Nikki Giovanni to Jamel Brinkley to Saeed Jones have credited Morrison with shaping their literary vision, calling her a "literary mother."[10] I myself have been deeply shaped by Morrison's unrivaled commitment to writing about the vulnerabilities of Black life. It was my first reading of *Beloved* that gave me permission to see the ghosts looming in Black life, the ones that were always there but were rarely talked about or acknowledged. Like many Black girls, I found in Morrison's stories a sort of affirmation of my own messy present and its tether to my ancestors and our past. The spirituality and magic in her stories all revolved around Black women and girls who believed in themselves, in their God, and in their communities. These women were incredibly powerful not because they oppressed other people or exploited their authority but because they were perfectly imperfect. They were mending, healing, broken but not irreparable. They weren't magical women. They weren't superheroes. They were Black women. That meant they could do literally anything, and it wasn't because of some preordained social order that made it so or some fairy dust granting them superhuman abilities. They could do anything because surviving a cruel, anti-Black, misogynistic world taught them how to harness their innate power. They had to work for it. They had to earn it. But it was theirs.

Not Black Women's Magic but Black Women's Power

In 2013, activist and organizer CaShawn Thompson created the hashtag #BlackGirlMagic and coined the iconic phrase "Black Girls Are Magic." The term was meant to uplift and empower Black women and girls, who are frequently our own cheerleaders because we have to be. "Sometimes our accomplishments might seem to come out of thin air, because a lot of times, the only people supporting us are other black women," Thompson told the *Los Angeles Times* back in 2015.[11] Essentially, because Black women's successes, beauty, and talents are so frequently recognized and acknowledged only by other Black women, it always looks like magic to community outsiders. Mostly because they just aren't paying attention. Thompson created the saying for Black women to encourage other Black women. It was an internal, community-based mode of encouragement that promoted positive imagery of Black women and girls and their accomplishments. After the popular phrase went viral, many people outside of Black women's immediate communities began to use the term as well, in some ways watering down its meaning and hearkening back to ideas of Black women's superheroism and imperviousness to harm or pain. Once again, Black women's efforts to name themselves and to create safe places to acknowledge our power were co-opted and corporatized for mass consumption.

Shortly after the phrase hit the mainstream, community outsiders of all races, creeds, and colors began to parrot the phrase in ways that actually harm Black women. For many people, this became a justification for exploiting labor from Black women rather than pouring into Black women's lives and protecting them. Their obsession with Black women's seemingly magical ability to overcome anti-Blackness and misogynoir at work, at home, at church, and in public shifted into an objectification of our experiences that left so many Black women unsupported by would-be "allies" and comrades. The perception from community outsiders, namely white Americans who see Black women as superheroes, minimizes the labor Black women must perform in order to survive every day. As I discuss in relation to Zora Neale Hurston's life and work, the overlooking of Black women's labor is inherent to a white supremacist society that oppresses people more the further they are from those in power. So, for Black women, who are both racial and gender minorities, they are vulnerable to not only being exploited but also being taken for granted. The ability to transcend these conditions is not about being "magical." It is about adapting to survive.

The notion of Black women's superhumanity or "magical" nature has long existed and dates back to slavery, when Black women were used as incubation systems for chattel slavery. As I discuss in reference to truth-telling and the legacy of Ida B. Wells, J. Marion Sims took advantage of these superhuman tropes about Black women when performing gynecological experiments on enslaved Black women without anesthesia. Sims pushed the pseudoscientific idea that Black women were impervious to pain. That idea remains today. There remain deep racial biases in medical science about Black people and pain tolerance.[12] Many white Americans believe that Black people are able to withstand more pain than other groups of people and that we somehow can tolerate higher temperatures, like extreme burning heat. Black Americans receive fewer prescriptions for pain and, when they do, they receive lower dosages. For Black people with uteruses (inclusive of cis and trans/nonbinary people), this has resulted in fewer endometriosis diagnoses even when Black women enter hospitals in immense pelvic pain.[13] It takes Black people with uteruses twice as long to receive an endometriosis diagnosis because of assumptions that they are more fertile or more sexually active. These beliefs permeate American culture and create harmful conditions for Black women and folks with uteruses. It also is a representation of the ways that magical beliefs about Black women put them at risk for neglect, misrecognition, and rejection. Believing that Black women are magical is a threat to our humanity and also to our livelihoods.

The myth of Black women's magic shows up in other insidious ways as well. Specifically, Black women are frequently called upon to save the United States from its political struggles. Meanwhile, Black women's concerns are rarely taken up as priorities by Congress. In fact, the concerns facing many poor and working-class Black women, like fair pay, equal access to housing and education, student loan forgiveness, and the expansion of healthcare to all, are frequently opposed by congresspeople concerned that these issues are too radical, too racialized, and too far left of center to justify the risk of doing something so unpopular. Nonetheless, Black women like Oprah Winfrey, First Lady Michelle Obama, Stacey Abrams, and Vice President Kamala Harris have had their accomplishments and potential compared to a magical superhuman ability to save us all. Every presidential election, reporters and political pundits throw these women's names around as potential candidates. Rarely do these commentators consider the immense risk it would be to become the first Black woman elected president of the United States. Evidence from our very recent past suggests that a Black woman in the White House would likely face immense threat, not just concerning the persistent racism in the country but for that individual. During President Barack Obama's time in office, many expressed increased concerns about his safety and about the potential for him to be assassinated. President Obama received a security detail eighteen months before the election, "the earliest of any previously unprotected presidential candidate, in part because of concerns about racially charged rhetoric that had been directed at him."[14] He frequently gave speeches behind bulletproof glass and surrounded by Secret Service agents who were fearful that his historic run for the presidency might result in racist violence. The dangers of the presidency loom large for non-white, non-male candidates and, since we have never had a woman as POTUS, the risks associated with that historic moment remain unknown.[15] But, even in the uncertainty, we should assume that a Black woman who isn't safe walking the streets in the United States wouldn't be any safer walking into the Oval Office at 1600 Pennsylvania Avenue.

This is part of the danger of the superhero narratives that many attach to Black women. They fail to fully account for the ways that this increased exposure and visibility puts Black women at unique risk for harm, harm that other racial and gender groups do not face. This propensity for white Americans to elevate Black Americans they deem worthy of saving all of us is a form of tokenizing that valorizes "respectable" Black people and objectifies those folks in the white gaze. Many white people see the Oprahs, Michelles, Staceys, and Kamalas of the world as characters rather than real people. The intersection of their Blackness and their perceived goodness has been called upon by white Americans who have sought a Black woman heroine to fly in with a cape and change the world. These women are mothers, sisters, aunts, friends, and comrades who are not beholden to white Americans. They do not owe white Americans anything. And they certainly aren't responsible for saving white people from themselves and their own choices.

This was never what Thompson meant by "Black Girls Are Magic." In an interview in April 2020, just a month after grade schools shut down across the country and we began living in something called "quarantine," I spoke with Thompson about what Black women were experiencing during the COVID-19 crisis. Specifically, I asked her what it meant to be a Black woman in a moment that was so complex, so fraught, and so clearly difficult for vulnerable people. I probed her on what she meant when she said Black women were magical. Thompson told me, "My definition of magical has nothing to do with the supernatural or a superpower as it stands right now." She continued, "I know that our magic lies just in our everyday being."[16] Thompson explained that people outside of Black communities ran with the term because it was more convenient for them to just write off Black women's accomplishments and abilities as magic than to simply give us credit for how hard we work.

Later in the interview, I asked Thompson what she wanted people to know about the experiences of Black women in 2020, just a year after Toni Morrison passed away and arguably one of the most difficult years any of us will ever experience. She said, "I want everybody to know that we are just as human as everybody else. That 'Black Girl Magic' is not a literal thing anymore because I am no longer five years old. And we are as vulnerable to illness, we are as vulnerable to mental health disorders, we are as vulnerable to stress, we are as vulnerable to loneliness and isolation, we are as vulnerable to confusion and uncertainty as anybody else is with this ongoing pandemic." It was a relief to hear Thompson affirm the humanity of Black women in such an intentional way. Since her hashtag went viral, Black women's humanity and the fragility of Blackness in the United States has seemed to fade a bit from plain sight. And I couldn't help but think about how Morrison would likely have agreed with every word. Thompson continued, "Don't look to us to save you. We're trying to save ourselves."[17] Thompson isn't describing what it means to be magical. Like Morrison's characters, she is explaining how Black women's experiences are manifestations and exhibitions of our power. Here, Thompson is vocalizing the same themes present in Morrison's works: that Black women don't have to be magical to have power. It is in the white gaze that we become something other than just humans who want to live, love, and be loved by others.

Perhaps Thompson's message is precisely what Morrison would have said if she were alive in that grueling year. The Black women of the House of Morrison were all working to save themselves. Sethe was trying to save herself from the memories of a child she killed. Denver was trying to save herself from a fate similar to that of her ghostly sister. And Sula and Pecola were trying to save themselves from the racial violence, sexualization, misogynistic gazes, and judgmental eyes of the larger world. These girls and women wanted to survive. The fact that they did seems like nothing less than sorcery. When everything was stacked against them, they existed despite the chaos, murder, and mayhem. And, sometimes, they even laughed, had sex, got married, went to tea, made friends, and fell in love. That's the power of Black women. It only looks like magic because so few people are really looking. They aren't focused enough to see the immense burdens behind our sleight of hand. They haven't studied the containers we use to chop ourselves in half in front of salivating audiences. They don't know about the hatch in the floor we use to escape danger. They think the rabbit in our hat is for them. They see us living and they believe we are performing. Because they are not ours and we are not theirs.

But Morrison saw us. She saw our magic and she knew it was power. It was thoughtful. It was intentional. It came from generations of Black women who had to use hope, prayers, and the energy of the earth to move mountains. Morrison knew that our magic was never for anyone else. It was just for us.

Horror, Trauma, and Black Life in the Words of a God

For Morrison, writing about Black people in the United States was inherently about writing through contention and complication. It was about unearthing and casting a light upon some of the most gruesome alleys and corners of modern American life that were riddled with racial hostility, violence, death, and deeply anti-Black sentiments. For example, her book *Beloved* is based on the experience of Margaret Garner. Garner was an enslaved Black woman in Kentucky who, at twenty-two years old, fled slavery with her husband and children to Ohio in 1856.[18] On the way, they were surrounded and were facing impending capture. Garner had pledged that she would kill herself and her family rather than return to slavery. And, as slave catchers approached, she stabbed her daughter, killing her. She attempted to kill her other children before she was captured.[19] Morrison was committed to telling this story and doing so in fiction. As Kristine Yohe says of Morrison, "While Toni Morrison's *Beloved* demonstrates a deep concern with the legacy of slavery in the United States, it also makes comprehensible for contemporary readers the dehumanizing personal experiences of enslaved individuals."[20] Morrison wanted to move beyond the trite and fleeting narratives about slavery to provide a deep and nuanced picture of what it meant to be enslaved and surviving in the United States. For Morrison, it was critical to articulate thoughtful and full visions of Black enslaved experiences to push back against the erasure of dominant culture. She took on this mantle knowing that, for many Black folk, her words were both a balm and an exposure of sorts. What's more, her work was an explication of the ways that horror, trauma, and Black life frequently weave together under the authority of a white supremacist State.

Many of Morrison's books focus on Black trauma and the horrors of Black life as allegories for the human experience. Books like *Song of Solomon* tell stories of Black self-actualization amid deep familial and intergenerational trauma. What is important about this masterpiece, though, is that it was Morrison's first project that focused primarily on the inner lives of Black men.[21] In a 1977 interview with WTTW's John Calla-

way, Morrison discussed why it was important for her to center the book around men and their desire for freedom, escape,
and triumph. She said, "I never really tried to become that intimate with a character, a man. To think about what it was
really like to think about dominion, power, those kinds of
things are alien to me in a way."[22] In the story, the protagonist
Milkman Dead moves through an immense personal struggle
in a Midwestern town as he searches for gold, a journey that
actually leads him to find himself. He is cared for by his mother
Ruth and his aunt Pilate. Milkman is both physically and spir-
itually haunted by the ghosts of his family's past. And, in an
effort to escape his present condition, he becomes obsessed
with the idea of flying away. But Milkman can never fly. Yet,
he searches for his ancestors who he is told were able to fly and
leave slavery. Over the course of the search for himself, Milkman journeys to his ancestral home in Shalimar, Virginia. The
novel ends when his own best friend, Guitar, shoots and kills
Milkman's dear aunt in a failed assassination attempt against
Milkman. Guitar, having grown up in poverty, holds a deep
hatred for white people and grows to use violence as a response
to the world around him. The novel ends with the words, "He
leaped. As fleet and bright as a lodestar he wheeled toward
Guitar and it did not matter which one of them would give up
his ghost in the killing arms of his brother. For now he knew
what Shalimar knew: If you surrendered to the air, you could
ride it."[23] This final line suggests that Milkman may have died
and that maybe flying away out of the conditions of one's life is
about crossing over to the other side and meeting one's ancestors. As we learn of freedom from the life of Harriet Jacobs,
the experience of being released from one's captivity, even

through death, has long been considered a viable and valorous way out for enslaved Black people. What is also hauntingly beautiful about Morrison's work here is that she mentions Shalimar, the town where Milkman's family comes from, to remind us of Black ancestry, of spirituality, and of the ways that even when we are alone, casting our faith out upon the wind, we are held up by those who passed on before us. This is a call to Black folk. This is a reminder that we remain connected to one another through energy and spirit. It is one of the many ways that Morrison haunts us—lovingly, but haunts us nonetheless.

I sometimes wonder if Morrison was haunted by her writing in the same ways that she haunted all of us. She wrapped words and letters around one another in ways that shifted the written word. She did so while spotlighting the parts of Black life that are frequently sequestered away from public sight. The parts of our lives that we are cajoled not to share in "mixed company," meaning "not around white people," those were the ones she put on the page, in full detail. In many ways, Morrison gave us all permission to be publicly Black even though doing so was frightening and threatening. While she centered the experiences and lives of all Black people and the traumas endured by Black women, she wasn't without her own struggles in doing so. In an interview in 1989, Morrison said, "I feel personally sorrowful about black-white relations a lot of the time because black people have always been used as a buffer in this country between powers to prevent class war, to prevent other kinds of real conflagrations."[24] Perhaps that is why Morrison feels like a horror writer for many readers. She managed to write fiction that so closely mirrored Black life that it seemed like an autobiography of sorts. For many of us, it felt like coming home. But there is something more than horror lacing Morrison's pages. There is something spiritual and ancestral. It's as though she were a vessel for a message that we were lucky to receive. Many of the hauntings in her novels are not of another world. Rather, they are tethered to feelings of shame and guilt or the long stench of death. While these sentiments are often avoided and deemed too taboo to expose to the light of day, Morrison reminds us that we, as Black people, are allowed to live fully in the light. There are no parts of ourselves that we are required to hide. There is nothing in Blackness that is inherently criminal, deviant, wrong, or stained. There is only beauty. Complicated beauty.

Toni Morrison is, for me and many others, the greatest writer of all time. As such, I struggled to find words for someone who made words exist and come to life in her mere utterings. Someone whose scribbles rocked me to my core and whose daydreams moved me to new lands. Someone who turned words into magic, music, and movement. Someone who wove together worlds that we could all see, touch, hear, and smell. Someone who physically touched me and my mother and my mother's mother through metaphysical energy. One thing I feel confident to write about is how Ms. Toni Morrison has made me feel. How she has changed my life. Sula, Denver, and Pecola were my best friends during seasons where I was afraid to leave my house for fear that I might not make it home again. They were confidants when I couldn't fully acknowledge how the butterflies in my stomach fluttered for the girls with soft, smooth skin and deep eyes. They were make-believe besties who emboldened and uplifted me even when no one else thought I deserved it. Sula, Denver, and Pecola were reflections of a gender-bendy girl who stared at the mirror for hours, wishing something else, something prettier, something "normal" would gaze back.

As we remember and rest in Morrison's legacy, we should reflect on that immense power she held to produce a form of "rememory" and revisiting of history that brought contemporary readers into a past forgotten. For Black people, who are frequently asked to leave pieces of ourselves behind, who are required to participate in institutions that oppress and exploit us, and who are pacified through political systems and law enforcement that are racialized and anti-Black, Morrison's writing has been a proclamation that we remain here. That we are unmoved. That we remember ourselves. And that we refuse to forget who we are or where we came from. Morrison wrote from a constant place of refusal. A refusal to ignore the nuances of Black racial and gender experiences, and a refusal to treat our experiences as though they only matter when told through a whitened or watered-down lens. This refusal invigorated generations of Black writers to do the same.

Morrison possessed the ability to capture all the pieces of me, of us. She did it with the tip of her little pen. She helped me find the parts of myself that I had not yet named, only lived in and with. Morrison wrote us alive.

That was her superpower.

CHAPTER 8

The Combahee River Collective Taught Me About Identity Politics

Identity is not inherent. It is shaped by circumstance and sensitivity and resistance to self-pity.

—*Dorothy West*

My identity is very clear to me now. I am a Black woman.

—*Lena Horne*

By identity politics we meant that Black women have a right to formulate our own political agendas based upon the material conditions we face as a result of race, class, gender, and sexuality. Unfortunately, the term has been maligned & distorted ever since.

—*Barbara Smith, Co-Creator of the Combahee River Collective*

It was my first time ever taking a course with a Black professor. She was an older woman, refined and well-dressed. She wore loafers and long skirts. She always kind of reminded me of the church women I grew up with. Her arms stayed neatly clasped behind her, crossed, or gently at her sides. Her hair was always elegantly pulled back like a school librarian's. It wasn't chemically straightened, so the little curly tendrils at her temples were always springing around the frame of her face. She wore glasses and never raised her voice. She seemed like she had come from some sort of wealth or esteem. And her demure attitude made me admire her. She seemed so much more feminine than the women I had grown up around. Dainty, even.

I was in my senior year of college and was starting to consider that a traditional engineering job might not be a good match for me in the long term. Not only that, the constant racism, sexism, and classism I faced from my engineering peers made me dread what getting out into "the real world" would be like for me. I knew I needed to make money, though. My family expected it. They were relying on me in so many ways, and I had a responsibility to them. So, I couldn't major in something "soft" like Sociology or African American Studies (at least that was what I thought). But when I got to college, those majors and courses were so interesting to me. I decided to pick up a minor in Sociology just so I would have a reason to go and think out loud about questions of gender, race, and class with other people who, as I assumed, wanted to know more about those things, too.

My sociology course was full of white students but had a smattering of Black, Latinx, and Asian students as well. Out of about thirty-five students, there couldn't have been more than five or six of us. That felt like a lot, since I was accustomed to being the only Black person in my engineering core courses.

The class was almost all women, and many were sorority girls with embossed and adorned sweatshirts. My predominantly white university seemed to have almost nothing but white women who looked like this.

I couldn't see the chalkboard very well with my impaired vision, so I usually sat in the very front row. The other Black girls would sit a few rows back. They didn't speak to me, though I later found out one of them was from the same city where I had grown up. I was the "hood" girl. I wasn't groomed for college. I was rough around the edges and spoke with a neighborhood accent. Many of the Black students on campus avoided me for these reasons. I was considered less than them, not marriageable, non-heteronormative, and just . . . different.

Being different in engineering classes wasn't serving me. People rarely wanted to study with me and assumed I wasn't as smart as them. I usually felt isolated and left out. I didn't get invites to hang out or go to parties. It was just kind of assumed that people like me weren't a part of the mainstream campus culture. We were visitors in an unknown land. I thought that taking classes outside of my major would help with some of that. I hoped to find some students, no matter their race or background, who would move beyond their racial biases to understand that we were all just young people trying to figure this adulting thing out. I chose to minor in Sociology because I wanted to learn about people and the world around me. I wanted to come out of college knowing more than how to build an aircraft, design bridges, or combine combustible materials in safe, non-hazardous ways. While I wanted to be an engineer, I also wanted to be able to speak with other human beings about life and society in knowledgeable ways. For me, that led to a minor in the social sciences.

The course was focused on race and racial issues. It was the one place where I was actually starting to acquire language to talk about all of the political and social issues happening in the world. It was the early 2000s, and we were very much still living in the aftermath of 9/11. There was an energy that felt implicitly antagonistic toward Arab and Muslim students, and really toward anyone who wasn't white. Heightened tensions with Middle Eastern countries and with our allies abroad meant that even college students tuned into the news to gather the latest information about the conditions of the world. The United States was still fighting the Iraq War and would be for another four years. Tensions were high all over the country, and campus was a microcosm of that atmosphere.

One day, while discussing the course readings on racism in the education system, we began talking about the differences in public school education access and the types of resources that are often intentionally withheld from inner city schools. When the professor began discussing inequalities in the modern education system, the class became less comfortable. She attempted to introduce the topic gently while acknowledging the role of race and racism in shaping these conditions. But this particular collection of students was set on debating the merits of her statements. A young white woman with sorority letters on her bag sitting in the very back of the class became very defensive. "I don't think we should blame students from wealthier areas just because they have better quality schools and less violence in their neighborhoods," she said. A few students responded about how they weren't blaming those students but that they were simply pointing out the differences in the ways that race, class, and neighborhood can affect people's life outcomes. "I get it but that's not super common. That's like, rare," she replied.

I raised my hand and the professor called on me immediately. Without turning around, I shared my personal experiences to round out the discussion. "Well, not really," I answered. "I know people who had metal detectors in their schools growing up. That's actually a thing where I'm from." I figured the conversation was over.

"Well, I'm sorry we didn't all grow up in the ghetto," the girl snipped, the word dropping like a brick. I immediately looked to the professor for comfort, or validation of what had just happened. She looked relatively unfazed. I glanced at the Black girl who I knew was from Oakland. She looked at me like she wanted nothing to do with me. I looked back at the professor again, hoping to see something that would help me not to feel alone here. "Okay, everyone. Let's settle down," she said, noticing the hurt and anger on my face. "Let's focus on the reading and not on each other." The professor turned her back to the class and continued speaking while writing on the board.

There was a quiet lull over the room as we all sat with the word: ghetto. It loomed in our classroom for the rest of the semester. I imagine that so many of my classmates had been thinking the word about others and about me, but she was the only one brave enough to actually say it out loud. This young white sorority girl had surmised from my looks, my walk and talk, my comments in class, and the metal detectors I expressed familiarity with that I was different from her. I was from a bad place that wasn't for people like her. She might not have known exactly what the "ghetto" was, but she knew she wasn't from it. What I didn't know then is that words like "ghetto" are often used by racists as a stand-in for the word "Black." It is one of those dog whistles in modern language that functions as a signal to white Americans that certain people, behaviors, and geographical locations are symbolic of Blackness and, often, poverty. By demarcating these phenomena as "ghetto," many white Americans find ways to distance themselves from Black people without overtly espousing racist ideas. It's a cloak for a whole host of anti-Black beliefs that are protected by the veil of whiteness.

The girl never apologized or even acknowledged the harm in what she had said. We all simply moved on, or at least we pretended to. But what happened that day was a critical example of the ways that identity is often seen as the domain of people at the margins. It is often framed as if it is only Black, queer, trans, poor, working-class, disabled, and immigrant folks who hold identities. For us, it is the gaze of outsiders that labels us as having different and nefarious sets of politics that are predicated on our perpetual victimization. It is as if we wake up every day looking for a new aspect of ourselves to be marginalized, ostracized, excluded, or diminished. But the truth is: Every single person in public society has an identity. Each of us has a set of politics associated with that identity.

Our identities are the products of how we have been socialized and what messaging we have received over the course of our lives about our group membership, our selfhood, and our communities. Our identities are not just about the ways we feel left out, but they are also about the ways that we feel called in, held, and covered by other people who look like us, believe like us, and love like us. Our identities are more than what people read on our skin. They are more than how we are labeled by systems of power and institutions of authority. They are linked to our elders and ancestors. More than anything, they are an entry fee into public life. They are the price we pay to be a part of civic society, whether we like it or not.

Today, many people believe the term "identity politics" is negative. Because the term has been overused in public forums and, namely, in the news media, many have failed to learn its deeper meaning. Identity politics is often reduced to the idea that someone (usually of a minoritized group) is relying on their group membership to garner undue benefits, sympathy, or victimhood of some sort. The right has worked hard to encourage this posture with sayings like "don't pull the race card" or "identity politics cause divisiveness." These trite and frankly meaningless statements shift the burden of proof and responsibility to marginalized people and away from the systems that harm them. It is a tactic meant to delegitimize the experiences marginalized persons have under white supremacist heteropatriarchy, and it upholds a violent status quo. Additionally, the term "identity politics" has been thrown around on cable news channels like Fox News (just like the word "ghetto") to signal to white audiences that marginalized people engage in forms of political actions and redress that frequently hold our institutions of power accountable for past and present harms. Because whiteness is frequently seen as the "norm," it is often hard for white people to understand how they also hold identities. For many, it is hard to even understand how whiteness is a unique and privileged possession that acts as a global power structure and shapes nearly every racial hierarchy in the world. In many ways, the rejection of identity politics is just a confirmation of both the fragility of whiteness and the refusal many white Americans demonstrate to be held accountable for the ways they benefit from racial oppression.

What Black Feminist and queer theoretical teachings have exposed, though, is that these types of narratives are under-developed and out of touch with reality. More important, they are unrepresentative of the ways that folks of color, working class and poor people, disabled people, and many others are rarely empowered to step fully into their identities without being undermined. These narratives are meant to evoke shame and stigma rather than empower and support marginalized people as they move through systems of oppression. The Com-bahee River Collective, a collection of Black lesbians in Boston in the 1970s, was critical in naming this process and making space for the ways that Black queer women navigate their identities against those systems.

The reality is that identity politics, as a term and concept, was actually coined by Black queer feminists to describe the ways that our personal experiences and characteristics are po-liticized and socially constructed. These Black queer radical feminists called themselves the Combahee River Collective after the Combahee River Raid conducted by Harriet Tubman on June 2, 1863. On this particular expedition, General Tub-man led 150 Black Union soldiers through South Carolina to liberate seven hundred enslaved Black people.[1] This was the journey that became the moniker for the collective of Black lesbian women who would lay the foundations of intersectional feminism and our notions of identity politics. It was also symbolic of the fact that the members of the Combahee River Collective believed that no real lasting change could occur for Black women without significant radical political action.

The organization was created in 1974 by Barbara Smith, her twin sister Beverly Smith, Demita Frazier, and others.[2] The Smith sisters had already been engaging in anti-racist protests throughout the 1960s.[3] Frazier was a longtime organizer and had been a member of the Black Panther Party in Chicago. These women were intentional about their decision to break away from the mainstream race, gender, and queer movements to pioneer what would later be called "intersectionality." It was from their theorizing that we came to understand that oppressions are interlocking and exist simultaneously for Black women, especially those who are also poor and working class, queer, and trans. In 1977, these women penned "The Black Feminist Statement," a manifesto on the state of Black Feminist theory and praxis, movement-making, and the threat of outsiders seeking to end Black women's efforts to free themselves before they could even really get started. This manifesto outlines the key areas of focus for these queer Black activists and organizers, whose political beliefs stemmed from their own life experiences rather than theoretical exercises or mythical imaginings about how the world should one day be. Instead, these women believed that if we are to fight on behalf of anyone, it must be those who are most vulnerable and therefore least protected by or from the State.

As such, the term "identity politics" was created to denote the ways that Black women (especially those at the intersections of sexuality and class) often must take up the issues and concerns facing their communities alone. Existing at the intersections of race, gender, class, and sexuality meant that these women frequently found that their social and political needs sat outside the status quo and the limited imaginations of the white heteropatriarchal capitalist society we live in. For them, taking up the work of identity on a political scale meant confronting the systems that were working so diligently to erase, diminish, eradicate, and isolate them. They wrote, "We realize that the only people who care enough about us to work consistently for our liberation are us. Our politics evolve from a healthy love for ourselves, our sisters and our community which allows us to continue our struggle and work."[4] In this quote, it is clear what is often meant by the phrase "the personal is political." These women made sure to articulate the importance of advocating and organizing for oneself and one's community because they were keenly aware of the ways that community outsiders would often abandon Black women when convenient. Specifically, white women and Black men were frequently able to center themselves and their concerns even while asking Black women for education, labor, and support. These community outsiders created distractions and obstacles to Black women's organizing efforts. This means that Black queer women had come to acknowledge that even Black men, their racial comrades, would not consistently fight for their needs. As queer people, they would frequently be relegated to the borders and boundaries of the Black community due to compulsory respectability.

For the members of the Combahee River Collective, this moment was a call to action. It was an opportunity to refocus and recenter. It was a way to shift the modus operandi to prioritize the needs, concerns, and issues facing Black women, poor folks, and queer people, who were often excluded from racial justice movements focused on Black liberation. They wrote that "this focusing upon our own oppression is embodied in the concept of identity politics."[5] Essentially, identity politics was about centering one's own lived experiences and working to liberate oneself before taking up causes to liberate others. While this may sound like a selfish political agenda, it is actually a politic of reclamation for Black women, who are too often expected to fight on behalf of everyone else but ourselves. Though Black women have been central to every movement and uprising in the name of Black liberation and justice for all people, our needs regularly take a backseat. As we learn from Toni Morrison, Black women are not magical beings sent to Earth to protect and save everyone else but themselves. Rather, Black women are saving *ourselves*. The Combahee River Collective members continued:

> We believe that the most profound and potentially most radical politics come directly out of our own identity, as opposed to working to end somebody else's oppression. . . . We reject pedestals, queenhood, and walking ten paces behind. To be recognized as human, levelly human, is enough.[6]

In many ways, these women's focus on their own identities was an effort to more fully embody themselves and live in their personhood. It wasn't just about challenging systems of control. It was also about making space for the full range of Black women's experiences and concerns. Embracing and naming a set of identity politics was about being more human, less object.

In this brief yet powerful statement, the organizers of the Combahee River Collective remind us that the work of identity politics is not frivolous work. It is not work that is taken up out of boredom or lack of drive for greater purpose. Contrarily, the work of identity politics is risky and threatening work that challenges existing notions regarding whose lives truly matter and how we should marshal our resources to support one another.

Black Feminist Theorizing: From Identity Politics to Intersectionality

People familiar with my work are probably surprised that intersectionality hasn't come up more explicitly by this point. The truth is: This entire book is about intersectionality. We just don't usually understand that we are doing this type of analytical thinking unless we refer to it by name.

Many people have become familiar with the term "intersectionality" in recent years. Some would say that it has reached the point of overuse. But it actually isn't new. The term dates back to 1988 with an article written by legal scholar and preeminent Black feminist Kimberlé Crenshaw. In a sequence of two articles between 1988 and 1990, Crenshaw introduced the term for use in the contexts of both Black women's labor and issues like domestic violence. She says, "I discuss structural intersectionality, the ways in which the location of women of color at the intersection of race and gender makes our actual experience of domestic violence, rape, and remedial reform qualitatively different than that of white women."[7] While Crenshaw was focused on domestic and intimate partner violence in this article, her argument was generalizable to the totalizing experiences that many women of color (especially Black women) face with oppression in the United States. For Crenshaw, intersectionality was and continues to be an analytical device for understanding how power is organized and how it uniquely shapes the personal, professional, and political lives of women of color, especially Black women. Rather than being a tool to "count up" our oppression points or calculate how much more of a victim we are than someone else, intersectionality is meant to make visible what cannot be revealed using the eyes of the State. As Brittney Cooper writes, "Intersectionality makes the disciplinary apparatus of the state visible and theorizes the way legal constructions continually produce categories of bodies existing outside the limits of legal protection."[8] In essence, intersectionality spotlights the gaps left open by white supremacist heteropatriarchal institutions that were conceived within anti-Black frameworks. Rather than naming and analyzing the experiences of marginalized people from the perspective of preserving the violent and harmful status quo, intersectionality asks us to consider that marginalized people are the subject-matter experts on their own lives and, therefore, have the clearest knowledge of how legal frameworks and institutions fail to protect and support them. Intersectionality has also provided us a framework for understanding how marginalization is not about interpersonal experiences or ideas. Rather, it is about the full collection of policies, formal and informal institutions, and systemic models that regulate access to power and resources. However, this academic terminology grew from community-based organizing.

Before Crenshaw coined the term "intersectionality," many Black women organizers and scholars had already created models and frameworks for it. Many Black Feminist historians and thinkers date intersectionality theory back to Anna Julia Cooper's seminal text published in 1892 entitled *A Voice from the South*. Cooper was born into slavery and became the fourth Black woman to earn a doctorate in the United States. Her book was one of the first narratives to explicitly include the plight of Black women in the struggles facing all Black people. She challenged Black men to consider the fullness of Blackness as they led movements. In the genealogy of intersectionality theory, Frances Beal was the first to theorize the term "double jeopardy" to account for the ways that being both Black and female in the United States resulted in the subjection to misogynistic standards of womanhood meant to exclude Black women. Beal lay the foundation for Black Feminist conceptions of identity in the post–Civil Rights era. The Combahee River Collective provides the clearest, most comprehensive notion of intersectional theory in the "Combahee River Collective Statement," published in 1977. They explained that, as queer Black women, "The major source of difficulty in our political work is that we are not just trying to fight oppression on one front or even two, but instead to address a whole range of oppressions."[9] This acknowledgment of how a "range of oppressions" underlies Black womanhood signals that the struggle for Black women is always being fought on multiple battlefields simultaneously. It is never just about race, or gender, or class, or sexuality, or ability. Rather, it may also be about immigration status, country of origin, religious practices, or many other intersections that are frequently leveraged to minoritize Black women in public spaces. This statement shows that, for many Black women organizers, political commitments and community connections are wrapped up tightly with each other. Thus, the movements and social justice efforts that result from these connections are often inherently intersectional because they must account for the varying orientations to power that Black women bring with them to movement work.

One primary example of this is the formation of the Black Lives Matter movement by Alicia Garza, Patrisse Cullors, and Ayọ Tometi. In 2013, it was Alicia Garza who tweeted the words "Black Lives Matter." This would become the rallying cry for a burgeoning movement of young Black people all over the country and globe who were catalyzed by the not guilty verdict in the George Zimmerman trial for the murder of seventeen-year-old Trayvon Martin. Then, in August 2014, when Michael Brown was killed on Canfield Drive in Ferguson, Missouri (a suburb of St. Louis), and left there for hours, the Black Lives Matter movement reemerged as the mobilizing and unifying banner under which Black and youth-led organizations all over the country united.[10] These three Black women, who are queer, working class, and committed to their communities, were working in the legacies of the Combahee River Collective. They were critiquing the violence of the State while simultaneously demanding that the most vulnerable among us be recognized, regarded, and counted. It is imperative that we understand the work of identity politics as wrapped up in and entangled with the work of liberation because liberation is incompatible with limitation. It is impossible to achieve liberation along only one axis. Identity politics is the work of opening up those limitations. Black women social movement organizers understand this fact. In conversation with Janell Hobson in 2017, Garza once said, "Intersectionality has been around for a long time and has resurged as a core principle of what movements need to be effective." She continued, "And yet I see a lot of misunderstanding of what intersectionality is. In some ways, the identity politics of people like Barbara Smith, Audre Lorde and others is now being bastardized in a way that makes me angry."[11] Garza's anger was justified.

While celebrities and political leaders alike have taken to using the terminology and nomenclature of Black Feminist movements, many mainstream white feminists have been critical to displacing and degrading the intentions of our Black Feminist foremothers and thinkers. One such example comes from 2018, when then presidential candidate Kirsten Gillibrand, a Democratic senator from New York, tweeted about the future being "intersectional" and was met with immediate and striking backlash.[12] Gillibrand was attempting to use the mobilization and power of the Black Feminist movement to move her closer to the presidency: a historically violent, masculine, white, and patriarchal institution that has been pivotal in orchestrating all manner of harm against vulnerable people. Gillibrand has previously supported gun rights (a stance she changed in word but not so much in deed)[13] and fought for more deportations before deciding that she actually wanted to abolish ICE (U.S. Immigration and Customs Enforcement).[14] It is the privilege of sitting at the nexus of whiteness and womanhood that allows white women to flip-flop on their commitments to women of color, Black women in particular. And their shakiness on feminist movements is intentionally designed to put them in closer proximity to white men, closer to power.

In her co-optation of the #MeToo Movement, actress Alyssa Milano has frequently and repeatedly usurped the intentions of intersectional movement-making to center the concerns and needs of upper-class, white, heterosexual women. On International Women's Day in 2019, Milano tweeted, "I'm trans. I'm a person of color. I'm an immigrant. I'm a lesbian. I'm a gay man. I'm the disabled." After receiving criticism for actually being none of those things, Milano responded with "I'm glad this tweet invoked conversation. I'm so sorry it offended some. I see you and hear you," she said. The actress then suggested that she was trying to invoke the sentiments of Persian poet Jalaluddin Rumi, who once said, "This is a subtle truth. Whatever you love, you are."[15]

Twitter quickly responded to let her know that intersectionality is not an activity in caricature and co-opting. These actions were a part of a larger movement of white feminists seeking to attach themselves to the #MeToo Movement, which was actually started by activist and survivor Tarana Burke more than a decade ago.[16] Milano tweeted the hashtag to her followers and initially failed to recognize the work and labor of Burke, which had already lasted for years before Milano "discovered" the movement. It is this propensity of mainstream white feminism to center itself, to take credit from Black women, and to usurp movements that they often want nothing to do with until it is politically beneficial that makes identity politics so important. For these women, they can simply opt in and opt out on a whim. But for the rest of us, we are in a state of constant negotiation with the State. We are constantly struggling against the power that they maintain such close intimacy with.

By turning these terms into political fodder for mass consumption, "likes," and celebrity, many people have forgotten how tethered these political outlooks have been to Black women's survival. Moreover, they have cheapened the work of Black women co-strugglers for whom these terms and processes were integral in creating a new genus of political movement-making.

One of the most important lessons I've carried with me in regard to identity politics is that they show up in ways that we often don't intend. Specifically, there are aspects of our lives that are cloaked in the mask of public opinion, drenched in the affirmation of social normativity, and deemed acceptable merely because "that's the way things have always been." And, often, the most acceptable violences are those that hide in plain sight.

In recent years, many people in the public sphere have

started to pay attention to police and policing as sites of anti-Blackness and institutional racism. But it is important that we delineate the differences between "police" and "policing." Police are an armed and paid "protection" agency meant to ensure that property and white upper-class and middle-class people are shielded from outside agitation or threat. These political actors make executive decisions regarding who or what constitutes a threat at any given moment. They frequently do so by leaning on commonly held tropes about who looks "suspicious," "deviant," or "criminal." Police find their origins during the era of slavery, when their primary job was slave-catching and pacifying enslaved Black people through regulated terror.[17] In those times, serving on the slave patrol was required of all able-bodied men, and the entity functioned more like an organized militia than a formal occupation. These militiamen were empowered by the informal laws of the land to shoot to kill escaped slaves. Police militias were engaged in hunting Black people and punishing them for offenses like standing outside without a lantern, being in a group of more than three people, and moving through the town center unescorted. Modern policing, as we will learn in the Angela Davis chapter, has only grown in its forms of technological acuity and its surveillance of Black people in the United States.

Policing, on the other hand, is the process by which we, as community members and civic citizens, engage in surveillance, hypervigilance, and oversight of others in the public sphere. It is the culmination of the ways that we all demand an adherence to social norms and mores so that we can predict the behaviors and ideals of those around us. Policing does not require that police officers be present. We all engage in some form of policing. We have all been equipped with language about respectability. What's more, we have all been socialized to believe that who we are is not just about what traits and characteristics we bring with us into the world but the way we package those traits and how we present them to others. We engage in our own forms of community policing when we avoid certain neighborhoods because they seem "sketchy." Often, those neighborhoods are Black, Brown, and poor due to systemic violence and disinvestment from governmental agencies that do not prioritize the needs of poor people of color. We engage in policing when using words like "ghetto" and "thug" to describe people who look different, come from different communities, or have different experiences from our own. And, sadly, it isn't just white Americans who engage in policing of Black, Brown, and poor folks. Even middle-class Black people wield their power and proximity to whiteness to reinforce the idea that poor Black people are less valuable, less intelligent, and more criminal than other groups.

Policing lays the foundation for police as an institution because it promotes the idea that some communities require the patriarchal influence of outside enforcers to ensure their proper citizenship and accountability to civic society. The function of the police as an organization is not to protect people (because they don't prevent crime), but to respond to property damage or interpersonal confrontations after the harm has already occurred. Typically, the prevention that police attempt to engage in with Black people, whether at protests, in communities, or in their homes, escalates into catastrophic violence against Black Americans without remorse or regard. While many people silently agree with these notions, many Black Americans continue to experience police as violent, criminalizing, and life-threatening political actors. For so many of us, police are not a form of protection, but rather a form of intrusion.

While there are many motivators of Black Feminist organizing, protection (or the lack thereof) underlies the notion of "mattering." Protection from the State and from those who would seek to harm us is a baseline expectation under a laissez-faire capitalist system. Yet, for many Black Americans, it is the most persistently absent component of their civil rights. This is precisely what the members of the Combahee River Collective were talking about when they said that no one fights for Black women except Black women. In many cases, we only matter to ourselves. That means that we remain unprotected and un-cared for, even by institutions that are purported to "protect and serve." Those institutions were not created to prioritize the needs and concerns of Black women, however. So, inevitably, they reinforce a status quo that leaves Black women, and especially Black trans women, more vulnerable to physical and emotional violence.

For these reasons, we must consider that identity politics was born out of a frustration with the lack of mobilization from outsiders for Black women's issues and concerns and with the general lack of protection Black women receive under the status quo. But it isn't only cisnormative and heterosexual Black women who are susceptible to these inequities in care and protection. Black trans women have an average life expectancy of thirty-five years old.[18] Many of those who pass away at such a young age die from intimate partner and intracommunity violence at the hands of heterosexual Black men who act out in transphobic violence. These conditions of insecurity and unprotectedness are a reality for many people in queer and trans communities. As Barbara Smith notes in an article for *The New York Times,* "One in four people in the L.G.B.T.Q. community experienced food insecurity in 2017. Twenty-four percent of lesbians and bisexual women earn less than the federal poverty line. L.G.B.T.Q. youth have a 120 percent higher risk of experiencing homelessness than heterosexual, cisgender youth."[19] It's clear that identity is a formative metric determining the life outcomes and livelihoods of Black trans and queer people across the United States. These influences are social and political. This lack of protection of Black women, especially those who are trans, is a direct result of the notion that Black women's bodies, behaviors, and public lives belong to the State. It is a descendant of the slave code that established matrilineal enslavement as the condition of a Black child's slave status. As the Combahee River Collective shows us, it is the nature of being vulnerable and unprotected by the State that makes identity politics so much more important.

For many Black queer and trans people, poor people, and disabled folks, not only are they left unprotected by the State, but they are also systematically exterminated and terrorized by police, their "protectors." More than fifty years after the Stonewall Rebellion of 1969, Morgan Bassichis, Alexander Lee, and Dean Spade remind us that this uprising was about abolition and ending the policing of queer and trans people in New York City.[20] Many in the mass public gloss over the fact that Stonewall was started by Black trans and gender nonconforming women like Marsha P. Johnson and Stormé DeLarverie, who were tired of being constantly harassed, arrested, and surveilled by police. Not only that, but they were also rejecting the notion that their bodies were inherently criminal and should therefore be hidden from public sight. The police were acting as an extension of heteronormative ideas about gender and sexuality, and these women were unbothered and in a state of refusal. This trend continues into today. A 2013 study found that "trans people are 3.7 times more likely to experience police violence and 7 times more likely to experience physical violence when interacting with police than cisgender victims and survivors."[21] Sadly, a few weeks of Pride rainbows do not fully acknowledge this struggle. Nor is this violent history with police in the United States typically associated with Black queer and trans folks' experiences.

When we think about the work of Black Lives Matter to fight against the police brutality Black people face (among so many other concerns), we should understand that this struggle to "matter" is rooted in the larger struggle to recognize our identities as socially constructed and politically shaped. Our identities have been used to justify all manner of violence against our communities. For Black queer and trans people, especially those who are also poor and/or disabled, the risks of exposure to police violence are only heightened. They are more vulnerable than any other group. This is why Black-led movements are so important. This is why it is so critical for community outsiders to listen to the demands and concerns of those whose lives exist at multiple margins of identity. Vulnerable people are the experts on their vulnerability. Until we fully acknowledge and accept that fact, we will continue to fall short of the democratic liberation we hold so dear. The Combahee

River Collective members understood this implicitly. Because of their efforts, generations of activists and organizers now have the language to articulate what it means to advocate for ourselves against a current of anti-Blackness, transphobia, homophobia, and generalized discrimination. In doing so, these women, Black queer women, laid a radical political foundation for Black futures to come.

CHAPTER 9

Audre Lorde Taught Me About Solidarity as Self-Care

I wish to live whatever life I have as fully and as sweetly as possible, rather than refocus that life solely upon extending it for some unspecified time. I consider this a political decision as well as a life-saving one.

—Audre Lorde, "A Burst of Light: Living with Cancer"

Growing up in Oakland, the birthplace of the Black Panther Party, I was raised by parents and elders from the generation of Black Power–style social ideas. As a child, I learned about the free breakfast program the Black Panthers created in my own community. My own mother, who grew up poor in West Oakland and Berkeley, told me how there were days when she had food to eat because of that program. From my elders, I learned that community care was more important than community punishment. They taught me how important it was to have an orientation toward building up my own community before setting out to build others. As I understood it, that building included my spiritual life. My religious activities often bled into my social life. Churches were as much meeting places, local eateries, and community centers as they were houses of worship.

Being that our neighborhoods were highly segregated, with white people working hard to separate themselves from areas their elders had flocked to, we were extremely close knit. This closeness and mutual aim toward community survival created kinship between Black folks in my neighborhood. Melissa Harris-Perry calls this "fictive kinship," which exists outside of the normative boundaries of blood lineage to expand our notions of who matters to us and how families can be built. Rather than just friends and family, this ethos created a group of comrades. My comrades were my friends and family. What's more, my comrades were also my co-fellowshippers and believers. But they were also Black people I didn't know. The way I was raised, we were all in this together.

While I always knew what "all in this together" meant anecdotally growing up, it wasn't until I left my community for college that I truly came to understand why this concept was so important. It was then that I had my own experiences with anti-Blackness, misogynoir, queerphobia, and overt racism throughout college that started to frame how that notion would manifest in my own life.

It was a sunny day during my freshman year when I was walking back to the dorms from class. The afternoons in early fall in Los Angeles meant dry heat and incessant sun. Rushing to get out of the heat, I tried to enter a busy crosswalk at the intersection of the campus swimming pool and track. Quickly, a white guy on a skateboard came around the corner at full speed. I stopped abruptly, afraid that he was going to run into me. Suddenly, he swerved his skateboard, keeping himself from falling. Before passing me, he yelled, "Go back to Africa, you Black bitch!" I was stunned. I had been arrested before. I had been confronted by other Black people and non-Black people of color. But I had never really interacted with white people. Most of my neighbors were Black. And we didn't live in a neighborhood where white people mingled with everyone else. At that point, no one had ever really drawn attention to my race and gender as targets for my othering or exclusion. I was used to being all in this together.

After he yelled the slur, I stood there for a second, darting my head around to see if anyone else had heard. I laughed a little because he'd said, "Black bitch," and it just sounded like something only a racist white person would say. But then came the shame, the embarrassment. As a first-generation Black college freshman at an elite, mostly white university, I was swimming in a sea of white faces. They were just shuffling around like nothing had happened. The sense of betrayal was only outstripped by the severe loneliness I felt in that moment.

I raced back to my dorm, where I lived on the only "Black floor" on campus. It was called Somerville Place. There, everyone looked like me. They spoke the same language. They understood my gestures. They knew that, even though we were all Black, not all of us had been to the continent of Africa. I reported back the story to whoever would listen. I was angry. Enraged. There was a baseline social contract that, in my naivete, I felt had been broken. I knew these sorts of things could happen. I just didn't know that they happened so easily and so quickly. Or that they would happen with so little provocation.

Some of my dormmates sat with me, reliving and recounting their varied experiences with confrontations like these in the past. Others were in disbelief because they had yet to en-counter that type of aggression. Even though we weren't all best friends, and some of us weren't close at all, we were all in it together. I began to see that, in a white supremacist world that I had no choice but to confront every day of my life, there would only be a few safe places to land. Even when walking home turned into a racist confrontation, I would always have comrades and co-strugglers who would see me and mirror my experiences.

Over time, I also learned that these quotidian interactions with bigoted and sometimes violent white people did damage to me every time they occurred. They rocked me out of mo-ments of pure joy and safety. They reminded me that a mere phone call to the police or the suspicion that I was in the wrong place at the right time (or vice versa) could mean life or death for me. Even though I had comrades and confidants around me who could share a "Girl, I've been there" or a "Wow, that happened to me the other day," they would never heal all the wounds from the tiny cuts from every racist, sexist, classist, and gendered comment, action, look of scorn, or attempt to exclude me from the fullness of public life. To put me in my place.

I began to see that it would take not only leaning into my community of co-strugglers to ward against the violence of the anti-Black world, but it would also take me protecting my en-ergy writ large. I would have to stop putting myself into envi-ronments where I was the only Black person or where I was expected to translate Blackness and the intersections of my identities to community outsiders. Instead, I would need to in-sulate myself through both personal and social means to ensure that I was not overexposed to environments that were rooted in a hatred of my mere being, whether explicitly or implicitly.

The first time I heard the word "comrade" used in reference to a type of politics and social organizing was at the INCITE! Color of Violence 4 Conference in Chicago, Illinois, in 2015. Angela Y. Davis was the keynote speaker. It was the first time I heard an entire conversation about prison abolition. One evening, I listened to abolitionists like Mariame Kaba, Beth Richie, Tourmaline (previously known as Reina Gossett), Andrea Ritchie, and Rasmea Odeh. I watched Marissa Alexander share her experiences with incarceration after defending herself from her abusive husband with a single shot into her own ceiling. I listened to trans activist CeCe McDonald explain why her transness was so critical in understanding her experiences with the carceral system. As a second-year graduate student at an elite, predominantly white university, I was getting my first real exposure to the various ways that organizers and scholars were building entire universes from the lessons I had learned back home in Oakland. This conference was the first time I saw how my elders' lessons through word-of-mouth teachings, mutual aid practices, and restorative justice philosophies had instilled in me a proclivity toward justice for all people, especially all Black people. I wanted to learn more, to do more.

Though I had participated in protests, petitions, voter registration initiatives, and other community-based events throughout my life, I had never identified as an organizer until joining BYP100 in 2016. It's a social movement organization that was created in 2013 following the acquittal of George Zimmerman in the killing of Trayvon Martin. The organization is composed of Black Americans between the ages of eighteen and thirty-five, and they engage in direct actions and other forms of social demonstrations in the name of Black liberation. Between 2015 and 2016, the organization successfully led the #ByeAnita campaign in Chicago, which led to the ousting of State's Attorney Anita Alvarez after she took more than a year to arrest Chicago police officer Jason Van Dyke for killing seventeen-year-old Laquan McDonald in October 2014.[1] Invigorated by the work they were doing in Chicago, I wanted to be a part of a community that had such a profound effect on Black life.

As a member of the Chicago chapter of BYP100, I witnessed comradeship as a way of life and livelihood. I learned how to create spaces that were accountable to all Black people but that intentionally centered Black trans women. I struggled with my comrades as we built models to educate the broader community about topics like capitalism, intersectionality, gender normativity, patriarchy, power, and privilege. We also facilitated spaces for joy, rest, peace, and restoration. We laughed. We argued. We learned. We deliberated. We were all in it together.

BYP100 became my place to land softly.

This evolution in my social movement organizing and education taught me that solidarity and self-care were wrapped up together. If I was going to have safe places to land, I would also need to be a safe place for others. Being a safe place for others meant getting appropriate amounts of sleep for my body weight and age. It meant eating when I was hungry and drinking ample amounts of water. It meant not going to every protest if it would require walking for blocks and blocks on my already swollen feet. It meant admitting when my own disabilities put limitations on my ability to participate in certain types of organizing.

Solidarity with Black people means solidarity with ourselves. It means being at one with our bodies and mental health needs. It means being at peace with the larger world around us and setting out to have a healthy connection to our ancestors and spiritual energy. It means not just translating Blackness and Black being to white people but being Black in ways that exist outside of the gaze of white heteronormative capitalism.

When I think of comradeship and solidarity, I often think of poet, writer, activist, and warrior lesbian Audre Lorde. She was born in Harlem to West Indian immigrant parents. She didn't actually speak words until she was about five years old. What many people do not know is that Lorde was classified as legally blind at a very young age. She was a disabled child who was likely deemed eccentric, an experience to which I deeply relate. Despite her acute nearsightedness, Lorde taught herself to read and write just as she was learning to master the English language. She writes of her experience in kindergarten: "By the time I arrived at the sight-conservation kindergarten, braided, scrubbed, and bespectacled, I was able to read large-print books and write my name with a regular pencil. . . . Ability had nothing to do with expectation."[2] Lorde explains that she would have to sit in the front row at school in order to see the chalkboard, an experience that I, too, understand. I was a sight-impaired child. I ran into doors and walls. I bumped my head at least twice a week at school, and I frequently fell so people thought I was just clumsy. It wasn't until I was four years old that doctors discovered I was nearly blind in my right eye. This disability wasn't an excuse to perform any differently in school, however. I wasn't given any special accommodations (a concept that we were still figuring out in the 1980s). Like Lorde, I was just expected to get good grades and come home clean. Imagine being four or five years old and carrying the burden of expectation to perform at or above the level of your peers when you cannot even see the playing field. Imagine having to be a high-performing student while your disabilities are misrecognized, overlooked, and made invisible. I know from personal experience that this seeds loneliness and the feeling of being perpetually misunderstood, of being seen as deviant and out of line. It creates an environment where, even as a child, you have to learn how to prioritize the logic, comprehension, and priorities of able-bodied people because they "can't see" you. And, sometimes, you forget how to see yourself because you're so busy looking through the eyes of everyone else.

I imagine that these experiences socialized Lorde out of solidarity with herself. When you are told not to listen to your body, you soon forget what you even sound like. Pain becomes normalized, and struggling to complete daily tasks seems to be inevitable. I imagine that this experience taught Lorde, from childhood, that her disabilities were no reason or excuse for performing differently from anyone else. I imagine they taught her how to separate herself from her own body, from her own flesh. How to perform wellness and success for a world that wouldn't be impressed with her anyway. I imagine these narratives and norms created a version of her that wasn't truly who she was but who she had to be in order to survive. I can imagine all of these learnings because as a disabled, blind Black child in the United States, that is precisely what I was taught, over and over and over again. Sometimes by teachers, sometimes by classmates, sometimes by family, and sometimes by myself. I learned well. I made sure not to ruffle any feathers. I swallowed down painful moments when I was made fun of because my glasses were so big or because I couldn't see words on the bulletin board across the room. I learned to adapt to my disabilities to shield myself from shame and stigma. But it still stung all the time.

As Lorde grew up and stepped into her identity as a Black lesbian poet, mother, and thinker, she started to really grapple with the ways that Black women's efforts to reclaim ourselves from messaging like this are often misidentified as egotistical or arrogant. In fact, most people now associate Lorde with the "self-care" movement that has emerged on a mass scale in the last decade or so. This is a valid comparison to make. One of Lorde's most iconic quotes states, "Caring for myself is not self-indulgence. It is self-preservation, and that is an act of political warfare," so she clearly had explicit investments in the prominence of self-care in the lives of Black women, especially queer Black women.[3] However, what many do not understand is that Lorde's larger project where this quote is mentioned, "A Burst of Light: Living with Cancer," was written during Lorde's battle with breast cancer. Lorde was first diagnosed with the disease in 1978. After undergoing a mastectomy, she found out her cancer had metastasized to her liver, killing her in 1992. She was only fifty-eight years old.

In *A Burst of Light and Other Essays,* Lorde shares entries from her journal written between January 15, 1984, and December 15, 1986. These dates span Lorde's first three years living with liver cancer. The journal entries are gentle offerings and timely letters about the ways that cancer had become a focal point in Lorde's life. Moreover, living with cancer and trying to reclaim herself from the disease often mimicked Lorde's own efforts to find herself in the larger struggle for freedom and liberation for all Black people.

The full quote about self-care that so many people fail to put into context reads:

> I had to examine, in my dreams as well as in my immune-function tests, the devastating effects of overextension. Overextending myself is not stretching myself. I had to accept how difficult it is to monitor the difference. Necessary for me as cutting down on sugar. Crucial. Physically. Psychically. Caring for myself is not self-indulgence, it is self-preservation, and that is an act of political warfare.[4]

For Lorde, every single day of her survival was an act of political warfare because she was choosing not to use her energy, labor, and intellectual capabilities toward any objectives that were not singularly rooted in her Black Queer Feminist principles. She had seen the ways that overextending herself ravaged her body and dampened her ability to continue the struggle in the ways that she had once intended. And she was no longer invested in any conditions that would perpetuate her annihilation, even if those conditions came from overworking herself, overcommitting herself, and giving away too much of herself to the community she loved so dearly.

In the closing of the book, Lorde writes, "Living with cancer has forced me to consciously jettison the myth of omnipotence, of believing—or loosely asserting—that I can do anything, along with any dangerous illusion of immorality. Neither of these unscrutinized defenses is a solid base for either political activism or personal struggle."[5] This means that it was her struggle with cancer that reminded Lorde of the ways that her body could deteriorate and be worn from the world. The unique conditions facing Black women, especially the fact that Black women are more likely to be diagnosed with cancer than other women and are more likely to die as a result, situated Lorde at the nexus of personal and political struggle. She was fighting for her own life just as she was fighting for the lives of all Black women.

When we sit with Lorde's work, we must reckon with the fact that it is about her efforts to pour into herself after decades of pouring into large struggles for Black liberation, especially where it pertains to Black women. It is about her working to reclaim herself, to be an advocate for herself after having been trained to be everything else. Even as a child, she was conditioned not to listen to her own body and to ignore her disabilities so that she could align herself with the expectations of society. Thus, Lorde's self-care work must always be situated within the larger framework of her struggle toward Black liberation and the damage she encountered, the small cuts, bruises, and harms she picked up along the journey.

Doing the Lorde's Work: Solidarity, Difference, and Black Feminism

Lorde was a Black academic who worked most of her career writing about the types of injustices and exclusions she endured as an academic, mother, and speaker. White women at feminist conferences would frequently tune Lorde out or exclude her from conversations on race, gender, and class. In the larger academic space, Lorde sat at the intersections of gender, race, sexuality, and motherhood, positions that are not typically rewarded in academic settings. She was unapologetic about the ways that interpretations and projections related to her race, gender, and sexuality disadvantaged her among her peers and in the larger world. While Lorde cared a great deal about the politics of difference, she understood deeply that solidarity was a possibility for all of us.

In *Sister Outsider,* Lorde wrote, "As women, we have been taught either to ignore our differences, or to view them as causes for separation and suspicion rather than as forces for change. Without community there is no liberation, only the most vulnerable and temporary armistice between an individual and her oppression. But, community must not mean a shedding of our differences, nor the pathetic pretense that these differences do not exist."[6] This is one of Lorde's clearest articulations of the ways that difference matters for her life and for the work of liberation. Like the importance of identity politics and intersectionality, solidarity with ourselves and others requires that we first come into a state of self-knowing. Our inner selves can only be validated by intentional affirmation that our ways of being are valid and valuable. Unfortunately, for many Black women, we are forced into boxes and containers of womanhood and femininity that do not fit us because they were never made for us. Lorde rejected this idea wholesale.

Lorde was constantly considering both the racial and gendered frames through which she and her colleagues and co-conspirators viewed the world. Moreover, she was keenly aware of the fact that white people, across gender, had been socialized to "not see" differences like race, gender, sexuality, and ability. Thus, in their not seeing, they would frequently feel challenged and aggressed when these differences were acknowledged. She elaborated that white women feminists had failed to truly grapple with race, class, gender, and the like in social life. For Lorde, white women, even those who were well meaning, were key in upholding white supremacy, thus preventing solidarity between white women and Black women.

For Lorde, the only way to build a healthy and restorative community was through an acknowledgment and regard for our differences. This may seem counterintuitive to some, but in fact, it makes complete sense. For those of us whose identities and experiences are already and always seen as criminal, deviant, "fringe," and outside of the norm, we often walk into public and social interactions carrying the burden of translating those identities and experiences to others in dominant groups and others outside of our communities. We do this not because we just enjoy explaining ourselves every day. Rather, we do this because it promotes our survival. By presenting ourselves as non-threatening, non-violent, non-intimidating, and docile, we signal to others that it is okay to embrace the differences we bring along with us. We also, hopefully, send that message that we are not there to be aggressive. Sometimes, we aren't trying to send a message at all. We are just trying to exist.

Some people signal these messages to institutions by engaging in forms of assimilation and respectability. Some people signal this by avoiding situations where they will be expected to perform for the white gaze altogether. These are all forms of self-care. And they are all valid.

Lorde's work is helpful in examining the role of and access to solidarity both internally and externally in Black communities. While Black women hold a sense of racial solidarity with Black men and a sense of gender solidarity with white women, they do not have true solidarity with any one group except other Black women. Lorde's writings about her identity as a lesbian highlight the tension that she often experienced during her constant struggle to promote and support the work of Black Feminism while having to be in close contact with the very people she was often harmed by.[7] Not only that, Lorde's commitment to recognizing difference lies at the heart of her notion of the possibility of solidarity.

In many ways, Lorde's self-care work and her work on solidarity are one and the same. She spent her entire life working in community with Black folks trying to get free. It was in the sunset of her life that she really began reflecting on what it meant to work in community with herself. Whenever I think about this conundrum, I reflect on what my best friend Alysia told me back in graduate school. I, a Black, disabled, queer mother of three, had been working myself to the bone every day trying to graduate, feed my family, and struggle for Black liberation. The toiling had resulted in multiple fainting episodes, including one where I fell into the snow and trees, losing consciousness for a few moments. I had fallen down stairs and bruised the cartilage in my right knee, resulting in a six-week bout of crutches and rehabilitative training. After all of this, I was still pushing myself, pulling all-nighters, extending my already-disabled body beyond my limits. And, one day, in my exasperation, I told her, "I just really love Black people."

She replied softly, "Well, Black people includes you, Jenn."

I realized exactly what she meant. Being in solidarity with Black people meant also and always holding space for myself. Not just waiting until after the race was run, but also running it in such a way that did not put me in an early grave. And if I was going to be committed to Black people in the ways I said I wanted to be, I was going to have to start with myself.

Beyond Allies and Toward Comrades

"Well, I think they're wearing a safety pin to show solidarity," my best friend, Jordie, was explaining to me. "It's symbolic," she said.

She and I were both in graduate school, working on degrees in Political Science. Recently, as racist acts against people of color all over the world had been increasing, (white) people had started using new methods of expressing "allyship" with Black people, LGBTQIA+ folks, immigrants, and other people at multiple margins of identity. The newest and most popular craze was the safety pin. People were fastening them to their lapels and collars. There were safety pin hashtags on social media and little safety pin images people were posting in their messages online. To understand the full breadth of this phenomenon, I went on Etsy and saw fancy, bedazzled safety pins. Some of them were large and others were small. In either case, they were meant to signal solidarity with someone. When worn on clothing, the safety pin was supposed to function as a small, nearly invisible gesture to signify that the wearers believed in . . . something.

"How am I supposed to see a safety pin when I'm in public?"
    I asked my best friend.
"Yeah, I don't know. Squint?"
"Also, what does it mean? Will they protect me? Will they
    stop voting for people who want to annihilate me?"
"No, probably not," Jordie told me.
"Help me understand," I demanded.
"I think a lot of people just want to do something. Anything.
    They aren't sure what to do. I know this is small. But,
    girl, I guess it's something," she sighed.

We were both in a state of exasperation at the idea, me maybe more so than my best friend. I was perplexed at the notion that a safety pin could somehow be the answer to the very real dangers so many of us were facing every day. Black people all over the country were organizing protests and other public demonstrations in response to the mass public school closures in Black and Brown communities, concerns over livable wages in poor neighborhoods, and ongoing contentions over police reforms and divestment in major cities all over the United States.

In the years that followed the killing of Trayvon Martin and the creation of the Movement for Black Lives, we watched Michael Brown's body lie in the streets in Ferguson, Missouri, for hours after Darren Wilson murdered him for looking like a "demon." We saw a video of and heard Eric Garner telling NYPD officers, "I can't breathe." We knew the names Tamir Rice, Sandra Bland, John Crawford III, Jonathan Ferrell, Korryn Gaines, Quintonio LeGrier, Bettie Jones, Laquan McDonald, and so many others. Amidst all this Black death and unrest, white people still were not sold on the Black Lives Matter movement. According to a Pew Research Center poll conducted between February and May 2016, 38 percent of whites who were familiar with Black Lives Matter said they didn't understand the movement's goals particularly well. Roughly 39 percent of white Americans polled said that Black Lives Matter would not be effective at achieving racial equality. And 28 percent of white Americans who took the survey opposed the movement altogether.[8] The social reactions to BLM made the safety pin movement all the more confounding.

It was 2016 and suddenly, because of the election of Donald Trump, white people were concerned about violence against non-white people. But it wasn't just white people who felt invigorated by this new performance of allyship. In *The New York Times,* a Filipino American graphic designer living in Brooklyn named Kaye Kagaoan told the publication, "It's a matter of showing people who get it that I will always be a resource and an ally to anyone and everyone who wants to reach out."[9] Kagaoan went on to say, "When I saw it on Facebook, it was so simple. It resonated with me." Maybe that was the part that made it hard for me and my best friend. Wearing a safety pin seemed so easy when our experiences with racism, misogynoir, classism, and so many other structural inequalities were a daily struggle. While Black women were birthing entire movements, crafting whole frameworks for racial justice, and supporting Black communities from the inside out, white people were haplessly donning safety pins and doing so while learning little about all the critical work Black women were already performing.

My introduction to allyship reflected the ways that white Americans often receive unearned credit for doing very little work to address racial inequality and injustice. It highlighted the stakes of white people's curiosity not being immediately met with quick, convenient, unchallenging answers. The safety pin movement signifies the pernicious possibilities of "well-meaning" white allies. There is no system of accountability in a volunteer fleet of safety-pin-wearing soccer moms.

While the word "ally" was relatively new to me in 2016, the way it's used today can be dated back to a book written by Anne Bishop in 1994 called *Becoming an Ally: Breaking the Cycle of Oppression in People*. This "is a book for men who want to end sexism, white people who want to end racism, straight people who want to end heterosexism, able-bodied people who want to end ableism—for all people who recognize their privilege and want to move toward a more just world by learning to act as *allies*."[10] The framework of allyship, for Bishop, functions as a way to confront oppression and take stock of one's own participation in it. Importantly, she works hard to help all people understand that they have a responsibility to end the oppression of others more vulnerable than themselves.

For Bishop, the issue of oppression stems from competition. Competition between oppressors and oppressed groups, for

Bishop, stems from class-based inequality and power over one another that she finds is rooted in economic opportunity hoarding. She says, "Class is both the result and the foundation of all other forms of oppression."[11] While Bishop acknowledges that oppressions are intersecting and interlocking, she still focuses on class-based oppression as an organizing feature of public life.

Part of the issue with an allyship based on class-based oppression is that it doesn't fully account for the ways that non-elites and non-class-privileged actors also contribute to and hold up systems of oppression against marginalized groups. W.E.B. Du Bois engages with this concept in his book *Black Reconstruction* when he explains that poor white Americans were crucial in maintaining American slavery. They often performed low-investment labor and menial tasks in the name of supporting plantations and slaveowners' wealth-building because they aspired to one day own slaves themselves. This aspiration to enter the ruling class undermined any potential solidarity between poor whites and Black Americans struggling for their freedom. After slavery ended, the strained relationships between Black Americans and poor non-Blacks, especially whites, remained tenuous due to the complex nature of race in America.

Likewise, white women frequently opt in and out of white supremacy and anti-Blackness when it is individually and systemically beneficial for themselves. When it comes to supporting oppressed communities, there is no one aspect of oppression that operates consistently with reference to other forms of oppression. The contexts and conditions of oppression are always changing. This means that allyship and the accountability structures therein will constantly be in flux as well.

Moving into the 2000s, especially after the horrible events of 9/11, we entered a "see something, say something" era of difference awareness. Neighborhood watch groups became all the rage. For many fearful white people, and even for Black people, the emphasis on terror from non-domestic actors shifted a focus toward the "other" as a potential unknown threat. This shift was dangerous for Black and Brown people. Surveillance, the patriarchal practice of watching over communities of color who are deemed less capable of caring for themselves, grew to be the primary mode of allyship. And the "see something, say something" aspect of this phenomenon frequently resulted in increased policing in communities of color deemed "criminal" and "suspicious."

Now, as the era of hypervigilance and policing has faced severe public backlash, white people and non-Black people of color have begun searching for new ways to signal that they are seeking solidarity with vulnerable communities, especially Black people.

As is often the case when movements grow and become more mainstream, language has become a bridge between new activists seeking to work on behalf of vulnerable communities and those who have long done this work. Unfortunately, coalition-building across distinct social groups often leads to complex naming practices like the term "ally." The term "ally" is highly problematic because it resists accountability and promotes the idea that privileged folks can simply elect themselves as safe places for Black people without doing the work. "Allyship" has become so sexy because it lets non-Black people feel as though they are "one of the good ones." Rather than being anti-racist, they may simply be non-racist. Unfortunately, that isn't enough.

Conversely, for many Black organizers, the word "comrade" has long come to mean both friends in love and friends in struggle. Embedded in the word is the expectation of linked fate but also linked success. Unlike the term "ally," it connotes insider status. And, unlike the word "accomplice," there is no assumption of co-guilt. The word "co-conspirator" also carries the connotation of criminal activity.

Terms like "ally," "accomplice," and "co-conspirator" have all been optioned as the appropriate indicator for the well-intentioned social justice efforts of concerned citizens who typically aren't directly affected by systemic racism and other inequalities they are fighting. In an effort to set themselves apart, to give themselves a proverbial "gold star" for working on behalf of "less fortunate" people, white people and non-Black people of color have been working to find new words that signify and valorize their existence.

By merely caring about Black people and thinking that racism is bad, white people can call themselves allies. This logic is problematic because it centers the goals and aims of people who are not the most marginalized. This is a cyclical process of searching for new words and practices every few years that help white and non-Black POC identify themselves as separate from community organizers and activists. It reinforces a hierarchy between groups engaging in social justice work. It also undermines any opportunity for coalition-building or developing social and political networks across race, ethnic, and other demographic groups.

What is probably most insidious about the ally movement is that it puts an undue burden on Black women, like Audre

Lorde, to constantly translate, lead, articulate, educate, and dictate to the masses about Black struggle. According to Lorde, "This is an old and primary tool of all oppressors to keep the oppressed occupied with the master's concerns."[12] It reduces us to involuntary mentors of white people who still sit in their refusal to fully acknowledge their own responsibility for the conditions we face each day. And, most important, it wears us down every single time we are expected to affirm white people in their willful ignorance about the world around them. This propensity of white Americans to appoint themselves as allies essentially turns us into Black Struggle Mammies: always joyful, always accommodating, always available to be used up, but never full human beings who also need support, affirmation, acknowledgment, and regard.

A Better Way: Lorde-ian Comradeship

We learn from Black feminists like Lorde that comradeship is the practice of possessing mutual aims as another. This concept is rooted in the idea that struggling toward liberation requires both a commitment to doing justice to one another *and* a mutual respect for one another's unique experiences, contributions, and orientations to power. Comradeship is neither a spectator sport nor the business of bystanders. Comradeship is rooted in social movement organizing and activism that has already been built over generations. It isn't self-congratulatory. Rather, it encourages curiosity but does so while providing tools and tactics to reduce harm. In this book, I'm looking back at the Black Feminist work of the past to give us direction about how to proceed. In doing so, I put forth a framework of comradeship as the optimal way. In order to ensure that those white and non-Black people of color who believe in justice stand in earnest solidarity with the most vulnerable, they must first decenter themselves as allies and disabuse themselves of the notion of scheming or criminal intent.

Comrades seek justice for justice's sake. They are partners in successes and in failures. And, most important, comrades are fundamentally tethered to one another by the content of the goals of the movement rather than the egos of individuals. That matters. One important thing to note about comradeship is that it isn't a term one can embody on one's own. No one can simply call themselves a comrade. It is a term that is earned through political action and solidarity. Comrades are affirmed in community with one another, which runs counter to the logic of self-ordained allyship. Comradeship, especially with Black women organizers and activists, means allowing space for Black women to heal. It means seeing that Black women's labor (which I discussed in chapter three on Zora Neale Hurston) is too often taken for granted, overlooked, and excluded.

What Does It Mean to Be Our Own Advocates, Allies, and Comrades?

I often wonder what it means that Lorde's focus on self-care (at least in her public writing) originates mainly from her struggle with cancer. It is pivotal that she provided us with so many lessons about how to have solidarity with one another, but that her life stands as a cautionary tale about what it means to struggle with having solidarity with yourself. Not only that, it's common.

For Black women to be our own comrades, we must allow ourselves to face our innermost hurts and vulnerabilities before they turn into malignant tumors and undetected strokes. We must allow ourselves space and time for rest, quiet, and peace. We must not see our stillness as laziness (as the world believes) but as time to restore the energy that has already been spent. We must allow ourselves to see community not as only extractive but as a site of implantation, newness, and rejuvenation. And we must fiercely defend our rights to own ourselves and our bodies.

Now, this is not to imply that the world will simply open up to us and remove the structural barriers that have long prevented these practices in the first place. Rather, I suggest that we must center ourselves when we center Black people *without* seeing that centering as haughtiness, selfishness, arrogance, or egotism. It is not ego to have the will and determination to live and live abundantly. But it is certainly ego to deny ourselves the opportunity to live because we do not have the courage to fight for ourselves.

> "The Master's Tools will never bring down the master's house," Lorde says.
> "We were never meant to survive," she reminds us.
> And if we believe her wisdom, we know that the master intends us dead.

Deceased, unmoving, stagnant, breathless, unfree, shack-
led, undone.

Poetry teaches us how to defeat that master.
How to wield those tools against the same systems that
would put us in our graves.

Poetry says that anything is possible.
That Black people can fly without wings,
That our Black skin sparkles and glows like the radiant
sun,
And that we, the collective we, will survive.

Poetry teaches us that Audre was right.
If we don't define ourselves for ourselves, we'll be
crunched into other people's fantasies for us
And eaten alive.

Poetry says we should never despair,
That our languishing is not the place but the process.

And it is in my children's sweet lessons that Lorde's words,
and the poetry of Black life, become most clear.
It was my eldest son who once taught me that, sometimes,
when we feel like there is nowhere else to move,
It is only because we must move from side to side.

Sometimes, the getting there, the surviving requires lateral
movement.

It's not necessarily forward progress
But it certainly isn't a setback, either.

Sometimes, the only way to move in our survival is left or
   right or nowhere at all.
Because, in the process of surviving this world, it's the getting there that truly matters.

We've never been there before.
But, if we believe Lorde, and poetry, and the lessons of
   Black children,
Then we know it is possible.
We know how to survive.

CHAPTER 10

Angela Davis Taught Me to Be an Anti-Racist Abolitionist

Abolition is about presence, not absence. It's about building life-affirming institutions.

—*Ruth Wilson Gilmore*

Nothing that we do that is worthwhile is done alone.

—*Mariame Kaba*

I am about life. I'm gonna live as hard as I can and as full as I can until I die. And I'm not letting these parasites, these oppressors, these greedy racist swine make me kill my children in my mind, before they are even born.

—*Assata Shakur,* Assata: An Autobiography

You have to act as if it were possible to radically transform the world. And you have to do it all the time.

—*Angela Davis*

"You look like Angela Davis," my mother called out to me from her bedroom. I could hear the smooth reverberations of her words ripple across the surface of her old waterbed. It sounded like the beach was stuck inside a giant balloon. She was looking through a *TV Guide* (a relic of a time when there was no "Guide" channel to help us select what to watch next). Her legs were crossed at the ankles, and she had her pink rollers atop her head with her shiny satin bonnet tied gently around them.

I was leaning toward the bathroom mirror in our tiny two-bedroom home. The house was so small that you could call out from any room and everyone else in the house could hear you. Her room was a direct shot from our one bathroom. I could look directly out from the door and see right into my mom's sacred place of escape. The door was open, as we typically kept it. So, she could see me from where she sat at the head of her bed. The house was kind of our hangout, the two of us girls.

"Who is Angela Davis?" I called back, picking out my afro in our ornate bathroom filled with plants, royal-blue carpet, linoleum, an old boom box, and a dusty electric heater that didn't work. When you turned the knob, the smell of soot and chemicals filled the air, and everyone knew you were messing with things you had no business messing with. I had been caught messing with that old heater a few times.

I was fifteen years old and had just done my first "big chop." I had seen so many other Black girls with my kinky hair texture talking about "going natural," and I just knew that I wanted to be done with the bimonthly permanent straightening chemicals that smelled like tar and burned my scalp. I wanted to discover what my own hair felt like and looked like. So, I just took my scissors to it and cut it down to one inch of new growth one day. I asked my older cousin Michon to put braids in until it got a little longer. Now, months later, I had a bona fide afro. On this particular day, my hair was blown out and conditioned. It was big and billowy. It was free and freeing. My mom loved it, and I could tell she envied me a bit. My courage. I was learning how to lean away from my hair as a crutch to define my beauty and use it to connect more deeply to my Blackness instead. Even in this journey toward self-reclamation, I still felt so incredibly awkward and masculine.

"Who is Angela Davis?" she repeated, dropping her jaw open
      for effect. "You know, Black Power."
She raised her right fist up in the air.
"All power to the people. Radical. Militant. She's amazing,"
      my mother cooed. She looked down into her slightly
      bent TV Guide, *smiling and nodding in agreement*
      with herself. She looked as if she knew Angela Davis
      personally.
"Angela Davis teaches right over here at UC Santa Cruz."
      She pointed her right finger around in a circle as if Oak
      land and Santa Cruz shared a common border. They
      don't. UC Santa Cruz was over an hour away and we
      only went there for all-day field trips at school. But I
      knew what she meant.
"I'm going to apply there one day!" I replied.
"Mhm, maybe you can take a class with her when you go to
      college."
I smiled back at her. "Well, she sounds hella cool."
"She wears that afro, too," my mom said. "Sometimes, she'll
      even put a little beret on it. It's tough."

In those days, "tough" meant stylish or regal. It was one of my mom's favorite words. My mom's use of the term signaled to me that, whoever this Angela Davis person was, she was impressive enough to get my mom fawning. This was no small feat. This is the same woman who wasn't impressed when my nearly perfect report card had two A-minuses in addition to the gaggle of A's I earned. Mama was a realist, and she also didn't allow the fleeting fancies of the world to make her lose sight of who she was, where she came from, or what her values meant in her broader life. She raised me with the same lessons; she was my earliest Black Feminist teacher and organizer. I had never heard her talk explicitly about a Black Feminist thinker before. This was the first time I noticed her gushing admiration for a woman (a queer woman, by the way) who espoused a set of liberatory politics—militant, radical politics— that were against the status quo. I was intrigued.

My mom would go on to call me Angela Davis another several dozen times in my life. In time, it became much less about how I styled my hair and more about my ever-evolving politics around race, class, gender, sexuality, and the like. She'd remind me that I came from a city steeped in the traditions and practices of the Black Panthers, Black Power, and Black Radical Thought. Even though she was no expert on all things Davis, she was absolutely proud of the ways my identity had been shaped by her work. She started talking to me about how the breakfast program led by the Black Panthers had once fed her and how she had grown up respecting the work of the Black Panther Party for Self-Defense back in the '60s. This was where I learned about the social programs of the Panthers and how Davis's work had contributed to the longevity and uplift of my own people and community.

It was in graduate school that I started to dig into Davis's political stances, actions, and words. I read her commentary on the Moynihan Report, a document written by then Secretary of the U.S. Department of Labor Daniel Moynihan in 1965. Moynihan wrote this report entitled "The Negro Family: The Case for National Action," which essentially credited Black matriarchs with the downfall of the Black family.[1] Specifically, Moynihan blamed the perceived degradation of the Black family, and therefore individuals, for systemic issues of inequality in Black communities. Citing the numbers of single and unwed Black mothers, a purported crisis of absent fathers, and a masculinizing of Black women, he essentially stereotyped Black people as suffering from a "culture of poverty" that was in many ways their own doing.[2] From Davis, I learned that the Moynihan Report was a highly contested document that shirked a focus on systemic racism and anti-Blackness and instead focused on the symptoms of institutional racism that so many civil rights leaders and activists had been addressing for years.

The effects of the Moynihan Report were harmful and measurable. In many ways, the Moynihan Report is important because it set the tone for a number of inequalities that have stemmed from its creation. Public policy regarding vulnerable populations, including welfare reform, was based on his findings. His report also contributed to the "War on Crime" rhetoric of the 1970s and '80s. From Davis's writings and teachings, I learned how systems of inequality and institutions of power and control will work to justify themselves through public proclamations, official reports, and other acts of ceremony. These processes, she articulated, were part of the reason that we, as freedom fighters, would always have to be nimble, intentional, and thoughtful when engaging with the world. What is particularly concerning about the Moynihan Report is that Daniel Moynihan considered himself to be working on behalf of Black communities.

As I studied Davis's work, I realized that I wanted to meet her. Seeing my position at the University of Chicago as a key opportunity to achieve my goal, I angled to make it happen during graduate school. I finally met her in 2015 at a conference I never intended on attending. When I found out she would be giving the keynote just a few minutes from my campus, I made sure to be there. Davis told us how important we all were and how, as young people, we were uniquely poised to do the work of anti-racism and abolition. After her talk, the large ballroom erupted in applause. We all stood up, out of awe and, I imagine, reverence for our foremother. It wasn't about fangirling or worshipping her. Rather, it was about feeling honored to share the space, to be seen and held by our comrade. Davis was gracious, letting all of us young zealots hug her and take gratuitous pictures. I was nervous, afraid to walk up to a woman I had been compared to since adolescence. When I walked up, she just smiled at me, hugged me from a real place, and said, "Do you want to take a picture?" It would be a few more years until I would be able to bring my mom along to one of these conferences.

About two years later, I packed my family into the minivan, and we drove from Chicago to Baltimore for a conference where Davis would once again be giving the keynote. With my mom, children, and partner in tow, I had no expectation of speaking to her again, but I was hopeful that I would at least bump into her in the hallways. During the conference, I did bump into her. I saw her walking with her partner and team at Starbucks, I saw her chatting in the lobby, and I witnessed her vibing with my advisor and friends from Chicago. Davis was floating around the conference hotel, living her absolute best life.

After one of her talks, I saw Davis pick up speed and head out. I thought nothing of it. I was on my way to visit my family. So, I dashed out to the minivan where my partner, kids, and mom were waiting. And, out on the roundabout, I saw Davis again. This time, I was going to bring my two Black Feminist teachers together.

"There's Angela Davis, Mama," I said with half of my body
    leaning in through the sliding door.
"Where?" She peered around.
I pointed her out, and my mom's eyes lit up.
"She's amazing," my mother said with a huge grin on her
    face.
"Do you want to meet her?" I asked.
My mom just looked back at me timidly. I imagine she was
    asking herself questions like: Really? Do I get to meet
    Angela Davis? Is this really happening?
Rather than waiting for a response, I grabbed my mother's
    hand and guided her out of the car. We floated over
    toward Davis, both of us anxious.
"Ms. Davis," I said in a quivering voice as I saw her heading
    toward a vehicle. "Hi, I'm so sorry to bother you. But

*can my mom introduce herself? She loves you and she
    has always wanted to meet you."*
*I saw the preeminent thinker on race and abolition pause,
    exhale, and think it over a bit. I could tell she was tired.*
"Sure," she said reluctantly.
*I beckoned my mother over as she hung back a bit, afraid to
    approach Davis without permission.*
*"I love you," my mother said as she slunk up to Ms. Davis.
    "You're amazing. Thank you for everything you've ever
    done."*

These were two women who had never met in real life but
whose choices and lessons had already met in me. Ms. Davis
reached out and embraced my mother, a dark-skinned Black
woman who has fought cancer for two decades, who raised her
kids without their dads, who worked outside of the home each
day and taught her latchkey kids how to fend for themselves if
necessary. My mother is the kind of woman that Daniel Moynihan had written about. She was bringing up Black children in
a society that saw her reproductive and birthing choices as inherently deviant, amoral, and potentially damaging to the
Black family. In some ways, I believe those two women trans-
mitted that understanding when their eyes met.

There was a certain consideration that these two women
had for each other, a level of recognition that I noticed in their
eyes. And while I couldn't fully understand it, I felt it. It was
care. It was a genuine acknowledgment that might have
emerged from a set of generational experiences I may never
understand. In that moment, it seemed as though whatever
both of those women were intending to do (Davis running be-

tween conference events and my mom hanging out with her grandkids in the car) could be placed on hold for a bit, left suspended in space, so that they could perceive and honor each other's presence. In seeing them together, part of me was made whole. Bringing together two parts of my Black Feminist journey felt like an immediate achievement. I was grateful that I could be the bridge between them.

In every moment that I've witnessed Davis, I've seen her speak and move in such a way as to be in alignment with her core principles and with her written words. She exhibits a deep care in the movements she supports and takes up. She also exhibits care for herself in setting boundaries and limitations about how she will engage in issues and dialogue on race and racism. In Davis, I have had the opportunity to witness a thinker and scholar who believes in our future and believes in her own future, too.

Angela Y. Davis was born on January 26, 1944. Davis was raised in Birmingham, Alabama, during the civil rights era, at a time when to be Black in the South was to live in constant peril. She recalls with great familiarity when the city was referred to as "Bombingham"[3] because white supremacists would frequently bomb churches, homes, and other landmarks to terrorize Black Americans. Davis knew the young girls who were killed at the Sixteenth Street Baptist Church bombing in 1963 by a homemade bomb planted in the girls' bathroom. Carole Robertson, Cynthia Wesley, Denise McNair, and Addie Mae Collins were little girls who were attending their Sunday church services when the bomb went off. Robertson and Davis had been longtime family friends. Robertson was Davis's sister, Fania's, best friend, in fact. Wesley was a neighborhood girl.

Davis's mother had taught McNair in first grade. While Davis didn't know Collins personally, she knew of her from the neighborhood. These were four little girls who were known and loved in their community. And they were targeted. The community had to witness the girls' dismembered bodies strewn about the wreckage of the blast. It was a vision, I imagine, that those community members never forgot.

Davis recalled that young people in her community at this time were actively working to help end segregation and to activate against the macabre violence they were facing at the hands of white supremacist forces in the South. Thus, the bombing at the Sixteenth Street Baptist Church was not random. The site was not selected without intention. Davis once told Amy Goodman of Democracy Now!, "There is deep symbolism in the fact that these four young girls' lives were consumed by that bombing. It was children who were urging us to imagine a future that would be a future of equality and justice."[4] This desire to imagine a future of equality and justice was one of the earliest ways that Davis articulated how her community was working to create a new world. It highlights the Black Radical Tradition within which Davis is squarely situated. For Davis, anti-racism and abolition (though they likely were not explicitly named as such) were hallmarks of her childhood and upbringing because the conditions of her life necessitated Black struggle against overt white violence and racism.

The Black families in Birmingham knew that they were at risk of violence and potential death because of the hatred of white supremacists. Yet, they sought to move freely in public and establish lives for themselves anyway. In her autobiography, Davis writes, "Every so often a courageous Black family moved or built on the white side of Center Street, and the simmering resentment erupted in explosions and fires."[5] She explains that, under Police Chief Bull Connor, there was specific and intentional terrorizing of Black families, as he would sometimes "announce on the radio that a 'nigger family' had moved in on the white side of the street."[6] Taking the threat lightly, Connor would predict bloodshed for all to hear. It was a regular occurrence that made the terrorizing of Black people in Birmingham as normal as the sun rising. "So common were the bombings on Dynamite Hill that the horror of them diminished," Davis writes.[7] People just didn't care. For Davis, this was one of the earliest ways that she witnessed the power of whiteness to facilitate public control and authority. It wasn't just about the anti-Blackness she and her community faced. It was also about the power so many white leaders and locals exercised to keep Black people fearful and pacified.

Davis's firsthand experiences with terror in her childhood led her into social movements and mass protest in her adulthood. It was in college that she began to work through the immense grief of having witnessed the dismemberment of those four little girls back at the Sixteenth Street Baptist Church. She attended Brandeis University for her undergraduate studies, where she was frequently one of the only students of color. When she attempted to share her experiences with her white colleagues and peers, it became clear to Davis that they just didn't understand how racism and anti-Blackness had shaped so much of her adolescence and how the long arm of white supremacy was very much still shaping the lives of Black people all over the country. I remember thinking that so many of her experiences in higher education recalled my own experiences in classrooms and in corporate America in my twenties. I remember being asked to "leave my identity at the door" when entering predominantly white spaces in higher education and at work, even when those spaces felt violently anti-Black, homophobic, misogynistic, classist, and ableist. "No matter how much I talked, the people around me were simply incapable of grasping it," she writes. "They could not understand why the whole society was guilty of this murder—why their beloved Kennedy was also to blame, why the whole ruling stratum in their country, by being guilty of racism, was also guilty of this murder."[8] As Davis explains, these murders were an indication that the white supremacist terrorists did not care about Black people's lives, and neither did the people who allowed their actions to become the norm.

What those murderers cared about was squelching the movement to protect Black lives before it could grow. By bombing that church, like the bombings of so many other Black churches and so many Black homes and so many Black businesses in the 1960s, white supremacists were targeting Black communities in their most intimate and vulnerable places. They wanted Black people to feel insecure, uncared for, unprotected, and exposed to the threat of physical violence at every turn. Those four little girls were, as Davis writes, "incidental to the main thing."[9] The "main thing" was white dominance and the exercise of power over Black people. Those four little girls, like so many Black people who have died because of white supremacist violence, were killed because of the larger systems of anti-Black violence that have come to define both our history and our present.

While Davis has long been associated with her life in Birmingham, she might be most well known for the fact that she was incarcerated by the United States government in the 1970s. At the time, Davis was an assistant professor at the University of California, Los Angeles (UCLA). Politically, Davis was also actively organizing with the Black Panther Party (BPP) and the Student Nonviolent Coordinating Committee (SNCC). She gained prominence in these organizations before encountering the complexities of holding multiple identities in a Black-led movement space. Specifically, Davis had started to experience issues with both SNCC and the BPP relating to gender and their treatment of women. These male-dominated organizations frequently delimited the opportunities for women's issues and voices to be centered or foregrounded in the work. Moreover, especially in the case of the BPP, some of the male leaders were often violent toward women in their ranks and communities. For these reasons, socialism and the Communist Party (CP) became a better political fit for Davis.[10] For Black women activists and feminists between the 1930s and 1970s, the CP grew to be a viable political organization for the advancement of gender and racial justice. Unlike many other civil rights organizations, many Black women were able to reach relative prominence in the CP while maintaining a focus on women's rights and concerns. Moreover, they frequently pushed back against the politics of respectability that were so often expected of Black women in the post-Reconstruction and Civil Rights eras.[11]

Davis's political engagement soon became a risk for her livelihood. In 1969, she was fired from her job at UCLA once she revealed that she was a member of the CP. Davis came under suspicion due to her proximity to George Jackson,[12] a Black revolutionary and member of "the Soledad Brothers," who was charged with murdering four people (including one police officer) after taking over a Marin County courthouse.[13] Davis was accused of providing weapons to Jackson. She was forced into hiding before being captured by U.S. authorities after being labeled a terrorist by her own government. They added her to the FBI's Top Ten Most Wanted Fugitive List. She was the third woman to ever be added.[14] Davis spent eighteen months in prison across three institutions (mostly in solitary confinement) before being acquitted in 1972.

During her incarceration, Davis was once again exposed to the violence, disregard, and anti-Blackness of the State. Davis's firsthand account has been critical to the abolitionist movement writ large. A fellow Black female CP member and comrade Charlene Mitchell wrote about how Davis "spent more than 16 months in one jail cell after another on framed-up charges of murder, kidnapping, and conspiracy."[15] Mitchell had also run as the CP's presidential candidate in 1968, becoming the first Black woman to run for president of the United States. Mitchell was one of many organizers who fought to get Davis free from detention. The chairman of the CP's all-Black Che-Lumumba Club, Franklin Alexander, helped organize a national campaign to free Davis, co-led by Fania Davis Jordan, Davis's twenty-three-year-old younger sister.[16] Later, Davis explained how her time in detention deeply informed her ideas about abolition and feminism. These experiences continued to fuel her work to end these systems of harm in all their forms. Through her lived experiences, Davis had direct evidence that the status quo of mass incarceration was inadequate in providing reparative justice or rehabilitation for incarcerated people. Moreover, the prison system reproduced violences against women and gender minorities that went unnoticed and unaddressed by those in the mainstream and other civic citizens. This is the critical harm of prison: The damage it inflicts on women and poor, Black, Brown, disabled, and immigrant people happens away from public sight. It is particularly insidious because the invisibility of the carceral state creates a symbiotic relationship between the public and the system of corporal punishment. In many ways, the public tacitly buys into the system by accepting it as it is. Most important, the cloak of darkness and secrecy around the inner workings and capitalistic underpinnings of the American prison system render the lives of incarcerated people incredibly vulnerable.

What Is Anti-Racism?

To understand the roots of abolition, we must first think through the motivations behind anti-Black racism. Davis's lifelong work shows us that the systems that underlie modern prisons are anti-Black and structurally racist. But they are rarely recognized as such. In her book *Are Prisons Obsolete?*, Davis explains how race has always been a central feature in the presumption of criminality: "After the abolition of slavery, former slave states passed new legislation revising the Slave Codes in order to regulate the behavior of free blacks in ways similar to those that had existed during slavery."[17] This recapitulation of enslavement meant that Black people, while legally free, were expected to comport themselves to fit a racial caste system where they still, in many respects, belonged to propertied white people. All white people had a vested interest in maintaining this social order. This form of anti-Blackness and criminalization also worked to make public spaces especially fraught terrain for Black people. Davis writes, "The new Black Codes proscribed a range of actions—such as vagrancy, absence from work, breach of job contracts, the possession of firearms, and insulting gestures or acts—that were criminalized only when the person charged was black."[18] The most well-known example of this codified expectation of Black subservience to white people is that of Emmett Till. In 1955, the fourteen-year-old was accused of whistling at and sexually grabbing a white woman named Carolyn Bryant. The teenager, who was visiting family in Mississippi but was from Chicago, was then brutally murdered by Bryant's husband and his brother. The two made the boy "carry a 75-pound cotton gin fan to the bank of the Tallahatchie River and ordered him to take off his clothes. The two men then beat him nearly to death, gouged out his eye, shot him in the head and then threw his body, tied to the cotton gin fan with barbed wire, into the river."[19] Nearly six decades after Till was murdered, Bryant admitted that she falsified her story: Till never grabbed her or made any sexual advances.[20] These encounters were par for the course for Black Americans following the official end of slavery. Throughout the mid-twentieth century, lynchings and public murders of Black people, like the bombings Davis witnessed as a child, were a part of the American social landscape, just like drive-in theaters and Frank Sinatra films.

Even after the formal abolition of slavery with the passage of the Thirteenth Amendment to the U.S. Constitution in

1865, there was intentional wording to ensure that freed Black Americans could still be captured and possessed by the State. The exact wording of the Thirteenth Amendment is as follows:

> Neither slavery nor involuntary servitude, except as a punishment for crime whereof the party shall have been duly convicted, shall exist within the United States, or any place subject to their jurisdiction.[21]

This loophole, which returns Black Americans into political servitude if they are "duly convicted" of a crime, is the subject of many contemporary projects, like Ava DuVernay's movie *13th*[22] and Douglas Blackmon's Pulitzer Prize–winning book *Slavery by Another Name: The Re-enslavement of Black Americans from the Civil War to World War II*.[23] In his book, Blackmon refers to debt peonage, or the system of selling free Black Americans into involuntary servitude for undefined periods of time, as a "neoslavery system [that] exploited legal loopholes and federal policies that discouraged prosecution of whites for continuing to hold black workers against their wills."[24] These loopholes were created and preserved with intention. To maintain a white supremacist system of order, powerful white leaders maintained the status quo through de jure (by law) and de facto (by fact) norms that regulated society. Essentially, white property owners and ex-slave owners seeking to recoup their perceived losses after slaves were freed used legal statutes to re-establish Black people as property using incarceration as a looming threat. Legal scholar and critical race theorist Cheryl I.

Harris describes this process as "whiteness as property." She writes:

> In ways so embedded that it is rarely apparent, the set of assumptions, privileges, and benefits that accompany the status of being white have become a valuable asset that whites sought to protect and that those who passed sought to attain—by fraud if necessary. Whites have come to expect and rely on these benefits, and over time these expectations have been affirmed, legitimated, and protected by the law.[25]

Thus, systemic and institutional racism refers to the sum total of the structural and societal methods and models that systematize and regularize anti-Black and white supremacist ways of being and the criminalizing of all Black people. Racism is rooted in law. It is embedded in every institution in this land. It is all around us all the time and it orders all of society.

Anti-racism, as Davis teaches us, therefore, will always be about dismantling and removing the systems that allow racism to grow and persist. This includes not only eradicating the legal institutions that perpetuate racism, but also acknowledging that society has been rooted in anti-Black racism and white supremacist underpinnings since its inception. "Racism can be discovered at every level in every major institution—including the military, the health care system, and the police," Davis wrote in her book *Freedom Is a Constant Struggle: Ferguson, Palestine, and the Foundations of a Movement*.[26] "This is why it's important to develop an analysis that goes beyond an understanding of individual acts of racism and this is why we need demands that go beyond the prosecution of the individual perpetrators."[27]

This is the framework that we must think about when considering what it means to be anti-racist in the United States. We must consider that racist processes and institutions are not just about interpersonal interactions, personal biases, internal bigotry, and the like. Eradicating racism can never be just a personal endeavor rooted in changing hearts and minds, thinking differently, or being "socially conscious." It has become sexy to talk about anti-racism as simply choosing not to think racist thoughts and working through our own racist beliefs without actually working to remove the barriers and obstacles that racist institutions create for racial minorities. Unfortunately, this model of thinking is rooted in privilege and the lack of will to take on the political risk of actually challenging the status quo. For many white Americans, taking on political risk is optional, while for those of us who fall outside of whiteness, we have no choice but to confront challenges to our mere existence every day. Overwhelmingly, white Americans choose to change their Facebook profile picture to a Black Lives Matter logo, wear a safety pin on their collar, or quietly believe themselves to be "allies" to victims of racial violence without engaging in overt rebellion against the harms facing those victims. Sadly, academics, commentators, and activists alike have offered this watered-down approach to anti-racism as a viable method to address the deep systemic problems in this country. But those of us who have been doing this work know that strategy will lead us nowhere we haven't been before.

What Is Abolition?

In its simplest form, abolition is the return of care to communities as opposed to outsourcing that care to institutions and police authorities. Abolitionists firmly believe that the world can exist and people can thrive without corporal punishment as it exists today. Most important, many abolitionists hold the opinion that communities, especially those at multiple margins of identity, possess the expertise and know-how to care for themselves.[28] What they often need is financial support and resources to assist and support them in living healthy and full lives. Abolition is frequently extended to consider not only the end of policing in the United States but also the end of prisons. Both of these institutions normalize the surveillance of poor, Black, Brown, disabled, and immigrant people who are frequently deemed to be outside of the acceptable bounds of citizenship. Yet, there remains a great deal of public confusion and resistance to eliminating police and prisons wholesale. Some of that resistance is related to a general lack of formal knowledge about abolition. Much of it is related to the sentiment that there are no alternatives to the status quo. Perhaps that is where Davis's work is most helpful.

Davis is credited with creating the term "Prison Industrial Complex" (PIC) in her book *Are Prisons Obsolete?*[29] This term refers to the "extent to which prison building and operation began to attract vast amounts of capital—from the construction industry to food and health care provision."[30] The goods that corporations provide to prisons include items like soap, furniture, clothing, food, and other supplies that create a codependent relationship between private industry and private prisons. Davis argues that as prison construction increased in the 1980s and '90s, corporate interest in prisons transformed incarceration into an industry that has expanded mainly because of a promise to reduce crime and bring more jobs into impoverished areas. Over time, prisons have worked to hyper-criminalize Black communities and benefit off of their unpaid labor. Meanwhile, this entire process remains largely hidden from society. For Davis, this is not only a breach of freedom and liberty, but is also anti-democratic and rooted in capitalistic exploitation. She credits global capitalism and the commodification of individualistic identity with the growth of individual cells in prisons for "personal reflection" and rehabilitation. One of the most important reminders Davis offers us is that the modern prison system is actually the result of reform. She notes that our existing model of rehabilitation stems from many previous failed attempts at punishment that were so vile and depraved that our current model looks like an improvement. Originally, American prisons mimicked the torture systems handed over from British rule. They were gruesome and cruel. While we continue to reform and chip away at existing institutions and create more technologically advanced prison systems, we fail to imagine our world without those prisons at all. The arguments that "this is the way we have always done it" and that "we have no other examples to follow" keep us in a vicious cycle of reproducing the same violence generation after generation. Davis challenges us to understand that it is our job to imagine a better future for ourselves and for our comrades. She implores us to see abolition not as a method of tearing down but as a process of building up.

In their workbook "Fumbling Towards Repair: A Workbook for Community Accountability Facilitators," Mariame Kaba and Shira Hassan describe Prison Industrial Complex abolition using a definition created by Critical Resistance.[31] It was at the Critical Resistance conference that I first met both Davis and Kaba.

The definition goes as follows:

> Prison Industrial Complex (PIC) abolition is a political vision with the goal of eliminating imprisonment, policing, and surveillance, and creating lasting alternatives to punishment and imprisonment.[32]

This definition is critical as its focus is not just on prisons and police but also on the larger culture of surveillance that convinces so many people that they are necessary. "An abolitionist vision means that we must build models today that can represent how we want to live in the future," Kaba and Hassan write.[33] Rather than focusing on tinkering with the system in place today, abolitionists ask us to envision what the ideal world without prisons would look and feel like. When we begin building toward that vision, we start to move away from the oppressive and exploitative violence inherent to the PIC and the culture of acceptance surrounding it. In the workbook, which is designed to help train community care workers engaging in transformative (techniques rooted in addressing the root causes of societal ills) and restorative (techniques rooted in Indigenous practices of harm reduction, community healing, and personal accountability) justice practices, Kaba and Hassan include a quote from Davis from 2003: "Our most difficult and urgent challenge to date is that of creatively exploring new terrains of justice where the prison no longer serves as our major anchor."[34] That is precisely why abolitionist ideals are frequently deemed too radical and too far-fetched to be considered realistic. Their roots in exploration, imagination, and the uncertain process of discovering alternative ways of being are so often the justification for disregarding abolition as a possibility at all.

Perhaps this notable lack of imagination around abolition is why Davis offers so many alternatives to the existing system of incarceration. She suggests that we should focus on the relationships that have been created between private institutions, corporations, the government, health services, education, and prisons to understand how we can remove those relationships and create a world without them. Rather than get hung up on what has been, she implores us to believe that any system we have built, we are capable of tearing down. Davis provides a constellation of alternatives, including destroying the stigma around issues like drug use and treatment, mental health, alcohol use, and immigration rights, which carry different stakes and penalties for folks who are Black or deemed other. She also suggests the decarceration of schools (by removing punitive measures like pseudo-arrests, in-school suspensions, and hypersurveillance that create the school-to-prison pipeline) and focusing on the ways that there is an ethics of social domination that moves throughout society and works to justify the growth of the modern prison system.

Anti-Racism, Abolition, Anti-Capitalism

One of the most common responses I remember hearing about race and racism while I was growing up was "That was so long ago. Why are you all still talking about it?" It was almost always said by a white person who did not "see" race or who was "post-racial," and they would discourage me from acknowledging how racism and anti-Blackness still shaped my day-to-day life. Like those college peers Davis encountered, they displayed an overt disregard of and inability to empathize with my experiences that often left me feeling as though my grief was invalid or unjustified. It often felt like I cared too much or cared for the wrong things. Now, as a professor who teaches young people about the long arc of slavery and the systemic violence associated with capitalism in the United States, I am sometimes still surprised at the parts of our history that confound my students. For example, students are shocked when they first learn about the critical roles Black women played in ending slavery and rebelling on slave plantations, or about the fact that access to voting in the United States was not fully universal for Black people until after the Voting Rights Act of 1965—and still, previously incarcerated people are frequently disenfranchised even after "serving their time." Times like these remind me that there remains a great deal of confusion over the chronological impacts and intergenerational consequences of anti-Blackness, slavery, and racism in the United States. This intentional lack of historical training and anchoring has made it nearly impossible for non-Black people, especially white Americans, to understand how today's conditions are deeply informed by—and indeed, explicitly in line with—the white supremacist machinations of generations past.

Perhaps the most important lesson I seek to teach my students about this particular political moment is the centrality of racial capitalism in shaping our day-to-day lives. This is where Davis has been and remains a critical interlocutor and thinker. Since Davis is a Communist, many of her core theories about injustice are also deeply rooted in an economic analysis that requires an end to capitalism. Davis writes, "The fact, for example, that many corporations with global markets now rely on prisons as an important source of profit helps us to understand the rapidity with which prisons began to proliferate precisely at a time when official studies indicated that the crime rate was falling."[35] Prisons have been monetized and so have prisoners. The system as it stands today is one that continues the financialization of poor, Black, Brown, disabled, and immigrant bodies in the name of profit margins. As such, Davis explains that these obvious connections between anti-racism, abolition, and anti-capitalism are central to any liberationist politic. Not only that, but we, as organizers and freedom fighters, cannot do this work without paying attention to all three simultaneously.

Davis has always been clear that racism against Black people and all forms of injustice are tethered to labor exploitation and the proliferation of capital among a very wealthy few. In 2020, in an exclusive interview with Al Jazeera, Davis said, "Capitalism is racial capitalism, and I think we need to confront that today and move in the direction of envisioning and hopefully building a socialist society."[36] In effect, we cannot divorce capitalism from race, nor can we divorce our struggle against racism from our struggle against capitalism. Every financial crisis is a racial crisis as well. It is under this oppressive, hetero-capitalistic model that Black people around the world during the COVID-19 crisis were among the most vulnerable to the disease.[37] Many of these folks found themselves not only more susceptible to contracting the virus but also more vulnerable to job losses, more likely to receive inadequate healthcare, less likely to have proper safety nets to buoy them during potential financial emergencies, and generally less prepared to survive such a catastrophic global tragedy.

One of the greatest gifts we have been given as organizers and believers in justice is the fact that Davis has lived to see such a vast passage of time. Angela Davis's work and witnessing has been essential in bridging the gap between a time many would like to forget and the present day. And in her position between the ugliest parts of our history and the most hopeful glimmers of our future, Davis has helped to draw lines directly from the violent bomb-makers and KKK members to the police officers who shoot down Black people in the streets all over this country today. Her work is a living archive connecting us to a past that is too often misunderstood, whitewashed, and erased. In this moment, as scholars, activists, and thinkers of all races, creeds, and stripes emerge to publish their books, give their speeches, and create their TikTok videos about anti-racism and abolition, Davis has endured as a queer Black woman who has actually lived this work publicly and at grave risk to herself. We don't deserve Angela Davis. We don't deserve the care she confers upon us. Nor do we deserve the violence she has had to carry in her body as she has struggled to make us all a little freer.

I'm so grateful for her deep love for us. And for her.

CHAPTER 11

bell hooks taught me how to love expansively

> A culture of domination is anti-love. It requires violence to sustain itself. To choose love is to go against the prevailing values of the culture.
> —*bell hooks, "Love as the Practice of Freedom"*

There's something a bit neglectful about love. It doesn't necessarily require an imperative action or reaction. It doesn't materialize in our day-to-day lives without an explicit cause (like someone saying the words "I," "love," and "you" in perfect sequence). And, unless it's the kind of love that exists between a parent and child, it doesn't actually ask us for much, if anything at all. Perhaps that is why we use the word so lazily and why we so often fail to show up in loving ways for our comrades, communities, and ourselves. Perhaps that is also why true agape love (a divine love that transcends human knowing and believing) seems so unreal to many people, even those who consider themselves deeply loving.

I can't pretend like I'm above it, either. I have fallen into the trap of offering mediocre and lackluster love to the community members who bore and raised me. I have taken my foremothers and forefathers for granted. I imagine they're disappointed in me even when they haven't said so. At times, I haven't shown up in ways that honor my own integrity and do justice to those in my various communities who have sacrificed for me. And I secretly, quietly feel shame about it. Since the global pandemic has altered the landscapes of our lives, I have committed these grievances even more. I've struggled to make phone calls because the weight of the world prevented my hands from dialing. I've canceled plans because I had little to no energy left after surviving another week as a Black queer woman in America. I've failed to respond to emails and text messages from people I loved even when I had the best intentions of doing so.

I still feel sensations of failure and regret when I look at the unanswered email from my dear friend Lauren Berlant, who passed away in 2021. On February 3, 2020, Lauren sent me a link to a guide on situating ourselves intentionally within a classroom setting. The article and associated exercise were a call to educators to provide dedicated space within the learning environment for students and instructors to critically engage with their own knowing, the work they do, and the people and communities that brought them to the classroom in the first place. Lauren would always send me links like this. Sometimes, after I had secured a tenure-track position at Syracuse University, they'd mail me a book to "the 'Cuse," as Lauren lovingly called it. Though they were a white Jewish queer human, Lauren always centered Indigenous and Black Feminisms in our challenging discussions. But our regular correspondences became fewer and farther between during the COVID-19 crisis as Lauren continued to struggle with cancer. I noticed the change, but I was holding so many burdens that my arms were full.

Lauren and I met when I was a graduate student at the University of Chicago. They were the professor whom all the students wanted to meet. I was the Black woman graduate student who was skeptical of this thin woman and their verbosity. Frequently wearing long-sleeved forest-green and gray knit shirts, black jeans, and other monochromatic tones, Lauren was always carrying a La Croix in an obscure flavor like mango or coconut. I would make fun of them for drinking a beverage that tasted like someone had already placed it in their mouth and swished it around before spitting it back into the can and sealing it for mass production.

Upon our first meeting, I remember Lauren sitting quietly and looking at me through their round glasses as our peer spoke intently. I was on the opposite side of their messy desk in a campus building that looked like a house from Harry Potter's adventures. I was to be their teaching assistant for a course of Feminist Theory. Lauren was tentative about me.

"What classes have you taught before?"
"I've been teaching since 2012, right after I finished my master's at Cal State Fullerton. I taught Black Politics and Intro to Statistics."
Their eyebrows rose to their curly gray hairline.
"Statistics?" Lauren questioned, leaving their mouth in the shape of an "S."
"Yeah, I love math and Black people."
Lauren nodded slowly and giggled a little. "I like you," was their reply.
"I like you, too."

After that day, we spent hours together, mostly in the classroom. Lauren, though they were an academic megastar, showed up for me in so many other ways. They came to my panels, sometimes serving on them with me. Lauren encouraged me to apply for grants and teaching opportunities that fit my research and personal interests. They checked on me when I seemed overwhelmed or otherwise stressed out by the relentlessness of graduate school. On several occasions, I brought my youngest children to campus with me because childcare was too expensive a burden on our single-income household. Lauren gladly entertained them. One year, for Lauren's birthday (which appropriately fell on Halloween), they gave my kids stress balls that looked like orange snot wrapped in black netting. Every time the stress balls were squeezed, they made a gross fart sound that my children adored. I still squeeze that stress ball from time to time. Giggling.

When it was time for me to go on the job market, Lauren (who wasn't even on my dissertation committee) was all hands on deck. They wanted to hear my "elevator pitch," the brief canned description I would use to sell myself to whatever universities might be interested in hiring me. They came to my practice job talk and told me I was selling myself short. They were right. And, when I received three job offers my first time out on the market, Lauren said, "Of course they love you. You're a star."

I left Chicago in a frenzy to move to upstate New York. I immersed myself in the culture of being a first-year faculty member. Lauren kept sending me notes here and there. I always sent a birthday message, making sure to tell Lauren they were my friend. More than anything else, we were friends.

And, when I received news that Lauren had passed, all I could think was "Wow, I never emailed them back." The February email was opened and never returned. I felt wholly inadequate. I felt like a fraud. I didn't feel like I had been a good friend.

What never crossed my mind until I put this experience to paper was that Lauren's email came through as the world was facing a new crisis: COVID-19. We spent months hearing about the virus and watching cases worsen around the globe. Meanwhile, friends and family in other states and countries were likely experiencing a totally different political and social moment than we were. Those early days were most characterized by uncertainty, misinformation, and general confusion. In March, my three children were sent home from school without any real guidance on how I would become their homeschool teacher while continuing to educate college grads and undergrads in my first year on the tenure track. I had two courses on my schedule and had just helped facilitate student social organizing on campus when we were told all teaching would be moving online. The details were unclear. Most of my colleagues and comrades at other universities were experiencing wage losses, potential delays in their tenure processes, and new holds on academic positions for which they had been interviewing for months. Some graduate programs halted admission. Outside of Academia, my family and friends were already facing decreased hours on their jobs and work closures that left them essentially unemployed overnight. Globally, markets were starting to be affected by the news. COVID-19 was all anyone was talking about. To say that we were facing a global emergency was a grave understatement.

Thinking about it now, I'm sure Lauren didn't hold it against me. The world was in utter crisis. They may not have even noticed that I never replied. But, beyond that, they were an incredibly forgiving person who was steadfast in their commitment to not give a shit so much that life was no longer fun. Lauren would frequently fan off student concerns about language and diction in class because they wanted students to be real, to be themselves, to be present. But, because those irregular, weirdly worded, sometimes sent-from-the-hip emails had become our love language, I worried that Lauren hadn't gotten the message. That I hadn't performed the act of loving them in the way they deserved.

I imagine much of Lauren's flippancy about the little things stemmed from their confrontation with their own mortality. In *The Cancer Journals,* Audre Lorde describes the ways that her breast cancer diagnosis set her into a perpetual presentness because the future was so incredibly imaginary. She explained that facing her own mortality had made her less sensitive to the little things. Instead, she was constantly seeking joy, lightness, and the parts of her life that made her feel real. She was no longer hung up on what she couldn't control. Nor was Lorde invested in wasting any energy on negativity, pain, or unhappiness. I can't know if that's how Lauren felt before they passed. But I imagine so.

I imagine Lauren was spending their days reading all the books they had intended to read for decades. They were probably inviting friends over to eat with them and their partner, enjoying fine wines and laughing over board games. I would like to imagine Lauren as being so light and carefree that my lack of response was the furthest thing from their mind in their final days. I will never know if my imagination is betraying me. I have no way of ever confirming any of this. But I know Lauren.

The email I never sent haunts me. I will likely carry that weight with me for the rest of my life. Along with it, I will carry the reminder that real loving is in the doing and it is in the doing right now. This is the lesson that is likely the hardest for us to truly get. Unfortunately, it takes failures at loving well for us to know where we've fallen short and how to be better at loving.

That's part of the reason I carry the same weight of regret when I reflect on the fact that I originally drafted this book with no chapter about bell hooks. I debated it. I considered writing one. But, I thought, she was still very much alive. I thought she had so much more time. She had written so many works of her own, many that gave me words for experiences that I had not yet articulated to myself, let alone to the world. So many scholars, activists, and thinkers had written about bell hooks. She was the feminist that inspired a generation of feminists. She was a household name. Who was I to perform an act of loving her when she had performed the act of loving herself so well? When so many worthy others had long been loving her in public even before I had knowledge of her work or language to articulate the impact it had on my own? Who was I to think that I had a right to love her at all?

These are silly questions when I think about them now. They posit love as a finite resource or as something that has direction and magnitude. This structuring of love suggests that only certain people—people with emotional maturity and bandwidth, patience, and inherent goodness—should be out there doing the loving. This framing of love suggests that if someone gets enough of it, they will never need to be loved again, or better, or more than they are. It also reflects my own fragility, my fear of loving a Black woman who was the expert at love. Or maybe it reflects my fear of loving at all.

Living through COVID-19 has taught me a lot about love. For one, love persists even when our lives end. The grave human losses and countless tragedies we've all endured have never eradicated the energetic connections we have to one another. Two, love expands as we learn more about who we are. As we self-actualize and see ourselves as a part of a broader community, we gain a greater capacity to love ourselves and others. Last, the most important thing I have learned about love during this COVID-19 moment is probably that love requires a great deal of boundary-setting and intention if it is to truly be rewarding for those who give and receive it.

I credit bell hooks with naming those lessons. Love is boundless, ever-reaching, out of this world, and bigger than our imaginations. That's likely why it has come to denote our feelings about romantic partners, children, family members, hobbies, foods, destinations, and so many other facets of human life. We love love.

And yet, we still fail to offer it in genuine ways to those who have shaped us so deeply and critically. We frequently withhold love from people closest to us as a form of punishment or to express our own hurts. We run away from love when it feels too big or overwhelming. We abandon love. We give up on love. We disbelieve love. Or, sometimes, we just don't do it. The loving.

I reflect on my relationship with Lauren Berlant, and it was clearly loving. It was the kind of love where you don't have to say it or even see the person for a while, but you both know it's there. Yet, that last email has cast a shadow I can't shake. Now, as both Berlant and hooks have passed on, both of them ancestors who animate these words, I offer love as a eulogy. I offer my love as a repast. I offer my love as mourning, memory, and edification. I offer my love, as meager and fledgling as it feels for me. I do so while flummoxed by my own failure. A failure I will likely never get over.

It is this failure that has really made me reflect on the types of love we offer our foremothers and the types of love that we, as Black women, accept from our lovers, friends, family, and comrades. What is it about our feminist foremothers that encourages us to look them over, forget them, and fail to honor them in life, yet still call that love? What is love without acts? I can't answer these questions yet. But I'm trying.

bell hooks came from loving kin

In the months since her passing, I have thought a lot about how hooks wrote about her family and about the ways that she learned how to love herself and her comrades. In her book *Sisters of the Yam: Black Women and Self-Recovery,* hooks writes about how her upbringing in rural Kentucky enveloped her in the caressing love of kin whose connections to the earth, ancestors, and spirits protected her family. One of the most poignant reflections hooks shares is a conversation that happened repeatedly with her "baba," her mother's mother, before her passing. Every time, her grandmother would ask how hooks could live so far from her people while continuing to do her work. In response, hooks writes, "She was asking how it was I could live without the daily communion and community of ancestors, kin, and family—how I could sustain my reason for living since I had been raised to believe that these connections gave life substance and meaning."[1] hooks says that she hung her head so that her grandmother "could not see tears" in her eyes. At this point, hooks had not yet formed new community and kinship ties to affirm her experiences. What's more, she had been isolated in predominantly white spaces that reminded her of her difference and left her even more isolated from the spirits, ancestors, and community that she had cultivated throughout her childhood.

After growing up in the segregated South and attending segregated schools, hooks, known by her comrades and family as Gloria Watkins, had grown deeply embedded in the poor and working-class Black community from whence she and her people came. Each of her books has commented not only on the centrality of her racial and gender identities but also on the critical importance of her class experience in shaping her feminist values and ethics. I often reflect on how growing up poor and working class orients us toward community-building that moves away from compulsory self-reliance and what hooks calls "narcissistic individualism." She writes, "The focus on building community necessarily challenges a culture of domination that privileges individual well-being over collective effort."[2] In this way, building community with other Black, poor, and working-class people is not just about fellowship and togetherness. Rather, it is also a way to challenge anti-Black systems of oppression that privilege white, middle- and upper-class, heteronormative culture and the ways that those systems have maintained a chokehold on the political and economic resources we all rely upon for our survival. I saw this illustrated in my community growing up. Most of the families I encountered in my community were combined and extended. Grandmothers, aunts, uncles, cousins, and half-siblings (which, in my community, were just siblings) were all a part of the "nuclear" household. There was no explicit emphasis on the "traditional family" with two heterosexual, gender-binary parents, two and half children, and a white picket fence. Instead, our community was often organized around raising and supporting children, even those who belonged to us not by blood but by bond. Nieces, nephews, and niblings[3] were constantly being fostered and adopted. With the constant police violence, incarceration, and other forms of harm in our communities, building expansive kinship networks was a type of scaffolding, a structural barrier to protect the next generation of Black children from the ravages of white supremacy before they had the tools to fight it themselves.

hooks came from my kinds of people. And, in her writing and speaking, she frequently articulated why these types of experiences were deeply formative for her political ethics and her orientation toward others. For hooks, healing was a communal project. She writes, "Now, I am more confident that community is a healing place."[4] Healing just couldn't be done alone. At least not completely. This is especially true when the wounds run deep due to the actions of the people we love, like parents, lovers, family members, and comrades. Central to the project of healing that hooks communicates is love: love for the self and for others.

a hooksian conception of love

Cornel West once said that "justice is what love looks like in public."[5] I used to accept that definition wholesale. I rarely challenged it and instead felt assured that if someone so prolific had made such an assertion, it had to be the final word on the matter. Rationally, I can accept private love as an intimate endeavor rooted in the self and decoupled from state institutions. Thus, if justice is what happens when we love in community, then perhaps that is why we have never really *seen* justice. In either case, since growing in my own self-actualization and figuring out who I am as a lover, both romantically and platonically, I have become deeply concerned with how justice shows up in our loving endeavors. Specifically, when loving, how do we do justice to ourselves *and* to others? hooks expands on the connection between love and justice when she discusses the ways that we all learn love in our childhood. Likewise, we learn the injustices of possession, abuse, and the violence of love from parents who sometimes cause harm. She writes, "Care and affirmation, the opposite of abuse and humiliation, are the foundation of love. No one can rightfully claim to be loving when behaving abusively."[6] For hooks, love must include a full accounting for the lessons we have brought with us from our various upbringings, lessons that too often center punishment without reconciliation. She pushes us to realize that these logics rarely prepare us for building loving romantic or platonic relationships. In fact, they set us up to replicate and reproduce the same patterns that left us feeling hurt as children. hooks argues that part of loving justly is teaching children that they are not property, that they have rights and deserve respect, so that when they grow up, they expect the same treatment in their adult relationships. As she says, "Without justice there can be no love."[7]

While I agree with West that publicness shapes the texture and tenor of love (especially for us queers, who often long to be affirmed under the warmth of the sun's rays), there is something about love in community that reaches beyond mere public exposure. Love in and with community is about vulnerability and finding affirmation in knowing that your people have you covered. There is an understanding when being loved in, by, and with a community that mistakes are forgivable, misunderstandings are repairable, and people don't have to be disposed of when they are confused or perceived as different. These types of love aren't subject to immediate cancellation at the first sight of turmoil or disagreement. Love in community provides a soft place to land where learning can happen without the fear of being ostracized and cast out. While no community is perfect, those who we consider close comrades and kin are typically amenable to these central suppositions. This is why the concept of "chosen family" has become so important for young queer and trans people, who are frequently excluded from their biological families once they are discovered to be non-heteronormative and non-cisgender. As bell hooks writes, "Communities sustain life—not nuclear families, or the 'couple,' and certainly not the rugged individualist. There is no better place to learn the art of loving than in community."[8] The learning that is required to love properly must happen without the fear that a misstep will result in permanent rebuke. It must be accompanied by the assurances that, as long as we remain in good relation and intention with one another, always centering accountability for any harms we commit, we will not be criminalized, marked, or otherwise excommunicated. White supremacy and anti-Blackness in the larger world create an environment where Black people are so often asked to be perfect, to be angels without flaws, that the possibility of making a mistake in public feels like a catastrophe waiting to happen. hooks asks us not to bring these models into our loving relations with one another. She asks us to move beyond the paradigm of love as punishment or retribution and toward love as learning, as art. A hooksian conception of love is a love that never strives to be perfect but instead works to be affirming, present, healing, and restorative. It is meant to redress the violences of the world by reassuring Black people that they matter simply because they do.

In her book *Communion: The Female Search for Love,* hooks writes most explicitly about the possibilities of loving outside of normative boundaries. She notes that her experiences in her early twenties as she encountered feminism taught her that there were alternatives to heterosexism (the idea that it is "natural" for men and women to romantically couple with one another). She writes, "As a young feminist, fully embracing the idea that I could choose as a partner a woman or a man gave me a sense of personal power."[9] Obtaining this power, she notes, is critical for young women seeking to engage in loving romantic and platonic relationships that do not reproduce gendered and sexualized hierarchies. hooks connects the desire to build loving and intimate (nonsexual) relationships with women in our communities to a feminist effort to reclaim ourselves from heteronormative dynamics that leave us unfulfilled. For many women, these relationships uphold gender expectations that are harmful and limiting. hooks asserts as much when she writes that, "Women loving women who choose paradigms of mutuality and reciprocity over domination and subordination are acting in resistance to everything they have learned about the nature of romance. Usually this will to resist has been forged in radical political movements for social justice or efforts to come to terms with unhappiness in other relationships."[10] While hooks's theorizing here seems rather straightforward, it is extremely non-traditional and taboo. This is especially so for those of us who grew up in conservative church environments where we were groomed to meet the men of our proverbial dreams. The social expectations around nuclear family-building and the preeminence of heteronormative coupling—as seen on nearly every television show and movie depicting a romantic couple—are often so burdensome and onerous on young women like us that the mere thought of queerness or non-monogamy seems like an invitation for a lifetime of woe. Or worse, exclusion and exile. Even developing friendships that involve deep love, passion, and romance may be considered threatening to the societal norms that surround us from birth. hooks notes, "Romantic friendships are a threat to patriarchy and heterosexism because they fundamentally challenge the assumption that being sexual with someone is essential to all meaningful, lasting, intimate bonds."[11] In many ways, developing loving platonic relationships that are not about sex or marriage challenges the idea that Black women are unlovable, undesirable, and beholden to men for providing our source of admiration and care. Moving beyond this paradigm allows us to find alternative ways to love others and ourselves. And, as hooks so clearly describes, it gives us back power over who and how we love in community.

non-monogamy as a site of community and healing

Monogamy is the practice of romantic coupling with only one other person at a time. It is often a compulsory expectation that is projected onto children from birth. It is rooted in age-old capitalistic structures of kinship that re-create the nuclear family as a microcosm of prefab units of labor production. These units of labor perpetuate notions of belonging and citizenship that are anti-Black, queerphobic, transphobic, classist, and ableist. They function in this way because, historically, the family was the first location where children learned how to function in modern society. It was expected that parents and caregivers would teach children not only how to grow up and be responsible laborers, but also how to build families of their own. All of these lessons were aligned with white capitalist heteropatriarchy and its necessity to categorize, label, delimit, and name. While monogamy itself is not inherently bad (there is nothing wrong with loving one person or building a life with one individual), the culture around monogamy is inherently violent toward those of us who fall outside of this paradigm. For us queer-loving people, monogamy culture (which is also wrapped up in heteronormativity) frequently leaves us to be measured by our romantic relationships or lack thereof. It results in stigmatization of unwed women and shaming of queer folks who choose not to assimilate into nuclear models of family-rearing. This framework sits in direct opposition to the model of love and community that hooks presents. She says, "Love is meant to extend ourselves so that we are mutually responsible for the spiritual growth and development of others. It is 'akin to work.'"[12]

I am polyamorous, which means that I am capable of and interested in romantically loving multiple people simultaneously. Polyamory falls under the ethically non-monogamous umbrella, meaning that it is a form of transparent and open non-monogamy (unlike cheating) wherein my partners and I clearly communicate about our agreements, expectations, and plans with respect to our various relationships. I am also a relationship anarchist, which means that I do not place a premium on romance over platonic love. My platonic life partners are just as important to me as my romantic life partners. In naming someone my partner, I make a commitment to not only *do* life with another Black person but to *build* a life with them. This is the foundation of community. It is the notion that, whether we are in one another's lives for the long haul or just for a season, we are present with the purpose of working through and beyond the limitations and obstacles placed around us by systemic violence and oppression. We are there to not only love one another through grief and loss and cheer one another on during career and life successes, but also to design lives that best serve us and our purpose. What our ancestors and forefolks have taught us is that building and maintaining community is the only way to heal ourselves beyond white supremacist violence. Raising children together, working through grief together, traversing our life journeys together, it all matters. Being in community with other Black people is inherently about taking full stock of the ways that the world bears down on us but knowing that, by working together, we have the resources, know-how, and capability to transcend anything if we are willing to work at it.

As a polyamorous relationship anarchist, I reject the idea that we are made to find someone who completes us. I reject the idea that there is only one person out there who can walk with us through the complexities of this world's violence. I reject that because that, too, is white supremacist violence.

loving as a queer androgynous polyamorous black woman

The type of expansive and non-monogamous love hooks articulates is rooted in the notion that Black women's capacity to love others and ourselves provides us with the possibility to overcome domination and the violences against us. She writes, "Understanding love as a life-force that urges us to move against death enables us to see clearly that, where love is, there can be no disenabling, disempowering, or life-destroying abuse."[13] This is likely why hooks focused so intently on love as a reaction of radical rebellion against anti-Blackness and white supremacist violence during her lifetime. For hooks, love was never just about sex, desire, or marriage. It was also a corrective to racist violence. Love was always an opportunity to heal harm that generations of neglect, dispossession, objectification, and oppression had caused. Likewise, loving Black people beyond binaries is a way to explicitly counter the effects of those systems with intention. These frameworks shape precisely how I view my love choices. As a Black queer androgynous genderflux woman who at times feels no gender at all, I love expansively. I subscribe to the idea that love is not a limited resource. Expansive visions of love are defined by the fundamental ethos that there is enough love for everyone. If we can hold love in our hearts for our parents, children, friends, and community, then we can also hold love for multiple romantic partners simultaneously. I love non-monogamously because I am made to love all Black people. Black people who are deemed unlovable or outside of care are still very much deserving of my love. Loving under a white supremacist framework does not typically allow all Black folks to be loved into liberation. Monogamy culture usually requires that we exclude some Black folk from our love (the deviants, the poor, the disabled, the romantically "undesirable"). Terms like "unmarriageable" remind us that, according to dominant logics, lifelong coupling is reserved for those with steady paychecks, respectable habits and practices, normative ideas about their gender, and socially acceptable ways of navigating the world. For many Black queer people this is particularly violent. It also inhibits the healing we must all engage in to overcome the harms we face each day. This is also the work of love.

My upbringing was riddled with lessons about monogamy and its inherent rightness. I saw messages on television about how we were all meant to find the right person of the "opposite sex" to complete us. At church, I was frequently encouraged to learn how to "find a good man" one day. Rather than cultivating my intellectual goals and aspirations, many strangers would first engage my non-male body in terms of how I could best position myself as someone's future wife and mother. I've had people tell me I had "childbearing hips" since I was twelve years old, a nod to the ways that my physical self was evaluated not by my character but by my perceived utility to men. As a queer Black woman who was once a queer Black child, these messages reinforced for me that monogamy would always surround me even if it wasn't a fit for my vision for myself. The weight of other people's expectations around my love and sex life often rendered my private self so public that I felt like I belonged to the monogamous world around me. I often felt that, by being queer and polyamorous (which I knew I was by fifteen years old), I was somehow failing at loving in accordance with my broader community and the people I loved within it. I struggled. I felt ostracized at times. I hid those parts of myself (both my queerness and my non-monogamy) from plain sight for fear that they would draw more attention to a body that I already wanted men, in particular, to stop noticing.

Now, as an adult, I often feel that I am failing at love, at least at the kinds of love that hooks wrote about. I am a Black lesbian. I'm polyamorous and my life is dedicated to loving Black people. But that doesn't mean that I feel like I'm very good at it. I love anxiously at times. I love without regard for societal judgments and respectability (which many of the people in my life still very much care about). I love women who sometimes do not love me back. I love women who choose to love me in ways that hurt me or leave me feeling taken for granted, abandoned, lonely even when I am not alone, and isolated. I have loved abusers. I have mistaken abuse for love because I didn't know any better. I have sometimes made excuses for people who pretended to love me to get close to others. Just like I felt like I failed at loving Lauren, I sometimes worry that I am not measuring up to the love I imagine, desire, and envision for all of the Black women in my life. I know I can't be perfect. But I can continue to use these experiences to work at what hooks calls "the art of love." I use these lessons and experiences in raising my own children. I just hope they know it. That they feel it.

For me, building a loving and open community is a way to teach my free Black children another way of being. It is meant to model for them the type of love that hooks writes about missing as a child. A love that was missing in my childhood, too. In reflecting on her childhood and versions of love we have all dreamt of, hooks writes, "We can never go back. I know that now. We can go forward. We can find the love our hearts long for, but not until we let go grief about the love we lost long ago, when we were little and had no voice to speak the heart's longing."[14] I know that longing well. I remember lying in bed and wishing to be truly seen and held by someone who looked like me. I remember telling boys I was dating that I had developed an interest in someone else but that I wanted to stay in a romantic relationship (which never worked out). I remember all the girls who liked me in secret but avoided me in public for fear that someone might realize we were more than "just friends." I remember how deeply hurt I was every time I attempted another loving relationship with a girl, only for it to turn into a rejection, a denial, and another notch in my growing list of love's failures. I want nothing more than to never have my children experience that pain and loss. My sincerest hope is that they never will.

how do we (black women) love ourselves and others in justice?

Actress and activist Beverly Bond founded the organization Black Girls Rock! in 2006.[15] Every year, the organization, which centers the worth and self-love of Black girls, hosts an awards show to spotlight Black women and girls all over the globe. And, every year, for almost a decade, Bond has come under attack on social media by critics who have accused her of engaging in "reverse racism" for focusing only on Black girls. Besides the fact that "reverse racism" is neither real nor possible, the accusations that critics have deployed are deeply rooted in white supremacy, anti-Blackness, and misogynoir. Specifically, Twitter users felt so strongly about this "exclusion" that they started a hashtag in response: #WhiteGirlsRock.[16] While the reaction seems trite and petty on its face, it is actually quite sinister. The effort to undermine the public's affection for and admiration of Black women and girls because there is supposedly not enough to go around suggests that any efforts to center or acknowledge the beauty, accomplishments, and worth of Black women and girls is inherently violent to everyone else. Instead of seeing love and admiration as expansive and thereby broad and capacious enough to supply love and admiration for all women and girls, this framework ends up leaving Black women and girls subject to a status quo that rarely regards them as valuable or worthy of care and affirmation. As a Black lesbian, a lesson I have learned well is that we encounter violence when we love Black women publicly. Loving Black women out loud is often met with a critical eye and scrutiny. Many of us have internalized that negativity, normalized it, and grown to expect it. This shapes not only how we love others but also how we love ourselves.

Many Black women don't love themselves justly. We don't love ourselves toward freedom and out of the domination we've endured over the course of our lives. We don't love ourselves beyond the harms we encounter. Why? Because loving Black women is incredibly lonely. Instead, I'd argue that we love ourselves by heading to an early grave. We love ourselves by spreading ourselves so thin that we serve everyone's needs but our own. We love ourselves into the lives and livelihoods of everyone around us because we frequently think that is the only way we will receive love in return. Our love becomes the lifeblood used to raise children, build churches, start social movements, and rescue Black folk from police violence and all manner of systemic discrimination. If this book has shown nothing else, it shows that Black women's love for Black people knows no bounds. And maybe that's part of the problem. Black women's love is so used up, so extracted, and so relied upon by everyone except us that there is rarely any leftover for us to keep for ourselves.

I have grown to believe—especially after writing this book and reflecting on the countless Black women whose lives have ended abruptly and painfully due to exhaustion, overwork, and physical exploitation—that loving Black women requires beautiful things. It requires softness, gentle words and touches, peaceful moments, loving glances, and the quietness of a persistent joy. Loving Black women and loving ourselves justly requires that we stop giving ourselves away to prove our worth and value. Loving us requires that we stop substituting presence for care and niceness for nurturing. It necessitates patience, grace, second and third chances, and the boundaries that move us all toward harmony and peace in our lives. We have to build communities and comradeship that don't require that our cups be empty before they seek to fill us back up.

a reflection on loving the dying and the dead

I started writing this book as my maternal grandmother, Lucille, was dying. I finished it a few months after she passed away in January 2021. She was a beautiful and loving Black woman whose presence in my life had grown to feel permanent, even though I knew it was temporary. She was a North Star in my life that I had tried to never take for granted. I tried to call her often, send money to help with medical bills, visit as frequently as graduate school and child-rearing would allow, and buy groceries on occasion. But as the distance between me and my North Star continued to grow, with me moving first to Los Angeles, then to Chicago, and then to Syracuse, I felt a deep disconnectedness from a critical anchor in my life. When my ancestors and spirits spoke to me in summer 2020, they told me it was time to head home and visit my grandmother for her birthday. They told me it would likely be my last time seeing her. I was afraid to travel during the COVID crisis. I hadn't been on a plane at all, but I knew what was being spoken into my heart. So, in October 2020, I pushed past my jitters, boarded a plane, and went to see my grandma in Oakland, California, one last time. It was the last time I saw her earthside. I took her to a beautiful restaurant on the water, treated her like a queen, and escorted her like she was born on the River Nile, because to me, she was. That day, I shared with my grandma that I was queer and polyamorous. I explained that I dated other people outside of my fifteen-year marriage, a marriage she had presided over herself. She looked at me and said, "Are you happy?"

I smiled at her, my eyes becoming wet, and said, "Yes."

"That's all that matters, sweetheart," she told me.

We ate fried chicken with my mother and my then partner. We shared cake and laughed on a beautiful fall day in my hometown. My mother and grandmother looked over the water, and in that moment, I felt a deep lightness and peace. My grandmother said it was the best birthday of her life. That was the last time I touched my grandmother's soft hands. It was the last time I carried that oversized leather purse and helped her pick out a meal on the menu. That day was the last time I smelled my grandmother's perfume or saw her crooked smile. That was it. Just a few months later, one of my tethers to this earth was cut. I felt like I was billowing in the wind. Lost to the gusts.

My grandmother had spent months stuck in her home during COVID-19. She was relatively immobile, and her little legs moved much slower than they had in the years before. She required a cane for most of her walking but was working on building strength by climbing a short hill outside her apartment every day. She was living in Section Eight housing that could only be described as overfull. Her hoarding tendencies had only worsened over the years, leaving the two-bedroom, first-floor unit looking like a messy gift shop. At times, the place was so full of things (excess toilet paper, stuffed animals, wigs, butterfly figurines, etc.) that she was too ashamed to let anyone besides me or my mother in. If they had come in, they likely wouldn't have been able to navigate the space without turning sideways or stepping over objects on the floor. My grandmother struggled with poverty her whole life, and her final days here were likely harsh reminders of her childhood. Fixed income constraints and medical emergencies were the norm. I, the grandchild she lovingly called "her baby," was across the country where I couldn't take care of her. Perhaps that was why this last trip home was so important to me. For years before that trip, I had sensed that my time with her was slowly ending. That she was slowly dying. Leaving me in a world without her. For years, I warned my immediate family that we needed to start planning for end-of-life care, sounding an alarm in an empty parking lot where no one could hear me. Screaming in a crowded room in a language no one could decipher. When the end came, I wasn't surprised. I was deeply saddened, hurt to my absolute core. But I wasn't surprised.

In early 2021, I fell into a deep depression after the loss of Grandma Lucille. Hours felt like days, days like months, and months like the years we hoped to forget. It felt like one of the longest years of my life. Losing my grandmother left me without words for myself and for the people I had grown to love. I spent months, maybe even a year, looking for myself, chatting with her at my altar, asking her to be with me because I just missed her so much. I talked to her about her last birthday. I laughed with her about all my relationship drama, since she now knew I'm completely gay and poly. And, later on, she started visiting me in my dreams. She hugged me. She giggled with me. And, on special occasions, she flashed that crooked smile.

It took me months to face her being gone. Even as I write this, I can't control the emotions. Tears are all that welcome me. I've only been able to go on because I know what love is and what it does. I believe we are still connected and that our love is expansive enough to transcend time, space, and even death. I believe that our love can never dissipate, that it just turns into a new energy between she and I. Because we love each other, and we always will. The same energy exists between Lauren and me. While I sometimes worry that I failed them both, Lauren with my unresponsiveness and Grandma with my moving away, I hold tightly to the energy that endures. It's the same energy every loving Black woman has with her comrades and kin. I have to believe this is true. I know it. These words would not exist if it weren't.

Conclusion

I Taught Myself About Patience

When I was four years old, my mom put me in a local preschool at a house run by a lovely Black woman named Ms. Ruby. I loved it there. At preschool, I spent a lot of time doing a few things. I played on the seesaw (my favorite aerobic activity), I cared for the little babies (like I was on staff), and I played every hand-clapping, waist-wiggling, foot-stomping game a Black girl could play. From songs about the mailman needing to "do his duty" because of the size of a woman's booty to "Ring Around the Rosie" (which I would one day learn was about the plague) to the "Shabooya Roll Call" games we would play on the foursquare before dodgeball, I soaked up the old Black folktales in the traditional word-of-mouth, rhythmic ways I witnessed other Black kids do it. My favorite hand-clapping game was Miss Mary Mack. The lyrics said:

Miss Mary Mack, Mack, Mack,
All dressed in black, black, black,
With silver buttons, buttons, buttons,
All down her back, back, back.
She asked her mother, mother, mother,
For fifteen cents, cents, cents,

To see the elephants, elephants, elephants,
Jump over the fence, fence, fence.
They jumped so high, high, high,
They touched the sky, sky, sky.
And, they never came back, back, back,
'Til the fourth of July, -ly, -ly.

Back then, I had no idea who Miss Mary Mack was or why she needed money to see these elephants. Nor did I understand why those elephants possessed such limber knees as to jump into the sky for some unknown period of time. But something about this nursery rhyme stuck with me.

It was only recently that I learned that this might be a song that was sung by enslaved children about the USS *Merrimack*, a ship used in the Civil War.[1] The silver buttons down Mary's back are said to be a reference to the metal rivets on the ship, and the elephants are thought to be the original Republicans, the party of Abraham Lincoln, who "freed" the slaves. Jumping over the fence is thought to signify them crossing the Mason-Dixon Line to free the slaves once and for all. Back then, enslaved people would have had to cloak their celebrations of Union army efforts and their passing along of the stories of the war in clever songs and riddles. So, it doesn't surprise me that Miss Mary Mack wasn't actually about a young girl who just liked to go see the jumping elephants. But what has struck me about this story is that now, in the 2020s, I am still very familiar with the words and hand gestures of enslaved Black people. Our culture was passed down to me in the sweetest and most subtle ways so that even my childhood pastimes, my moments of joy and respite, were moments of cultural production, knowledge transference, and community-based learning. While I may not have understood the significance or the salience of those lessons in that moment, I certainly grew to understand and appreciate them in time.

For me, that has been my experience discovering Black Feminism as well. In many ways, it's like these teachings, theories, and frameworks have long shaped my life since before I even knew these women's names or the unique histories that animated their purposes. This is the nature of being Black in America, of creating countercultures and subcultures meant to preserve our ways of being and our inner knowing, protecting them from the white gaze and co-optation. I'm grateful for those hidden meanings and cloaked narratives only exposable by living in the light.

Growing into Black Womanhood

Now, at thirty-eight years old, I look back over so many lessons in this book that I wish I had picked up on sooner. I never became the perfect, petite, small-voiced woman who moved through crowds with grace and poise. I never turned heterosexual or became the proper Corporate America woman with the briefcase, solid-color pumps, and pencil skirts. Instead, I grew into my height, learning to speak louder and louder. I adorned my skin with tattoos and piercings, dying my hair every color of the rainbow until I finally cut it all off because it felt like involuntary drag. I stopped wearing long sleeves in summer to cover my stretch-marked shoulders, evidence of my weight gains and losses and my life with Marfan syndrome. After all these lessons, the explicit ones and the implicit ones, I stopped hiding from everyone. But most important, I stopped hiding from myself. Instead, I shifted my focus toward finding people who would love me not for who they hoped I would become or who I had the potential to be but for who I truly was at my core. I fell in love with myself after thirty-eight years of fighting to fit into boxes that were not made to fit me. It didn't happen until the global pandemic, when I shaved my head and told the world that I am an androgynous, genderflux lesbian. And, in 2020, my thirty-sixth birthday felt like my first. It feels so freeing now.

Patience Without the Long-Suffering

While this book is about recognizing and centering the work of Black women foremothers and thinkers, it also tells another story. A story of becoming. Through my engagement and encounters with the works of my Black Feminist ancestors and forefolks, I learned how to situate myself within a larger social world. I began to see myself more clearly and understand how my experiences in society were not by happenstance but absolutely by design. In many ways, I became a critical and self-actualizing subject because of the oral and written traditions archived by Black women. Women like my mother and grandmothers, who often lived on the tip of a needle, pointing their toes and moving nimbly through a world rampant with hidden dangers and overt violence, have been and remain my North Stars. They always point me back home.

When I read the words and experiences of these women, I began to understand myself as a part of a larger community, history, and narrative. I started to understand how my existence links up with the existences of those around me and those of so many people whom I may never meet. Black women taught me about living in community even before I knew I was doing so. They taught me love, for myself and for others, when I didn't know that love was radical. They taught me to steal every moment of joy as if it were my last despite an anti-Black world that continues to stamp out Black joy at every turn. Black women taught me that struggling for my own liberation and freedom was never a sign of failure but rather an indication that I was dissatisfied with a harmful status quo. That I believed in a better future. A future that, despite the beliefs of the world, I saw myself in.

It's no wonder to me, then, that I became a teacher and a nurturer of future generations of Black people. I started at a very young age. In preschool, I would stay inside during breaks and sneak into the nursery. There, I would help make bottles, dump dirty diapers into the aluminum pails, and gently comfort infants who were missing their parents. A part of me was waiting for the day when I would be a mother, or at least a caretaker.

"You're going to be a great mother one day," Ms. Ruby, my daycare teacher, once told me. I was only about three or four. I was rocking one of the older toddlers in my arms.
"Me?" I asked.
"Yeah, you got the gift. It's all over you." She smiled as she laid a smaller infant in the crib. "But don't rush it, though. Be a kid first," she said.
I didn't quite understand what she meant. Maybe it was the Virgo in me. Maybe it was the early stages of my perfec-

> *tionism and overachieving peeking through. Either way,*
> *I knew she was giving me a bit of knowledge. She was*
> *clueing me in on a lesson I would need to hold for the*
> *rest of my life.*
> "*Now, go on outside with the big kids and play.*" *She shooed*
> *me off with a wave of the back of her right hand.*
> *I opened my arms, releasing the toddler, who had been awake*
> *the entire time, and trotted outdoors.*

I always had a sense of disappointment that I wasn't "there" yet. That I didn't have all the answers, that I wasn't in charge, that I wasn't a grown-up. Sometimes I hated that I wasn't the person making the decisions and that I had to wait until I was big enough, old enough, educated enough, or just brave enough to accomplish the tasks set out before me. It would take me years to understand that my calling and my gifts would manifest in my life in their own ways, in their own time, and along whatever guidelines they saw fit. I actually had very little control over the process. What's more, I was ill prepared to manage my own journey. Instead, it was my job to be a student of the world. To allow myself the grace to make mistakes. To give myself all the time I needed to struggle and languish (if needed) under the weight of this work. The work of Black Feminist struggle and a liberatory politic often requires that we center time, never expecting ourselves to be fully formed. Never requiring our own doneness, because doneness encourages complacency. Instead, I have learned to be deeply, completely, and unwaveringly patient with myself.

Here are five lessons this process taught me:

1. Sometimes you have to build the world you want to see.

I often chuckle about the fact that, to this very day, I have never taken a formal course on Black Feminism. I've attended elite universities that promised top-tier education systems and access to every type of knowledge one could dream up. I took extra classes outside of my undergraduate engineering major to try to enrich myself in courses on social psychology and racial history in the United States. I've essentially done all the things one would expect of a person seeking formal training on anything about race, gender, and class in the United States. So, it isn't lost on me that the thing I've had so little access to is Black Feminist theories and writings. These classes were rarely available. Rather, it took years of digging through syllabi that were publicly available from other universities, directly emailing professors for book recommendations even when I couldn't enroll in their courses, and scouring the citations in books I already owned to build a collection of books, speeches, and teachings from Black Feminist scholars. And the work still isn't done. I am still actively seeking out the labor and intellectual contributions of these women as I write this.

Why? Well, because in most of these women's times, their work wasn't valued or deemed academically rigorous. Even in recent years, Black Feminist thinkers and educators have found their work diminished and considered "not rigorous enough" to count in traditional social science disciplines. Their works and words were often marginalized both in the academy and in public discourse and were deemed to be unimportant or just too focused on race. So, now, reclaiming and recalling that work is a feat of contending with an incomplete and severely limited archive. An archive that intentionally writes out Black women scholars, activists, organizers, and thinkers.

In response, I write this book to add to an archive that is too often erased, ignored, and undermined in mainstream publishing. This book is not only a love letter to Black women, but it is also an effort to write against the erasures we too often encounter when attempting to fully express what it means to live at the intersections of Blackness, womanhood, queerness, and class.

2. Our trauma is not who we are.

One thread that has always drawn together the Black ancestors, elders, and foremothers in my life is that of racial trauma. For years, because racial trauma had been foregrounded when discussing the lives and livelihoods of Black people, I thought that my trauma was the only way I could enter conversations on Blackness and being. It took until my thirties for me to realize that this was the trickery of white supremacy, teaching Black folks to bare their vulnerability, to unmask ourselves in plain sight, to relinquish our privacy so that we could "earn" the benefits of citizenship that everyone else received just for merely existing. I went all the way through graduate school before I fully understood that I didn't have to become trauma porn in order to be worthy of human dignity, respect, and the abundance of the universe. The practice of centering trauma (rather than love or joy) in our collective struggle often reduces us to our pain. It equates Black people with the harms, violences, and aggressions we face. And, for those outside of our communities, it perpetuates the myth of a culture of poverty, suggesting that we are bereft of experiencing anything but strife and heartache. Unfortunately, our trauma is all too often weaponized and used as justification to terrorize and enact all manner of violence against us. And, by healing ourselves, we remove the opportunity for others outside our communities to use us in this way.

3. Scarcity isn't real.

One of the most insidious and dangerous ideas to ever come from white supremacy and capitalism is the notion of scarcity. It is the idea that there is not enough room or resources for all of us to thrive, or to have a voice, or to be seen. It stems from the supply and demand logics that treat everything as a linear model where consumers dictate the amount of goods available. Under this economic model, labor and production markets are superficially controlled to force more demand so that increased prices are justifiable. Capitalism doesn't just dictate economic behavior, but it is also embedded in the ways that many people in civic society view human interactions and social dynamics. With models like these, we have to choose one person, or a select few, who will "represent" us before the masses. It encourages us to compete and compare within our own communities. It also creates models of intragroup harm that stem from egotistical "brand"-building and other forms of credit-taking that are not rooted in Black Feminist principles.

The fact of the matter is: There is enough room for all of us. There is enough freedom for all of us. There is enough justice and enough love for all of us. And, when we begin to forget that, we start to reinscribe the same systems that we seek to destroy.

4. There is no time limit on learning.

The most common issue I have seen when introducing people to Black Feminism and the thinkers who birthed it is that people believe these ideas are outdated, irrelevant, and out of touch with present societal conditions. Every new generation behaves as if their experiences with oppression, othering, and violence are unique to them. What many fail to appreciate is the fact that, while situational contexts and characters might vary, so much of American life consists of ongoing struggles against the same systems of inequality and injustice that lie at the very heart of this land's foundation. Systems like racism, sexism, white supremacy, anti-Blackness, queer/transphobia, fatphobia, ableism, and the like continue to shape our daily lives in both visible and invisible ways. These systems simply transform as technology, globalization, access, and capital change. Thus, the contributions of Black women thinkers and activists remain all the more true today.

The frameworks and models that Black women have offered us are timeless. They are not tethered to the political situations or moments that birthed them. Rather, they are modes of justice-seeking and liberatory struggling that are rooted in the hope for the freedom of all people.

5. Black women are always teaching us. We just have to listen.

This book is a container, a container that is far too small to hold all the Black women thinkers and scholars who continue to shape me and shift my philosophical commitments. As such, I wanted to end the book with a list of recommended readings to get the reader started on the rest of their journey. Here are a few more Black women and folks whose work has left an indelible mark on my scholarship, writing, and teaching:

Cathy Cohen—Dr. Cohen is a political scientist and scholar whose work rests at the intersections of queer theory, young people's politics, and Black movements. She has written extensively on Black Feminism, queer political futures, and the possibilities of a queer transformative politics. Her first book, *The Boundaries of Blackness* (1999), is canon for thinking about the AIDS crisis and its impact on Black organizing. Her second book, *Democracy Remixed* (2010), is a deep dive into the political opinions, attitudes, and orientations of young Black Americans. In all, her work, words, and mentorship have been invaluable in shaping my own theorizing about the radical potential of young Black folks' politics and the ways that queerness intervenes in existing modes of oppression and domination in the United States.

Patricia Hill Collins—Dr. Collins is a sociologist whose theoretical contributions include such concepts as "othermothering" and "standpoint theory." Her book *Black Feminist Thought* (1990) remains one of the seminal texts situating Black Feminism in the contemporary moment. Collins has written extensively on intersectionality and how we can move beyond theoretical applications of this tool into praxes. Her work remains foundational to nearly all argumentation in Black Feminism today.

Brittney Cooper—I am deeply grateful for Dr. Brittney Cooper both as a thinker and a comrade. She is intellectually astounding. In addition to that, she is caring and kind. She loves us. Her article titled "Intersectionality" in the *Oxford Handbook of Feminist Theory* is likely one of the best things I have ever read that breaks down a concept that has grown to be greatly overused. Her books *Eloquent Rage* (2018) and *Beyond Respectability* (2017) continue to challenge us to be better Black Feminists.

Kimberlé Crenshaw—Crenshaw stands as one of the most influential Black Feminists today. She coined both "intersectionality" and "critical race theory." Crenshaw is one of the most important feminists of our generation. Her 1989 and 1991 articles on intersectionality are pathbreaking, and she continues to school us on the uses of intersectional theory in our day-to-day lives.

Melissa Harris-Perry—I'm not sure I would be here today without Dr. Harris-Perry's *Sister Citizen* (2011). Through that book, I was exposed to the notion of the "crooked room" and what it means to be a citizen on paper but to not truly feel citizenship in my heart. This book is so important, as it also helps to situate Black Feminism within the conversation on "natural disasters" and how they disproportionately affect vulnerable people.

Saidiya Hartman—Dr. Hartman is a prolific writer, scholar, and thinker. Hartman's *Scenes of Subjection* (1997) rocked me to my core in graduate school. It asks us to shift our focus to the various locations where slavery was made and remade and how those modes of making affected the selves of Black women. I have never read another book that so beautifully described and analyzed such an awful period in our past.

Mariame Kaba—Kaba is one of those thinkers who you just have to thank the Universe that you are allowed to witness in person. She has made the revolution delicious for many audiences and continues to do the work of abolition through her books on defunding prisons and police and her community organizing work to provide bail and bonds for incarcerated folks. There is nothing that Kaba has said or written that I do not recommend.

Janet Mock—Mock is one of those really important thinkers who does her work quietly and intentionally. Her first book, *Redefining Realness* (2014), should be taught on every feminism syllabus across the globe. And she continues to find ways to intervene in existing logics about Black and trans women through her film and TV work.

Barbara Ransby—Dr. Ransby has written about our prolific movement workers and continues to write about the nuances of the Black Lives Matter movement. Ransby is a movement historian whose work is critical in understanding how Black-led and youth-led movements shape today and tomorrow. Her book *Ella Baker & the Black Freedom Movement* (2003) has been critical to my thinking on the capacity of movement work to shape national politics. Her book *Making All Black Lives Matter* (2018) is mandatory reading for anyone looking for a thorough examination of the emergence, growth, and frameworks of the Black Lives Matter movement from its inception.

Beth Richie—Dr. Richie is a preeminent interdisciplinary scholar and researcher on sexual and gender-based violence in the United States. Her book *Arrested Justice* (2012) is a critical examination of the ways that violence against Black women is deeply connected to the creation and preservation of the "prison nation." Richie has also played a central and critical role in the development of abolitionist movements in Chicago and nationwide.

Dorothy Roberts—Dr. Roberts, lawyer and sociologist, continues to produce critical research on Black women's experiences with Western medicine and the racialization of medical systems in the United States. Her book *Killing the Black Body* (1997) takes on the racial and gender disparities wrapped up in the access to reproductive care and justice in the United States. Her work remains integral to our understanding of Black women's ongoing struggles with birthing justice and healthcare access.

Christina Sharpe—Dr. Sharpe is an English scholar of Black Studies, colonialism, and the long arc of slavery in the Americas. Her book *In the Wake* (2016) traces the "orthography of the wake," the ways that Black life is swept up in the afterlife of slavery. The concept of the wake has likely touched every work on Black life since its publication, and Sharpe's theorizing has moved all of our work forward. She is a gift.

Barbara Smith—Smith was a founding member of the Combahee River Collective and continues to work on behalf of Black, queer, poor, and working-class women. She is a walking anthology of a movement that she, her sister Beverly Smith, and so many comrades helmed. We are lucky to still have her here.

This list of Black Feminist thinkers is by no means exhaustive. Rather, it is a list of writers and scholars who have taught me along the way and whose work continues to teach me every day. Their work underlies my own, sometimes explicitly and sometimes implicitly. But it is always there. As I continue to build upon my own Black Feminist ethics and philosophical commitments, I return to these women who are, like me, building an archive beyond trauma and erasure. These women who are committed to writing Black women's lives into the annals of history are part of the reason I remain patient with myself as I continue to grow as a thinker. In their words, I see reflections of my own lived experiences, versions of my past selves and of selves I have yet to become. I'm grateful for their courage and their wisdom.

This is my offering. My love letter to them, and to us.

Acknowledgments

I'm grateful to so many people. I couldn't have written this book without all of the Black women who raised and shaped me. To my late grandmothers, Lucille and Clara, I am eternally grateful for your wisdom and patience with me. Thank you for modeling the kinds of love I intend to share with the world.

To my biological mother, Cynthia, who raised me largely on her own. The lessons you imparted in that tiny two-bedroom home will always rest at the foundation of who I am and who I intend to become. Thank you, Mom.

To my chosen mother, Jacqueline Thompson, I don't think you will ever know how much your light and your example have shifted the arc of my life. You are kind, generous, thoughtful, and caring, and, as you say, you don't "keep score." I believe it was the unconditional love I witnessed from you that has allowed me to understand the kinds of love I am willing to receive from and offer others. I love you and I am so grateful for you. Thank you for being my mother.

To my hosts of aunts, church mothers, and community mothers, thank you. Thank you for feeding me when I was hungry, for being a shoulder when I cried, and for making space for me to become who I am today.

To the only man for me, my closest friend, my greatest cheerleader, my bone marrow, Daren Wesley Jackson. I honestly do not think I would be alive without you. You came into my life at a time when I felt there was little to nothing left. You arrived when I needed you most and you've never left me. I love you in ways that words do not describe and beyond the containers we have for it. I will never stop loving you. Thank you for being my life partner, the most incredible father to our children, and the sweetest friend I could ever ask for.

To my three beautiful children, Logan, Camryn, and Jaelen, you are my lifelines. You keep me tethered to a world that I once believed had no space or place for me. But you have always and will always be home to me. You three are the most beautiful and perfect gifts I could have ever received. Thank you for letting me be your guide, your confidant, your mommy.

To my life partner and the woman who brought light back into my heart when it had been stamped out, Jamelle Thomas. You are the sweetest gift. You hold a deeply bashful kindness in your spirit, which always reveals how sentimental you are. I'm so glad you're "sweet on me." I'm so grateful for your love. Thank you for choosing me. Thank you for loving me whole.

To the sweetest boys, Nicholas and Sebastian, you have an incredible light and joy. You remind me that there is always time for laughter, a hug, or a chance to play Legos and race cars. Thank you for keeping me grounded in childlike imagination and the innocence of Black adolescence.

To my inner sanctum, my best friends (some of whom have read multiple versions of this book), Amber Butts, Jordie Davies, Bryce Henson, Marcus Pender, Kia Richards, and Alysia Mann Carey, you all are my oxygen. I love you so very much. You're my life vests. Y'all have rocked with me through all manner of self-sabotage, self-reflection, and self-actualization. When I was in my twenties, I prayed and prayed for a group of friends. I asked for five. I got six.

Amber, you are kind, honest, and a whole gangsta. You tether me to home in ways that are so healing.

Jordie, you are my bubbly Georgia potato. You are a shining light in my life and you always have been.

Bryce, you taught me about boundaries from a place of love and deep care. I am a better person because of you.

Marcus, you are my brother. You are my oldest friend. I know you will always have my back.

Kia, I adore your wisdom, your confidence, and your deep rootedness in your own self-worth. You have encouraged me every day of our sistership. I can't articulate how much that means to me.

Alysia, you are my sister. I am so grateful for your light and your spirit. You have always taught me to be gentle with myself. And, I'm so honored to be in your life.

To my mentor, friend, and academic auntie, Cathy Cohen, I love you. I would not be the scholar or thinker I am today without your careful (and very patient) wisdom and guidance. You and I have struggled through so much on this academic journey and I wouldn't change anything. Thank you for loving me as a person, thinker, and comrade (even though you feel challenged at times).

To my close friends, comrades, and interlocutors Uday Jain, Paul Cato, Causha Spellman-Timmons, Kei Williams, Cole

Armstrong, Ashley "Dr. Vivid" Elliott, and Malkia Devich-Cyril, thank you for the many loving, open, gracious conversations with me over the years. Thank you for the long talks while I was working through my emotional traumas and processing so many hurdles and losses. Thank you for being there, consistently.

To my writing and professional mentors Deesha Philyaw, Imani Perry, and Keeanga-Yamahtta Taylor, thank you for your wisdom which you each offered enthusiastically. You cheered me on at every stage of the writing process, through my tears and self-doubts. Thank you all for guiding and nurturing my craft and my voice.

I am eternally thankful to Marie Pantojan, who saw something in me back in 2018 when she invited me for lunch in New York City. At the time, I didn't even know I had a book in me. And now, here we are. Marie, you are incredible and I hope that you know, though your job may be mostly thankless, this Black girl from Oakland rocks with you. You helped me find parts of my story that I didn't even know were mine to tell. This is the book of my dreams. Thank you for helping me dream it to life.

To my graduate research assistant, Andrea Constant, who was both a support and interlocutor in the earliest days of this book. Deepest thanks.

To my current and past students. My students, I love you all so very much. I learn from you every day. I am constantly in awe of your talents and your courage. Thank you for letting me learn with and from you. Thank you for teaching me.

I am grateful to my remaining early readers, community of

writers and co-strugglers, informal mentors, and everyone who poured into me while I wrote this book.

Lastly, to the people who told me I would never become anything, mostly straight Black men, those who spoke negatively over my life when I was a small child. I'm grateful for your place in my journey. You showed me that, as Zora Neale Hurston once said, "all skinfolk ain't kinfolk." You prepared me for a world where my inclusion would not be guaranteed and certainly wouldn't be qualified by mutual similarity. Thank you for the part you played in my politicization and my personal awakening.

Asé.

Notes

Introduction: Black Women Taught Us

1. Audre Lorde, "The Master's Tools Will Never Dismantle the Master's House," *Sister Outsider: Essays and Speeches* (Berkeley, Calif.: Crossing Press, [1984] 2007), 110–114.
2. Taylor Dunn, "Record 41 Female CEOs Among Fortune 500 Includes 2 Black Women for 1st Time," ABC News, June 2, 2021, abcnews.go.com/Business/record-41-female-ceos-fortune -500-includes-black/story?id=78046013.
3. Hunter Shackelford, "Ask Ashleigh: What Does Gap's Commercial Teach Us About Misogynoir in the Media?," April 7, 2016, archived at web.archive.org/web/20210729125956/https://www .wearyourvoicemag.com/gap-commercial-misogynoir-media/.
4. Justin Parkinson, "The Significance of Sarah Baartman," BBC News, January 7, 2016, bbc.com/news/magazine-35240987.
5. Caroline Elkins, "A Life Exposed," review of *African Queen: The Real Life of the Hottentot Venus,* by Rachel Holmes, *The New York Times,* January 14, 2007, nytimes.com/2007/01/14/ books/review/Elkins.t.html.
6. David Hearst, "African Woman Going Home After 200 Years," *The Guardian,* April 30, 2002, theguardian.com/world/2002/ apr/30/education.arts.

7. Mikki Kendall, "Of #FastTailedGirls and Freedom," *Rewire News Group,* December 3, 2013, rewirenewsgroup.com/2013/12/03/of-fasttailedgirls-and-freedom/.

8. Amie Koch and Arthi Kozhumam, "Adultification of Black Children Negatively Impacts Their Health: Recommendations for Health Care Providers," *Nursing Forum* 57, no. 5 (September/October 2022): 963–967, doi.org/10.1111/nuf.12736.

9. Carolyn M. West and Kamilah Johnson, "Sexual Violence in the Lives of African American Women: Risk, Response, and Resilience," VAWnet: The National Online Resource Center on Violence Against Women (National Resource Center on Domestic Violence), March 2013, vawnet.org/material/sexual-violence-lives-african-american-women-risk-response-and-resilience.

Chapter 1: Harriet Jacobs Taught Me About Freedom

1. "Family of the Inhabitants of the Edisto Island Slave Cabin Visit the National Museum of African American History and Culture," Smithsonian Institution, April 11, 2017, si.edu/newsdesk/releases/family-inhabitants-edisto-island-slave-cabin-visit-national-museum-african-american-history.

2. Harriet Jacobs, *Incidents in the Life of a Slave Girl* (Mineola, N.Y.: Dover Publishing, 2001), 8.

3. Ibid., 10.

4. Ibid., 11.

5. Ibid., 27.

6. Ibid., 48.

7. Ibid., 95–96.

8. Hortense J. Spillers, "Mama's Baby, Papa's Maybe: An American Grammar Book," *Diacritics* 17, no. 2 (Summer 1987): 72.

9. Lyrics to "Oh, Freedom" by the Golden Gospel Singers, balladofamerica.org/oh-freedom/.

10. Sydney Trent, "John Lewis Nearly Died on the Edmund Pettus Bridge. Now It May Be Renamed for Him," *The Washington Post,* July 26, 2020, washingtonpost.com/history/2020/07/26/john-lewis-bloody-sunday-edmund-pettus-bridge/.

11. Lisa Respers France and Taylor Romine, "Tory Lanez Found Guilty in 2020 Shooting of Megan Thee Stallion," CNN, December 23, 2022, cnn.com/2022/12/23/entertainment/tory-lanez-megan-stallion-verdict/index.html.

12. Anastasia Tsiouclas and Chloe Veltman, "Tory Lanez Sentenced to 10 Years for Megan Thee Stallion Shooting," NPR, August 8, 2023, npr.org/2023/08/08/1181702809/tory-lanez-megan-thee-stallion#:~:text=Rapper%20Tory%20Lanez%20was%20sentenced,home%20of%20celebrity%20Kylie%20Jenner.

13. Ashley Blackwell, "Tory Lanez Sparks Online Debate Ahead of Sentencing for Megan Thee Stallion Shooting as Public Predicts Outcome: 'This Man Going to Prison Because of Evil People,'" *The Jasmine Brand,* August 7, 2023, thejasminebrand.com/2023/08/07/tory-lanez-sparks-online-debate-ahead-of-sentencing-for-megan-thee-stallion-shooting-as-public-predicts-outcome-this-man-going-to-prison-because-of-evil-people/.

14. Alicia R. Isaac, Lettie L. Lockhart, and Larry Williams, "Violence Against African American Women in Prisons and Jails," *Journal of Human Behavior in the Social Environment* 4, no. 2–3 (2001): 129–153, doi.org/10.1300/J137v04n02_07.

15. Mariame Kaba, *We Do This 'Til We Free Us: Abolitionist Organizing and Transforming Justice* (Chicago: Haymarket Books, 2020), 92.

16. Azadeh Ansari, "Texas Teen Tackled by Police Officer at Pool Party Files Federal Lawsuit," CNN, January 5, 2017, cnn.com/2017/01/05/us/texas-mckinney-pool-party-officer-lawsuit/index.html.

17. Benjamin Fearnow, "Video: White Woman Calls Police on Black Family's BBQ for 'Trespassing' in Oakland Park," *News-*

week, May 10, 2018, newsweek.com/lake-merritt-bbq-barbecue
-video-oakland-racist-charcoal-east-bay-black-family-919355.

Chapter 2: Ida B. Wells Taught Me Radical Truth-Telling

1. Damon Mitchell, "The People's Grocery Lynching, Memphis, Tennessee," *JSTOR Daily,* January 24, 2018, daily.jstor.org/peoples-grocery-lynching/.

2. DeNeen L. Brown, "For Years, Newspapers Printed Hate, Leading to Lynchings and Massacres of Black Americans," *The San Diego Voice & Viewpoint,* December 26, 2021, sdvoice.info/for-years-newspapers-printed-hate-leading-to-lynchings-and-massacres-of-black-americans/.

3. Ida B. Wells-Barnett, *On Lynchings* (New York: Humanity Books, [1892] 2002), 29.

4. Ibid., 30.

5. Paula Giddings, *Ida: A Sword Among Lions: Ida B. Wells and the Campaign Against Lynching* (New York: Amistad, 2008), 1.

6. Wells-Barnett, *On Lynchings,* 31.

7. "NAACP," *History.com,* March 29, 2023, history.com/topics/civil-rights-movement/naacp.

8. "About NAACP," NAACP, naacp.org/about.

9. Paula Giddings, "Missing in Action: Ida B. Wells, the NAACP, and the Historical Record," *Meridians* 1, no. 2 (2001): 1–17, jstor.org/stable/40338447.

10. Giddings, *Ida: A Sword Among Lions,* 231.

11. Wells-Barnett, *On Lynchings,* 27.

12. Ibid.

13. Darlene Clark Hine, "Rape and the Inner Lives of Black Women in the Middle West," *Signs: Journal of Women in Culture and Society* 14, no. 4 (1989): 912–920.

14. Ibid., 915.

15. Sarah Zhang, "The Surgeon Who Experimented on Slaves," *The Atlantic,* April 18, 2018, theatlantic.com/health/archive/2018/04/j-marion-sims/558248/.

16. Esha Ray and Denis Slattery, "Protesters Demand Removal of Central Park Statue of 19th Century Doctor Who Experimented on Women," New York *Daily News,* August 20, 2017, nydailynews.com/new-york/manhattan/protesters-slam-nyc-statue-doctor-experimented-slaves-article-1.3426690.

17. "Mission & Values," Chicago Torture Justice Center, chicagotorturejustice.org/mission-values.

18. "*Unapologetic:* Team," Unapologetic, unapologeticfilm.com/team.

19. Terry Gross, "Uncovering Who Is Driving the Fight Against Critical Race Theory in Schools," NPR, June 24, 2021, npr.org/2021/06/24/1009839021/uncovering-who-is-driving-the-fight-against-critical-race-theory-in-schools.

20. Russell Vought, "Memorandum for the Heads of Executive Departments and Agencies: Training in the Federal Government," White House, September 4, 2020, whitehouse.gov/wp-content/uploads/2020/09/M-20-34.pdf.

21. Tyler Kingkade, Brandy Zadrozny, and Ben Collins, "Critical Race Theory Battle Invades School Boards—with Help from Conservative Groups," NBC News, June 15, 2021, nbcnews.com/news/us-news/critical-race-theory-invades-school-boards-help-conservative-groups-n1270794.

22. Char Adams, Allan Smith, and Aadit Tambe, "Map: See Which States Have Passed Critical Race Theory Bills," NBC News, June 17, 2021, nbcnews.com/news/nbcblk/map-see-which-states-have-passed-critical-race-theory-bills-n1271215.

23. Katarzyna Mierzejewska, "Online Harassment, Physical Threats: The Cost of Reporting for Women Journalists," *Ms.,* October 21, 2020, msmagazine.com/2020/10/21/online-harassment-physical-threats-the-cost-of-reporting-for-women-journalists/.

24. Carrie Mott and Daniel Cockayne, "Understanding How Hatred Persists: Situating Digital Harassment in the Long History of White Supremacy," *Gender, Place & Culture: A Journal of Feminist Geography* 28, no. 1 (September 2020): 1–20, researchgate.net/profile/Carrie-Mott-2/publication/344836738 _Understanding_how_hatred_persists_situating_digital_harass ment_in_the_long_history_of_white_supremacy/links/5f998fc 4299bf1b53e4bda66/Understanding-how-hatred-persists-situating -digital-harassment-in-the-long-history-of-white-supremacy.pdf.

25. "Henrietta Lacks: Science Must Right a Historical Wrong," *Nature,* September 1, 2020, nature.com/articles/d41586-020 -02494-z.

26. *The Immortal Life of Henrietta Lacks,* HBO, hbo.com/movies/ the-immortal-life-of-henrietta-lacks.

27. "User Clip: HIV and AIDS in the Black Community," C-SPAN, October 5, 2004, c-span.org/video/?c4558877/user-clip-hiv-aids -black-community.

28. "HIV & Black Women," National AIDS Treatment and Advocacy Project, natap.org/2006/HIV/031506_03.htm.

29. Mary C. Curtis, "In Appreciation: Gwen Ifill, 1955–2016," *Andscape,* November 18, 2016, andscape.com/features/in -appreciation-gwen-ifill-1955-2016/.

30. Sherrilyn Ifill, "Remembering Gwen Ifill: Truth Teller and Exemplar of Civility," *The American Prospect,* December 3, 2016, prospect.org/culture/remembering-gwen-ifill-truth-teller -exemplar-civility/.

31. Giovanni Russonello, "Read Oprah Winfrey's Golden Globes Speech," *The New York Times,* January 7, 2018, nytimes.com/ 2018/01/07/movies/oprah-winfrey-golden-globes-speech-tran script.html.

32. Janell Hobson, "Black Women's Histories and the Power of Truth-Telling," *Black Perspectives,* African American Intellec-

tual History Society, January 16, 2018, aaihs.org/black-womens
-histories-and-the-power-of-truth-telling/.

33. Katie Shepherd, "Trump Berates 'PBS NewsHour' Reporter
for 'Threatening' Question, Hits 'Nice' Question out of Park,"
The Washington Post, March 30, 2020, washingtonpost.com/
nation/2020/03/30/coronavirus-yamiche-alcindor-trump/.

34. Ej Dickson, "Journalist Yamiche Alcindor on 'Bringing the
Hard Truth to America,'" *Rolling Stone,* February 22, 2021,
rollingstone.com/culture/culture-features/yamiche-alcindor-pbs
-donald-trump-1127664/.

35. bell hooks, *Sisters of the Yam: Black Women and Self-Recovery*
(Cambridge, Mass.: South End Press, 2005), 12.

Chapter 3: Zora Neale Hurston Taught Me About the Reclamation of Our Labor

1. Zora Neale Hurston, *Their Eyes Were Watching God* (New
York: Amistad Books, 2006), 14.

2. Christa Smith Anderson, "Power of Prose: African American
Women," PBS, 2005, pbs.org/speak/seatosea/powerprose/
Hurston/.

3. Claudia Roth Pierpont, "A Society of One," *The New Yorker,*
February 9, 1997, newyorker.com/magazine/1997/02/17/a-society
-of-one.

4. Zora Neale Hurston, *Dust Tracks on a Road: A Memoir* (New
York: Harper Perennial, 2010), 1.

5. Lisa Page, "Zora Neale Hurston Was Once Forgotten. A New
Book Reminds Us Why Her Voice Must Be Heard," *The Washington Post,* January 21, 2022, washingtonpost.com/books/2022/
01/21/zora-neale-Hurston-new-book/.

6. "Alice Walker Shines Light on Zora Neale Hurston," PBS, pbs
.org/wnet/americanmasters/alice-walker-film-excerpt-walker
-puts-zora-neale-Hurston-back-in-spotlight/2869/.

7. Alice Walker, "In Search of Zora Neale Hurston," *Ms.,* 1975, 79.

8. Ibid., 79.

9. Ibid., 85.

10. Ibid., 89.

11. Ibid., 89.

12. Hurston, *Dust Tracks,* 227.

13. Ibid., 227.

14. Emma Rothberg, "Marsha P. Johnson," National Women's History Museum, 2022, womenshistory.org/education-resources/biographies/marsha-p-johnson.

15. Elyssa Goodman, "Drag Herstory: A Drag King's Journey From Cabaret Legend to Iconic Activist," *them,* March 29, 2018, them.us/story/drag-king-cabaret-legend-activist-storme-delarverie.

16. Reiss Smith, "Who Threw the First Brick at Stonewall? A Final and Definitive Answer to the Internet's Favourite Question," *PinkNews,* May 27, 2020, thepinknews.com/2020/05/27/who-threw-the-first-brick-at-stonewall-uprising-riot-pride/.

17. Sarah Pruitt, "What Happened at the Stonewall Riots? A Timeline of the 1969 Uprising," *History.com,* June 13, 2019, history.com/news/stonewall-riots-timeline.

18. "About MPJI," The Marsha P. Johnson Institute, marshap.org/who-we-are/founders-message/.

19. Aisha Becker-Burrowes, "In Conversation with Elle Moxley, Founder & Executive Director of Marsha P. Johnson Institute," *Feminist* 1, feminists.co/feminist-zine-01/elle-moxley.

20. Sewell Chan, "Marsha P. Johnson, a Transgender Pioneer and Activist," *The New York Times,* March 8, 2018, nytimes.com/interactive/2018/obituaries/overlooked-marsha-p-johnson.html.

21. Michele Wallace, *Black Macho and the Myth of the Superwoman* (New York: Warner Books, 1980).

22. Ibid., 103.

23. "Racial and Ethnic Disparities Continue in Pregnancy-Related Deaths," Centers for Disease Control and Prevention, September 5, 2019, cdc.gov/media/releases/2019/p0905-racial-ethnic -disparities-pregnancy-deaths.html.

24. Nina Martin and Renee Montagne, "Black Mothers Keep Dying After Giving Birth. Shalon Irving's Story Explains Why," NPR, December 7, 2017, npr.org/2017/12/07/568948782/ black-mothers-keep-dying-after-giving-birth-shalon-irvings -story-explains-why.

25. Maya Salam, "For Serena Williams, Childbirth Was a Harrowing Ordeal. She's Not Alone," *The New York Times,* January 11, 2018, nytimes.com/2018/01/11/sports/tennis/serena-williams-baby -vogue.html.

26. Robin Bleiweis, "Quick Facts About the Gender Wage Gap," Center for American Progress, March 24, 2020, americanprogress .org/issues/women/reports/2020/03/24/482141/quick-facts-gender -wage-gap/.

27. "Black Women's Equal Pay Day 2021," Equal Rights Advocates, 2021, equalrights.org/events/black-womens-equal-pay-day -2021/.

28. Valerie Wilson and Melat Kassa, "Black Women Workers Are Essential During the Crisis and for the Recovery But Still Are Greatly Underpaid," Economic Policy Institute, August 12, 2020, epi.org/blog/black-women-workers-are-essential-during -the-crisis-and-for-the-recovery-but-still-are-greatly-underpaid/.

Chapter 4: Ella Baker Taught Me Why We Should Listen to Young People

1. Barbara Ransby, *Ella Baker and the Black Freedom Movement* (Chapel Hill & London: The University of North Carolina Press, 2003).

2. Jenn M. Jackson, "Martin Luther King, Jr Was Radical: We

Must Reclaim That Legacy," Al Jazeera, January 18, 2021, aljazeera.com/features/2021/1/18/martin-luther-king-jr-was-radical-we-must-reclaim-that-legacy.

3. "Montgomery Improvement Association," *Martin Luther King, Jr. Encyclopedia,* Martin Luther King, Jr. Research and Education Institute, kinginstitute.stanford.edu/encyclopedia/montgomery-improvement-association-mia.

4. "Montgomery Bus Boycott," *Martin Luther King, Jr. Encyclopedia,* Martin Luther King, Jr. Research and Education Institute, kinginstitute.stanford.edu/encyclopedia/montgomery-bus-boycott.

5. Daniel Perlstein, "Teaching Freedom: SNCC and the Creation of the Mississippi Freedom Schools," *History of Education Quarterly* 30, no. 3 (Autumn 1990): 297–324, jstor.org/stable/368691.

6. "Freedom Schools," SNCC Digital Gateway, snccdigital.org/inside-sncc/culture-education/freedom-schools/.

7. Ella Baker, "Bigger than a Hamburger," *Southern Patriot,* June 1960, historyisaweapon.com/defcon1/bakerbigger.html.

8. Barbara Ransby, "Ella Baker's Legacy Runs Deep. Know Her Name," *The New York Times,* January 20, 2020, nytimes.com/2020/01/20/opinion/martin-luther-king-ella-baker.html.

9. Julian Bond, "SNCC: What We Did," *Monthly Review,* October 2000, monthlyreview.org/2000/10/01/sncc-what-we-did/.

10. Baker, "Bigger than a Hamburger."

11. Hands Up United, November 1, 2014, web.archive.org/web/20141101140725/http://www.handsupunited.org/.

12. Lois Beckett, "Ferguson Protest Leader Darren Seals Shot and Found Dead in a Burning Car," *The Guardian,* September 8, 2016, theguardian.com/us-news/2016/sep/08/ferguson-protest-leader-darren-seals-shot-dead-burning-car.

13. Barbara Ransby, "Black Lives Matter Is Democracy in Action," *The New York Times,* October 21, 2017, nytimes.com/2017/10/21/opinion/sunday/black-lives-matter-leadership.html.

14. "Who Was Ella Baker?," Ella Baker Center for Human Rights, ellabakercenter.org/who-was-ella-baker/.

15. Erhardt Graeff, Matt Stempeck, and Ethan Zuckerman, "The Battle for 'Trayvon Martin': Mapping a Media Controversy Online and Off-line," *First Monday* 19, no. 2 (February 3, 2014), firstmonday.org/ojs/index.php/fm/article/download/4947/3821.

16. Matthew Wilson, Eric Huntley, Ryan Cooper, and Taylor Shelton, "Mapping Ferguson Tweets, or More Maps that Won't Change Your Mind About Racism in America," *Floating Sheep,* August 18, 2014, floatingsheep.org/2014/08/mapping-ferguson -tweets-or-more-maps.html.

17. Brian Fung, "Watch Twitter Explode Along with Ferguson," *The Washington Post,* August 14, 2014, washingtonpost.com/ news/the-switch/wp/2014/08/14/watch-twitter-explode-along -with-ferguson/.

Chapter 5: Fannie Lou Hamer Taught Me to Be (Un)respectable

1. Ms. Lauryn Hill, "Outro," *MTV Unplugged No. 2.0,* Sony Music Entertainment, Inc., May 7, 2002, open.spotify.com/album/ 22tn8fUpD1lurSga9yuqhM.

2. Ibid.

3. Melissa Block, "Yes, Women Could Vote After the 19th Amendment—but Not All Women. Or Men," *Morning Edition,* NPR, August 26, 2020, npr.org/2020/08/26/904730251/ yes-women-could-vote-after-the-19th-amendment-but-not-all -women-or-men.

4. Olivia B. Waxman, " 'It's a Struggle They Will Wage Alone.' How Black Women Won the Right to Vote," *Time,* August 14, 2020, time.com/5876456/black-women-right-to-vote/.

5. Oliver Laughland, "Claudette Colvin: The Woman Who Refused to Give Up Her Bus Seat—Nine Months Before Rosa

Parks," *The Guardian,* February 25, 2021, theguardian.com/
society/2021/feb/25/claudette-colvin-the-woman-who-refused
-to-give-up-her-bus-seat-nine-months-before-rosa-parks.

6. Kay Mills, *This Little Light of Mine: The Life of Fannie Lou
    Hamer* (Lexington: University of Kentucky Press, 2007), 8.

7. Debra Michals, "Fannie Lou Hamer," National Women's His-
    tory Museum, 2017, womenshistory.org/education-resources/
    biographies/fannie-lou-hamer.

8. "Freedom Riders," *History.com,* February 2, 2010, history.com/
    topics/black-history/freedom-rides.

9. DeNeen L. Brown, "Civil Rights Crusader Fannie Lou Hamer
    Defied Men—and Presidents—Who Tried to Silence Her,"
    The Washington Post, October 6, 2017, washingtonpost.com/
    news/retropolis/wp/2017/10/06/civil-rights-crusader-fannie-lou
    -hamer-defied-men-and-presidents-who-tried-to-silence-her/.

10. Mills, *This Little Light of Mine,* 21.

11. Michals, "Fannie Lou Hamer."

12. Fannie Lou Hamer, "Letter to Northern Supporters," Civil
    Rights Movement Archive, September 30, 1963, crmvet.org/
    docs/hamer_letter.pdf.

13. Fannie Lou Hamer, "I'm Sick and Tired of Being Sick and
    Tired—Dec. 20, 1964," Archives of Women's Political Com-
    munication, Iowa State University, July 17, 2019, awpc.catt
    center.iastate.edu/2019/08/09/im-sick-and-tired-of-being-sick-and
    -tired-dec-20-1964/.

14. Ibid.

15. Isaac Chotiner, "The Buried Promise of the Reconstruction
    Amendments," *The New Yorker,* September 9, 2019, newyorker
    .com/news/q-and-a/the-buried-promise-of-the-reconstruction
    -amendments.

16. Hamer, "I'm Sick and Tired of Being Sick and Tired."

17. Maegan Parker Brooks and Davis W. Houck (eds), "'Nobody's
    Free Until Everybody's Free,' Speech Delivered at the Found-

ing of the National Women's Political Caucus, Washington, D.C., July 10, 1971," *The Speeches of Fannie Lou Hamer: To Tell It Like It Is* (Jackson, MS, 2010; online edition, Mississippi Scholarship Online, 20 Mar. 2014), doi.org/10.14325/mississippi/9781604738223.003.0017.

18. Mills, *This Little Light of Mine*.

19. Evelyn B. Higginbotham, *Righteous Discontent: The Women's Movement in the Black Baptist Church, 1880–1920* (Cambridge, Mass.: Harvard University Press, 1993), 187.

20. Ibid.

21. Matt Laslo, "Al Sharpton Is Struggling to Control the 'Black Lives Matter' Movement," *Vice,* December 18, 2014, vice.com/en/article/znw9y4/al-sharpton-is-struggling-to-control-the-black-lives-matter-movement-1218.

22. Rev. Jesse Jackson, Sr. (@RevJJackson), "This act of pillaging, robbing & looting in Chicago was humiliating, embarrassing &morally wrong. It must not be associated with our quest for social justice and equality," Twitter, August 10, 2020, twitter.com/RevJJackson/status/1292826658379096066.

23. Khaleda Rahman, "Black Lives Matter Chicago Organizer Defends Looting: 'That's Reparations,'" *Newsweek,* August 12, 2020, newsweek.com/black-lives-matter-chicago-defends-looting-reparations-1524502.

24. "'Cast Down Your Bucket': Learning Activities for Students Grades 5–7," National Park Service, nps.gov/bowa/learn/education/upload/Cast%20Down%20Your%20Bucket.PDF.

25. "Ferguson Protests: What We Know About Michael Brown's Last Minutes," BBC News, November 25, 2014, bbc.com/news/world-us-canada-28841715.

26. Josh Sanburn, "All the Ways Darren Wilson Described Being Afraid of Michael Brown," *Time,* November 25, 2014, time.com/3605346/darren-wilson-michael-brown-demon/.

27. John Eligon, "Michael Brown Spent Last Weeks Grappling

with Problems and Promise," *The New York Times,* August 24, 2014, nytimes.com/2014/08/25/us/michael-brown-spent-last-weeks -grappling-with-lifes-mysteries.html.

28. Erik Wemple, "*New York Times* Defends Michael Brown Jr. 'No Angel' Characterization," *The Washington Post,* August 25, 2014, washingtonpost.com/blogs/erik-wemple/wp/ 2014/08/25/new-york-times-defends-michael-brown-jr-no-angel -characterization/.

29. Robert Cherry, "The Difficult Childbearing Problems Facing Black Women," Real Clear Policy, April 30, 2020, realclear policy.com/articles/2020/04/30/the_difficult_childbearing_choices _facing_black_women_490362.html.

30. Daniel Geary, "The Moynihan Report: An Annotated Edition," *The Atlantic,* September 14, 2015, theatlantic.com/politics/ archive/2015/09/the-moynihan-report-an-annotated-edition/ 404632/.

31. William H. Chafe, "The Moynihan Report, Then and Now," Council on Contemporary Families, March 5, 2015, sites.utexas .edu/contemporaryfamilies/2015/03/05/moynihan-then-and-now -brief-report/.

32. Nico Lang, "Gen Z Is the Queerest Generation Ever, According to New Survey," *them,* February 24, 2021, them.us/story/ gen-z-millennials-queerest-generation-gallup-poll.

33. Cathy J. Cohen, "Punks, Bulldaggers, and Welfare Queens: The Radical Potential of Queer Politics?," *GLQ* 3, no. 4 (May 1997): 437–465, doi.org/10.1215/10642684-3-4-437.

Chapter 6: Shirley Chisholm Taught Me to Hold Whiteness Accountable

1. Jenn M. Jackson, "Black Feminisms, Queer Feminisms, Trans Feminisms: Meditating on Pauli Murray, Shirley Chisholm, and Marsha P. Johnson Against the Erasure of History," in *The*

Routledge Companion to Black Women's Cultural Histories (New York: Routledge, 2021), 289.

2. Debra Michals, "Shirley Chisholm," National Women's History Museum, 2015, womenshistory.org/education-resources/biographies/shirley-Chisholm.

3. Jackson, "Black Feminisms," 290.

4. Shirley Chisholm, *Unbought and Unbossed* (Washington, D.C.: Take Root Media, 1970), 93.

5. Jenn M. Jackson, "Congresswoman Shirley Chisholm's Historic Presidential Run Was 'Unbought and Unbossed,'" *Teen Vogue,* February 8, 2019, teenvogue.com/story/congresswoman-shirley-Chisholm-unbought-and-unbossed.

6. Chisholm, *Unbought and Unbossed,* 167.

7. Ibid., 168.

8. Ibid., 168.

9. Letter from Representative Shirley Chisholm to Chairman of the House Judiciary Committee Don Edwards, April 14, 1971, Legislative Bill Files of the Committee on the Judiciary for the 92nd Congress, Committee Papers, 1813–2011, Records of the U.S. House of Representatives, Record Group 233, National Archives Building, Washington, D.C., docsteach.org/documents/document/Chisholm-edwards.

10. Stephan Lesher, "The Short, Unhappy Life of Black Presidential Politics, 1972," *The New York Times,* June 25, 1972, nytimes.com/1972/06/25/archives/the-short-unhappy-life-of-black-presidential-politics-1972-black.html.

11. Jackson Landers, "'Unbought and Unbossed': When a Black Woman Ran for the White House," *Smithsonian,* April 25, 2016, smithsonianmag.com/smithsonian-institution/unbought-and-unbossed-when-black-woman-ran-for-the-white-house-180958699/.

12. Christopher Lydon, "Gloria Steinem Aids McGovern's Cause," *The New York Times,* February 12, 1972, nytimes.com/1972/02/12/archives/gloria-steinem-aids-mcgoverns-cause.html.

13. David M. Dismore, "Today in Feminist History: Gloria Steinem and Shirley Chisholm Take Chicago," *Ms.,* January 21, 2020, msmagazine.com/2020/01/21/today-in-feminist-history-gloria -steinem-and-shirley-Chisholm-take-chicago/.

14. Jennifer Steinhauer, "2019 Belongs to Shirley Chisholm," *The New York Times,* July 6, 2019, nytimes.com/2019/07/06/sunday -review/shirley-Chisholm-monument-film.html.

15. Gloria Steinem, "Gloria Steinem: I Did Not Abandon Shirley Chisholm," *The New York Times,* July 8, 2019, nytimes .com/2019/07/08/opinion/letters/gloria-steinem-shirley-chisolm .html.

16. "The Rise of the Congressional Black Caucus," History, Art & Archives: United States House of Representatives, history.house .gov/Exhibitions-and-Publications/BAIC/Historical-Essays/ Permanent-Interest/Congressional-Black-Caucus/.

17. Chisholm, *Unbought and Unbossed,* 158.

18. Ibid., 158.

19. Ibid., 159.

20. A. T. Geronimus, "The Weathering Hypothesis and the Health of African-American Women and Infants: Evidence and Speculations," *Ethnicity & Disease* 2, no. 3 (Summer 1992): 207–221, pubmed.ncbi.nlm.nih.gov/1467758/.

21. DeNeen L. Brown, "Emmett Till's Mother Opened His Casket and Sparked the Civil Rights Movement," *The Washington Post,* July 12, 2018, washingtonpost.com/news/retropolis/wp/2018/ 07/12/emmett-tills-mother-opened-his-casket-and-sparked-the -civil-rights-movement/.

22. Tony Harris, "One Year After Michael Brown's Killing, His Mother Vows to 'Never Forgive,'" Al Jazeera America, August 5, 2015.

Chapter 7: Toni Morrison Taught Me That Black Women Are Powerful

1. Jennifer Haliburton, "Remembering Toni Morrison," *Ohio Magazine,* August 2019, ohiomagazine.com/arts/article/remembering-toni-morrison.

2. Hilton Als, "Toni Morrison and the Ghosts in the House," *The New Yorker,* October 19, 2003, newyorker.com/magazine/2003/10/27/ghosts-in-the-house.

3. Hermione Hoby, "Toni Morrison: 'I'm Writing for Black People . . . I Don't Have to Apologize,'" *The Guardian,* April 25, 2015, theguardian.com/books/2015/apr/25/toni-morrison-books-interview-god-help-the-child.

4. Justin Kirkland, "Toni Morrison Broke Down the Truth about White Supremacy in a Powerful 1993 PBS Interview," *Esquire,* August 6, 2019, esquire.com/entertainment/books/a28621535/toni-morrison-white-supremacy-charlie-rose-interview-racism/.

5. David Streitfeld, "Author Toni Morrison Wins Nobel Prize," *The Washington Post,* October 8, 1993, washingtonpost.com/archive/politics/1993/10/08/author-toni-morrison-wins-nobel-prize/6077f17d-d7b7-49a3-ad90-8111cf8478d1/.

6. Edwin McDowell, "48 Black Writers Protest by Praising Morrison," *The New York Times,* January 19, 1988, nytimes.com/1988/01/19/books/48-black-writers-protest-by-praising-morrison.html.

7. William Grimes, "Toni Morrison Is '93 Winner of Nobel Prize in Literature," *The New York Times,* October 8, 1993, nytimes.com/1983/10/08/books/toni-morrison-is-93-winner-of-nobel-prize-in-literature.html.

8. Elizabeth Kastor, "'Beloved' and the Protest," *The Washington Post,* January 21, 1988, washingtonpost.com/archive/lifestyle/1988/01/21/beloved-and-the-protest/8bc8cb27-5607-4cad-a3e1-26a0b20e0608/.

9. "Toni Morrison Dies at 88," Penguin Random House, August 6, 2019, global.penguinrandomhouse.com/announcements/toni-morrison-dies-at-88/.

10. Hillel Italie, "Toni Morrison Was a 'Literary Mother' to Countless Writers," Associated Press, August 7, 2019, apnews.com/article/entertainment-ap-top-news-celebrities-toni-morrison-national-book-awards-1cd49bfd899e4ee5be64d963c7a476c6.

11. Dexter Thomas, "Why Everyone's Saying 'Black Girls Are Magic,'" *Los Angeles Times,* September 9, 2015, latimes.com/nation/nationnow/la-na-nn-everyones-saying-black-girls-are-magic-20150909-htmlstory.html.

12. Jordan R. Axt, Kelly M. Hoffman, M. Norman Oliver, and Sophie Trawalter, "Racial Bias in Pain Assessment and Treatment Recommendations, and False Beliefs about Biological Differences Between Blacks and Whites," *Proceedings of the National Academy of Sciences of the United States of America* 113, no. 16 (April 19, 2016): 4296–4301, ncbi.nlm.nih.gov/pmc/articles/PMC4843483/.

13. Megan Holohan, "'Collective Voice': Endo Black Empowers Black People with Endometriosis," *Today,* February 28, 2022, today.com/health/celebrate-black-history-3/endo-black-supports-women-color-black-women-endometriosis-rcna17991.

14. Kevin Johnson, "Scope of Obama's Secret Service Protection Proves Daunting," ABC News, December 15, 2008, abcnews.go.com/Politics/story?id=6464900&page=1.

15. Jelani Cobb, "Barack Obama's Safety," *The New Yorker,* October 2, 2014, newyorker.com/news/daily-comment/barack-obamas-safety.

16. CaShawn Thompson (founder of #BlackGirlMagic, educator, author), in discussion with the author, April 2020.

17. Ibid.

18. Rebecca Carroll, "Margaret Garner," *The New York Times,* January 31, 2019, nytimes.com/interactive/2019/obituaries/margaret-garner-overlooked.html.

19. Bruce Scott, "A Mother's Desperate Act: 'Margaret Garner,'"
     NPR, November 19, 2010, npr.org/2010/11/17/131395936/a
     -mother-s-desperate-act-margaret-garner.

20. Kristine Yohe, "Margaret Garner, Rememory, and the Infinite
     Past: History in *Beloved*" in *Critical Insights: Beloved,* ed. Mau-
     reen N. Eke (Ipswich, Mass.: Salem Press, 2015), 27–32,
     salempress.com/Media/SalemPress/samples/ci_beloved_sample
     pgs[1].pdf.

21. Vanessa Willoughby, "Why Toni Morrison Knew *Song of Solo-
     mon* Had to Be About Men," *Literary Hub,* September 1, 2021,
     lithub.com/why-toni-morrison-knew-song-of-solomon-had-to
     -be-about-men/.

22. "Young Toni Morrison Interview (1977)," YouTube, youtube
     .com/watch?v=_vgEhN4fypw.

23. Toni Morrison, *Song of Solomon* (New York: Plume, 1987), 337.

24. Toni Morrison, interview by Bonnie Angelo, *Time,* May 22,
     1989, content.time.com/time/subscriber/article/0,33009,957724
     ,00.html.

Chapter 8: The Combahee River Collective Taught Me About Identity Politics

1.   Helen Leichner, "Combahee River Raid (June 2, 1863)," *BlackPast,*
     December 21, 2012, blackpast.org/african-american-history/
     combahee-river-raid-june-2-1863/.

2.   Jaimee A. Swift, "Where Would Black Feminism Be Today If
     It Wasn't for Barbara Smith?," Black Women Radicals, black
     womenradicals.com/blog-feed/where-would-black-feminism-be
     -today-if-it-wasnt-for-barbara-smith.

3.   Ibid.

4.   Demita Frazier, Alicia Garza, Barbara Ransby, Barbara Smith,
     Beverly Smith, and Keeanga-Yamahtta Taylor, *How We Get*

Free: Black Feminism and the Combahee River Collective (Chicago: Haymarket Books, 2017), 18.

5. Ibid., 19.

6. Ibid., 19.

7. Kimberlé Crenshaw, "Mapping the Margins: Intersectionality, Identity Politics, and Violence Against Women of Color," *Stanford Law Review* 43, no. 6 (July 1991): 1245, doi.org/10.2307/1229039.

8. Brittney Cooper, "Intersectionality," in *The Oxford Handbook of Feminist Theory,* ed. Lisa Disch and Mary Hawkesworth (New York: Oxford University Press, 2016), 397.

9. Frazier et al., *How We Get Free,* 22.

10. Julie Bosman and Joseph Goldstein, "Timeline for a Body: 4 Hours in the Middle of a Ferguson Street," *The New York Times,* August 23, 2014, nytimes.com/2014/08/24/us/michael-brown-a-bodys-timeline-4-hours-on-a-ferguson-street.html.

11. Janell Hobson, "The *Ms.* Q&A: Black Lives Matter Co-Founder Alicia Garza on Getting Intersectionality Right," *Ms.,* November 16, 2017, msmagazine.com/2017/11/16/ms-qa-black-lives-matter-co-founder-alicia-garza-getting-intersectionality-right/.

12. Caitlin Flanagan, "Kirsten Gillibrand's Invocation of 'Intersectionality' Backfires," *The Atlantic,* December 21, 2018, theatlantic.com/ideas/archive/2018/12/kirsten-gillibrand-tweets-about-intersectional-feminism/578776/.

13. Robert Samuels, "How a Grieving Mom Changed Kirsten Gillibrand's Stance on Guns," *The Washington Post,* June 24, 2019, washingtonpost.com/nation/2019/06/24/grieving-community-changed-kirsten-gillibrands-mind-guns-it-didnt-change-much-else/.

14. Andrew Kacynski, "How Kirsten Gillibrand Went from Pushing for More Deportations to Wanting to Abolish ICE," CNN, January 31, 2019, cnn.com/2019/01/17/politics/gillibrand-kfile-immigration/index.html.

15. Carly Mallenbaum, "Alyssa Milano Gets Backlash for Tweet Saying, 'I'm Trans. I'm a Person of Color,'" *USA Today,* March 11, 2019, usatoday.com/story/life/entertainthis/2019/03/11/alyssa-milano-gets-backlash-im-trans-tweet/3135537002/.

16. Amy Grady and Laura Oxley, "#NotAllWomen: Intersectionality and the #MeToo Movement," University of Technology Sydney, April 15, 2019, uts.edu.au/partners-and-community/initiatives/social-justice-uts/news/notallwomen-intersectionality-and-metoo-movement.

17. Jill Lepore, "The Invention of the Police," *The New Yorker,* July 13, 2020, newyorker.com/magazine/2020/07/20/the-invention-of-the-police.

18. Alicia Garza, "Trans Women Don't Want Your Sympathy. They Want to Be Treated as Human Beings," *Marie Claire,* June 25, 2019, marieclaire.com/politics/a28169056/black-trans-women-murdered/.

19. Barbara Smith, "Barbara Smith: Why I Left the Mainstream Queer Rights Movement," *The New York Times,* June 19, 2019, nytimes.com/2019/06/19/us/barbara-smith-black-queer-rights.html.

20. Morgan Bassichis, Alexander Lee, and Dean Spade, "Building an Abolitionist Trans and Queer Movement with Everything We've Got," in *Captive Genders: Trans Embodiment and the Prison Industrial Complex,* ed. Nat Smith and Eric A. Stanley (Oakland, Calif.: AK Press, 2011), deanspade.net/wp-content/uploads/2010/07/Building-an-Abolitionist-Trans-Queer-Movement-With-Everything-Weve-Got.pdf.

21. Katelyn Burns, "Why Police Often Single Out Trans People for Violence," *Vox,* June 23, 2020, vox.com/identities/2020/6/23/21295432/police-black-trans-people-violence.

Chapter 9: Audre Lorde Taught Me About Solidarity as Self-Care

1.   Monica Davey, "Prosecutor Criticized over Laquan McDonald Case Is Defeated in Primary," *The New York Times,* March 16, 2016, nytimes.com/2016/03/16/us/prosecutor-criticized-over-laquan-mcdonald-case-is-defeated-in-primary.html.

2.   Audre Lorde, *Zami: A New Spelling of My Name (A Biomythography by Audre Lorde),* (Berkeley, Calif.: Crossing Press, 1982), 24.

3.   Audre Lorde, *A Burst of Light and Other Essays* (Garden City, N.Y.: IXIA Press, 1988), 130.

4.   Ibid.

5.   Ibid., 133.

6.   Audre Lorde, *Sister Outsider* (Berkeley, Calif.: Crossing Press, 1984), 112.

7.   "Audre Lorde," Poetry Foundation, poetryfoundation.org/poets/audre-lorde.

8.   Juliana Menasce Horowitz and Gretchen Livingston, "How Americans View the Black Lives Matter Movement," Pew Research Center, July 8, 2016, pewresearch.org/short-reads/2016/07/08/how-americans-view-the-black-lives-matter-movement/.

9.   Valeriya Safronova, "Safety Pins Show Support for the Vulnerable," *The New York Times,* November 14, 2016, nytimes.com/2016/11/14/fashion/safety-pin-ally-activism.html.

10.   Anne Bishop, *Becoming An Ally: Breaking the Cycle of Oppression in People* (Halifax, NS, and Winnipeg, MB: Fernwood Publishing, [1994] 2015), back cover.

11.   Ibid., 45.

12.   Lorde, *Sister Outsider,* 113.

Chapter 10: Angela Davis Taught Me to Be an Anti-Racist Abolitionist

1. Ta-Nehisi Coates, "The Black Family in the Age of Mass Incarceration," *The Atlantic,* October 2015, theatlantic.com/magazine/archive/2015/10/the-black-family-in-the-age-of-mass-incarceration/403246/.

2. Geary, "The Moynihan Report."

3. "'Terrorism Is Part of Our History': Angela Davis on '63 Church Bombing, Growing Up in 'Bombingham,'" Democracy Now!, September 16, 2013, democracynow.org/2013/9/16/terrorism_is_part_of_our_history.

4. Ibid.

5. Angela Y. Davis, *Angela Davis: An Autobiography* (New York: International Publishers, 1974), 95.

6. Ibid.

7. Ibid.

8. Ibid., 131.

9. Ibid.

10. Angela Y. Davis and Tony Platt, "Interview with Angela Davis," *Social Justice* 40, no. 1 (2013): 37–53, jstor.org/stable/24361660?mag=50-years-on-how-angela-davis-focus-changed-in-jail&seq=5.

11. Lashawn Harris, "Running with the Reds: African American Women and the Communist Party During the Great Depression," *The Journal of African American History* 94, no. 1 (Winter 2009): 21–43, jstor.org/stable/25610047.

12. Joy James, "George Jackson: Dragon Philosopher and Revolutionary Abolitionist," *Black Perspectives,* August 21, 2018, aaihs.org/george-jackson-dragon-philosopher-and-revolutionary-abolitionist/.

13. Nelson George, "The Greats: Angela Davis," *The New York*

Times, October 19, 2020, nytimes.com/interactive/2020/10/19/t
-magazine/angela-davis.html.

14. "Angela Yvonne Davis," Federal Bureau of Investigation, fbi
.gov/wanted/topten/topten-history/hires_images/FBI-309-Angela
YvonneDavis.jpg/view.

15. Charlene Mitchell, *The Fight to Free Angela Davis: Its Importance for the Working Class* (New York: New Outlook Publishers, 1972), 1, jstor.org/stable/community.31888239?mag=50-years
-on-how-angela-davis-focus-changed-in-jail&seq=2.

16. Sol Stern, "The Campaign to Free Angela Davis . . . and Mitchell
Magee," *The New York Times,* June 27, 1971, nytimes.com/1971/
06/27/archives/the-campaign-to-free-angela-davis-and-ruchell
-magee-the-campaign-to.html.

17. Angela Y. Davis, *Are Prisons Obsolete?* (New York: Seven Stories Press, 2003), 28.

18. Ibid.

19. "Emmett Till Is Murdered," *History.com,* August 24, 2022,
history.com/this-day-in-history/the-death-of-emmett-till.

20. Richard Pérez-Peña, "Woman Linked to 1955 Emmett Till
Murder Tells Historian Her Claims Were False," *The New York
Times,* January 27, 2017, nytimes.com/2017/01/27/us/emmett
-till-lynching-carolyn-bryant-donham.html.

21. "13th Amendment," Cornell Law School, law.cornell.edu/
constitution/amendmentxiii.

22. Juleyka Lantigua-Williams, "Ava DuVernay's *13th* Reframes
American History," *The Atlantic,* October 6, 2016, theatlantic
.com/entertainment/archive/2016/10/ava-duvernay-13th-netflix/
503075/.

23. Douglas A. Blackmon, *Slavery by Another Name: The Re-
enslavement of Black People in America from the Civil War to
World War II* (New York: Doubleday, 2008).

24. "*Slavery by Another Name: The Re-enslavement of Black Americans from the Civil War to World War II,* by Douglas A. Black-

mon (Doubleday)," The Pulitzer Prizes, pulitzer.org/winners/douglas-blackmon.

25. Cheryl I. Harris, "Whiteness as Property," *Harvard Law Review* 106, no. 8 (June 1993): 1713.

26. Angela Y. Davis, *Freedom Is a Constant Struggle: Ferguson, Palestine, and the Foundations of a Movement* (Chicago: Haymarket Books, 2016), 17.

27. Ibid.

28. "#8toAbolition," 8toAbolition, 8toabolition.com/.

29. Jenn M. Jackson, "Our Liberation Praxis Must Be 'Both/And,'" *Signs: Journal of Women in Culture and Society*, signsjournal.org/davis-dent-meiners-richie/.

30. Angela Y. Davis, *Are Prisons Obsolete?* (New York: Seven Stories Press, 2003), 12.

31. "What Is the PIC? What Is Abolition?," Critical Resistance, criticalresistance.org/mission-vision/not-so-common-language/.

32. Mariame Kaba and Shira Hassan, "Fumbling Towards Repair: A Workbook for Community Accountability Facilitators," (Chicago: Project NIA and Just Practice, 2019), 13.

33. Ibid.

34. Beth Potier, "Abolish Prisons, Says Angela Davis," *The Harvard Gazette,* March 13, 2003, news.harvard.edu/gazette/story/2003/03/abolish-prisons-says-angela-davis/.

35. Davis, *Are Prisons Obsolete?,* 85.

36. Steve Clemons and Angela Davis, "Angela Davis: 'Capitalism is Racial Capitalism,'" Al Jazeera, June 23, 2020, ajplus.net/stories/angela-davis-on-racial-capitalism.

37. Stephanie Soucheray, "US Blacks 3 Times More Likely Than Whites to Get COVID-19," Center for Infectious Disease Research & Policy, University of Minnesota, August 14, 2020, cidrap.umn.edu/news-perspective/2020/08/us-blacks-3-times-more-likely-whites-get-covid-19.

Chapter 11: bell hooks taught me how to love expansively

1. bell hooks, *Sisters of the Yam: Black Women and Self-Recovery* (Cambridge, Mass.: South End Press, 2005), 3.

2. Ibid., 117.

3. A gender nonbinary term for a sibling's children.

4. hooks, *Sisters of the Yam,* 115.

5. "Cornel West: Justice Is What Love Looks Like in Public," YouTube, youtube.com/watch?v=nGqP7S_WO6o&t=21s.

6. bell hooks, *All About Love: New Visions* (New York: William Morrow, 2001), 22.

7. Ibid., 30.

8. Ibid., 129.

9. bell hooks, *Communion: The Female Search for Love* (New York: William Morrow, 2002), 199.

10. Ibid., 202.

11. Ibid., 210.

12. hooks, *All About Love,* 110.

13. hooks, *Sisters of the Yam,* 97.

14. Ibid., x.

15. Black Girls Rock!, blackgirlsrock.com/.

16. Olivia A. Cole, "Why I'm Not Here for #WhiteGirlsRock," *HuffPost,* November 4, 2013, huffpost.com/entry/why-im-not -here-for-white_b_4214132.

Conclusion: I Taught Myself About Patience

1. "Miss Mary Mack," *Dictionary.com,* dictionary.com/e/pop -culture/miss-mary-mack/.

Index

PIC. *see* Prison Industrial Complex
Point of Pines Plantation, 4
police
    function of, 198, 199–200
    lack of protection for Black women
        by, 200–203, 207
    origins of in slavery, 198
    and Stonewall Rebellion, 78–79,
        201–202
    violence by, xii–xiii, 17–18, 127, 130,
        132–133, 148–149, 220
policing, 198–200, 223, 249
political office, risks for Black women,
    170–171
polyamory, 272–277
Possessing the Secret of Joy (Walker),
    xiii
Pride Parades, 79
Prison Industrial Complex (PIC)
    abolition movement, 25–26, 208,
        250–252
    defined, 249–251
Pulitzer Prize, 165
Pulley, Aislinn, 44

queer politics, 136–137

Racialicious (blog), xvi
racism
    anti-Black, 244–248
    author's experiences with, xii, xv,
        80–83, 148–149, 154–155,
        181–185, 205–207, 253
    capitalism and, 11–12, 254–255
    on college campuses, 99
    culture of dissemblance, 40–41,
        135–136
    dog whistle language, 184–185
    in education, 183–184
    institutional, 147, 198, 234, 247–248
    medical, 42–43, 122–123, 126,
        169–170

    in politics, 143–146
    respectability as a tool against,
        129–131
    "reverse," 277
    systemic, 47, 224, 234, 247–248
Random House, 166–167
Ransby, Barbara, 108, 295–296
Reconstruction, 15–16, 126
Redefining Realness (Mock), 295
Reese, Maggie, 40
reformative justice, 145
rememory, 179
resistance, secrecy as necessary for,
    40–42
respectability politics, 119–121,
    127–137, 189, 242
Rice, Tamir, 148–149, 220
Richie, Beth, 208, 296
Ritchie, Andrea, 208
Rivera, Sylvia, 79
Roberts, Dorothy, 296
Robertson, Carole, 238
romantic friendships, 270–271
Rose, Charlie, 165
Rumi, Jalaluddin, 196
Rustin, Bayard, 104

safety pin solidarity, 218–221
Salt-N-Pepa, 118
Sands, Mr., 6–7
Sapphire stereotype, xiv
scarcity, 291–292
Scenes of Subjection (Hartman), 295
school-to-prison pipeline, 101, 252
SCLC. *see* Southern Christian
    Leadership Conference
Seals, Darren, 107
Second Continental Congress, 19
secrecy, as necessary for resistance,
    40–42
"see something, say something" era,
    223
self-care, 209–210, 212–214, 217–218

About the Author

JENN M. JACKSON, PhD, is an award-winning professor of political science at Syracuse University and a columnist for *Teen Vogue,* for which they write the popular "Speak on It" column that explores how today's social and political life is influenced by generations of racial and gender (dis)order. A queer genderflux androgynous Black woman, Jackson researches Black Politics with a focus on Black Feminism, racial trauma and threat, gender and sexuality, and social movements. *Black Women Taught Us* is their first book.

jennmjackson.com
Twitter: @JennMJacksonPhD

About the Type

This book was set in Granjon, a modern recutting of a typeface produced under the direction of George W. Jones (1860–1942), who based Granjon's design upon the letterforms of Claude Garamond (1480–1561). The name was given to the typeface as a tribute to the typographic designer Robert Granjon (1513–89).